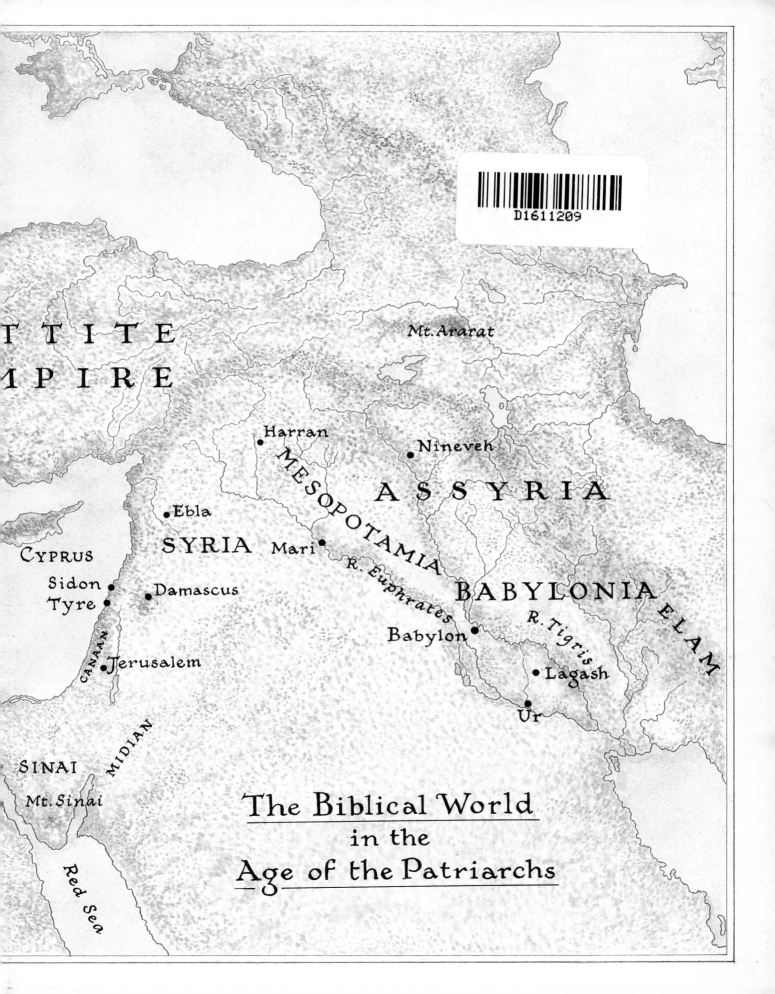

The Biblical World
in the
Age of the Patriarchs

People
from the
Bible

St. John's Episcopal Church
322 South Greer
Memphis, TN 38111

People
from the
Bible

Old Testament: Martin Woodrow
New Testament: E.P. Sanders

The artists

John Heseltine   Jack McCarthy
Pam Masco   Ted Mortelmans
                 Craig Warwick

MOREHOUSE-BARLOW
Wilton, Connecticut

ACKNOWLEDGEMENTS
The publishers would like to thank all those
who helped with and advised on the
archeological background and on the costume
and appearance of the people in the
illustrations; particularly Beatrice Teissier,
Professor E P Sanders, Dr Rupert Chapman
and Roberta Harris. The maps are by Peter
McClure.

BIBLE QUOTATIONS
Quotations from the Old Testament have been
translated from the Hebrew by the author,
although the references to chapter and verse
numbers follow the major English translations
of the Bible. In some instances, these will differ
slightly from Hebrew versions of the Old
Testament.
   The New Testament quotations are based on
the Revised Standard Version used in
conjunction with the author's own translation
from the original Greek texts. The references
given for these quotations apply to all English
versions of the Bible, although the wording will
differ between texts.

First American edition published by
Morehouse-Barlow Co., Inc.
78 Danbury Road
Wilton, Connecticut 06897

ISBN 0-8192-1460-4

Printed in Italy

A List of Books

A List of People

The Bible World

The people of the Bible are among the best known characters of all time. The events in which they were involved have been studied by scholars for centuries; the people themselves have been painted by the world's greatest artists and each generation has built up its own vision of what they were like. Until the last century, archaeology and anthropology were virtually unknown and an artist was free to use his imagination, to set the character in whatever period of time he chose, often setting them in an idealized landscape.

Today we are more concerned with the reality of life in the past; we try to find out how people lived, what they ate, what they wore, what happened to them when they were ill or old, how their lives may have been affected by everything from climate to political upheavals and war. Perhaps, above all, we wonder what they looked like.

It was to satisfy a very human curiosity that this book was conceived. The 100 portraits in its pages are not, of course, portraits in the literal sense for no-one can ever know exactly what these people looked like individually. But their racial characteristics, their physical features, the styles, fabrics and colours of their clothes, are based on up-to-date archaeological and anthropological evidence. In addition, the artists have taken into account the greatly varying conditions in which people lived, conditions which would have influenced their appearance, their attitudes and even perhaps their expressions.

With the portraits, is the story of the events which shaped their lives. Whether they were kings or prophets called by God, famous military leaders or very ordinary people caught up in great events these characters are seen in the Bible as real human beings, people with the hopes, fears, ambitions and problems that are common to us all.

The evidence

The period of time covered in the Old and New Testaments stretches from around 2000 BC to 100 AD; the area extends from the Fertile Crescent of Mesopotamia (modern Iraq) to Egypt and the Arab states bordering the Red Sea. Within it lie the biblical lands of Canaan, the Promised Land which became the centre of David and Solomon's empire and the homeland of Jesus of Nazareth. During the two thousand years from the time of Abraham to the birth of Jesus, the Bible lands saw wars and conquests as kings and warriors fought for local supremacy and the great empires of Egypt, Syria, Assyria, Babylon and Rome rose and fell. During all this time how did the people live? And how do we know it?

The first written records were official ones, consisting of inscriptions on monuments and buildings, archives carved onto wax or clay tablets or later written on scrolls; individual documents recorded historical events, commercial or legal transactions, religious matters or works of literature. Sculptures, reliefs, paintings and figurines provide pictorial evidence. Some records have survived by chance; others were intended for posterity but more for immediate descendants than for an audience living up to 4000 years in the future. They were certainly not made with us in mind. However, archaeologists have been working in the Near East since the middle of the nineteenth century and by combining the imagination and inspiration of past scholars with the scientific techniques available today, it is possible to piece together a great many facts about the lives and appearances of the people of the Old Testament.

The first important source is the Mari archives, palace records dating from the 19th—18th century BC. Mari lies in the Upper Euphrates, within the borders of modern Syria and its archives date from a time when some scholars believe the Patriarchs lived. They give extensive information not only on life at the Mari court and town but also on the tribesmen of the adjoining desert. Could this be how people such as Abraham lived?

An equally valuable source of information are the Amarna letters from Tell el-Amarna, Egypt. These are foreign office records of the Egyptian pharaohs of the 14th century BC (of whom Tutankhamen is the best known) and include information about Canaan before the Israelites arrived. Egyptian wall paintings such as those at Beni Hasan also illustrate visiting foreign traders and battles, recording both general appearance and methods of war.

The Assyrian empire grew to dominate the Near East in the 9th to the 7th centuries BC. Reliefs carved on their monuments show their campaigns in Syria and Palestine. The scenes show sieges, plunder, conquered peoples being led to captivity or offering tribute, all represented with careful details of dress, armour and equipment. These conflicts are also recorded in royal inscriptions, especially by Kings Sargon and Sennacherib in the later 8th century BC. An obelisk made from black stone shows the successes of King Shalmaneser III, with the king receiving tribute from Jehu, king of Israel, in 841 BC.

For the New Testament period there is an abundance of evidence of all kinds, though it does not always answer all our questions. Greek, Roman and Jewish historians wrote of both military and domestic affairs and the archaeological remains of classical Greece and Rome fill the museums of the world. From Egypt there are realistic portraits and Jewish synagogues of the 3rd and 4th centuries AD contain murals and mosaics which show human figures in considerable detail.

In the past, archaeologists tended to be interested mainly in the more spectacular sites and we know far more about life in palaces and temples than we do about the daily life of ordinary people. However, small town settlements have been excavated as well as the more imposing sites.

Villages were either grouped around a town on which they depended economically, or formed separate hamlets of farmsteads in the country. Conflict, in the form of skirmishes between tribes and city states or full scale battles between the major powers, were frequent occurrences and a constant threat. From around 2000 BC onwards, a large number of towns were fortified either with ramparts, moats or solid walls and multi-storied towers.

Outside the settled areas lived the nomads who are often referred to but who have left no archaeological record. Living in tents of skin and felt, they moved seasonally in tribal groups, visiting different pastures with sheep, goats and sometimes asses. Their economy was precarious and settled communities often felt threatened by encroaching nomadic groups.

Palestine was one of the earliest agricultural centres of the ancient Near East and agriculture based on sheep and cattle keeping, and the cultivation of wheat and barley was its main resource. In both towns and villages, food was provided mainly from locally grown produce. Organized industry such as smithing, pottery and weaving was carried out in particular areas either within the town or outside it. In towns these areas were much like the *suks* or bazaars of today, centres of barter where business was transacted and news (and gossip) circulated. Most people could not read or write and scribes were responsible for recording both legal and commercial business. The smith was an important member of the community, responsible for making weapons, tools, figurines and jewellery. Copper, tin and later iron were standard utility metals with gold, silver and bronze for jewellery.

The people of the Bible lands did not live in isolation from the rest of the world. The ancient Near East had widespread trade routes from a very remote period (around 10,000 BC) and by Solomon's time, Israel lay at the centre of the great overland trade route from Egypt to Mesopotamia. Solomon developed trade by sea down the Red Sea to Ophir (perhaps in modern Somaliland) and Sheban in modern Yemen. The merchant caravan routes were the principal means of communication, and travel, whether for commercial or personal reasons, was very much a way of life. Ordinary people travelled with the caravans for safety, either on foot or in ox-carts.

The clothing

The evidence for the kind of clothes people wore comes from the figures on monuments and wall paintings, from the remains of parts of spinning and weaving machines, vats where cloth was dyed, even from scraps of cloth itself. A variety of fibres (flax, wool, goat and camel hair) were used, dyed with colours derived from plants or, at the coast, with the mollusc dyes which gave the rich purple colour. Because of its expense, this was reserved for royalty and those with royal connections. Wool and cotton were easier to dye than linen, which was usually left white but could be stiffened and shaped for head coverings.

Garments could be richly coloured. Royal and religious vestments could have separate embroidered trimmings or be adorned with silver and gold. Costume indicated both a person's rank and where he came from. Colour was not exclusive to rank. Egyptian tomb paintings representing a contingent of Asiatic traders show them wearing brightly chequered and striped clothing, which contrast markedly with the plain white dress of the ordinary Egyptian. Joseph's 'many-coloured coat' may have been a particularly colourful version of the standard Canaanite tunic. The basic dress of the ordinary citizen consisted of a loin cloth, a long or short linen or wool skirt or robe, covered in a mantle or cloak. These could be trimmed with fur, or be fringed. On the Assyrian reliefs, the Israelites wear plain, round-necked tunics, sometimes with a fringed overgarment. Persians and Assyrians have more elaborate costumes, their rulers and officials wearing gold crowns or richly decorated robes. Many people went barefoot but those who could afford to wore leather or wooden sandals. Away from towns and cities, clothing was evidently plainer, but adorned with jewellery as a symbol of wealth. Skins and leather were used as protective garments. Head coverings were worn by both men (bonnets, twisted cloth, head bands) and women (veils) as a protection against the sun and as a mark of rank.

In the New Testament period the universal dress for both men and women was a close-fitting tunic (a simple slip-over garment), with a cloak. Cloaks were decorated by stripes down the front or around the hem and the few fragments of first-century Jewish clothing which have been uncovered by archaeologists show that the decoration was often elaborate. A belt was often worn over the tunic and was used to carry money (Matthew 10:9). The robes of Jews had fringes or tassels on the four corners, as commanded in Numbers 15:37—39.

The people

At first sight, the reconstruction of the faces of people from the Bible seems a daunting task. Hardly anything that can be called a portrait has survived from the Old Testament world outside Egypt and stone carvings and reliefs are more useful for clothing than for individual faces. They show general outlines of features which give an indication of a type of face (e.g. a fleshy nose, receding chin or forehead, broad cheekbones) and may have been exaggerated to give instant recognition—much as cartoonists today exaggerate the most identifiable feature of a person or type. It is possible to draw parallels with today's peasants and nomads but these, too, can only provide general guidelines for such things as skin and hair colour: time and history have inevitably brought changes as peoples have mixed and migrated.

There are, however, certain characteristics of people from biblical times which it is safe to guess at, and which help to fill in the human background. Their life span would have tended to be less than the three score years and ten allotted in the Bible and although many adults did survive into old age, they would have formed a smaller proportion of the populations than they do today. They would have become parents in their teens and grand-parents in their thirties. A hot, sunny climate and a life spent in the open air, dry out the skin rapidly, and the ordinary people, especially the nomads, would have aged rapidly, so that people often looked older than they really were. As in any community without access to modern medicine, deaths from illness or accidents we would consider minor would have been an ever present hazard and scars and deformities would no doubt have been a common sight.

Evidence from archaeology helps to build up the factual details. Small containers and spatulas show that cosmetics and ointments were used in a wide section of society, to beautify, for medicinal purposes, as insect repellents or to soothe irritations. Ochre and mineral pastes (galera, antimony) were used as face and eye colourants, crushed henna (not used by the Hebrews) to dye nails, hands, face and hair; aromatic resins (myrrh) and aloes for embalming, incense (frankincense, galbanum) for religious ceremonies. Oils and fats were used for anointing and perfuming the body and the hair.

Many of the carvings that show us how people dressed and wore their hair were made in stone, and the effect is often very stylized. Nevertheless, they do indicate the care that was taken in hairdressing by people of rank. Styling (tight or loose curls or ringlets) was common for men and women's hair. Beards were carefully groomed and trimmed. Head bands, ivory combs and pins were used as ornaments. Women usually wore their hair long, and men on average, shoulder-length. Some styles seem to have persisted for centuries among the Israelites. Egyptian wall paintings of Canaanites from Joseph's time show a characteristic pointed beard which is still the style centuries later among the kings of Israel. Barbers did exist, though metal razors are rare (iron rusts), suggesting that sharp stones and other methods may have been used in shaving. Bronze razors have been found in ancient Egypt.

For the New Testament period, reconstruction becomes easier, for in Roman times, sculpture became more realistic and painted portraits have survived from Alexandria, the major city of northern Egypt. The population there was very mixed, with not only native Egyptians, but also thousands of Macedonians, Greeks and Jews. Many people had their portraits painted on the lids of their coffins, and the variety of features shows that the portraits were realistic. Their features, hairstyles and jewellery were probably typical of the eastern and southern Mediterranean of the time.

The principal direct evidence for Jewish features, hairstyles and adornment is a synagogue in Dura-Europus, dating from the first half of the third century AD. Its walls and ceiling were covered with frescos and painted tiles, the murals showing biblical scenes. In general the clothing and hair styles are in typical Roman style.

In the Roman empire most men, apparently, conformed to the same style of hair and beard. The early Romans had worn beards but eventually adopted the practice of shaving daily. They used iron razors, but their use required great skill, and good barbers were much sought-after. The well-known style of Julius Caesar (clean shaven, with short hair brushed forward from the crown) prevailed throughout the empire and endured well into the second century AD. The style was so widespread that Paul thought that 'nature itself' teaches that men have short hair (1 Corinthians 11:14). It is this style that we see in murals, mummy tombs and sculpture for some centuries throughout the empire. Short beards, trimmed close to the face, are occasionally to be found, but never long hair. We must suppose that in rural areas people were less well groomed, and both hair and beard may have become ragged and a bit long. But the long, flowing beard and hair of popular imagination are most unlikely. Men whose hair became long enough to get in the eyes wore headbands, and those who worked outside may have combined a kerchief with a headband for protection against the sun.

Women's hair style and dress in the first century were quite modest. The hair was sometimes braided or made into a bun, and some form of headdress was usually worn. This might be a net, a headband or a shawl. Hair was unbound on festive occasions, and in certain religious rites women let down their hair. Paul urged the women in Corinth to cover their heads when praying (1 Corinthians 11.4—16), and it may be that unbound hair brought to his mind certain pagan practices.

This, then, is the background. For the five artists who have painted the 'portraits' in this book, it formed the starting point from which they could begin to understand the lives and characters of the 100 people whose faces they have imagined so vividly.

The Old Testament

PALESTINE
in
Old Testament
Times

SYRIA

Sidon

Damascus

Tyre

PHOENICIA

Hazor

BASHAN

Mediterranean Sea

Sea of
Galilee

Mt. Carmel

Endor

Ramoth~Gilead

Megiddo

Jezreel

Mt. Gilboa

ISRAEL

Samaria

River Jordan

GILEAD

Penuel

Shechem

Mahanaim

AMMON

Joppa

Shiloh

Bethel

Ramah

Michmash

Gibeon

Jericho

Jerusalem

Gath

Bethlehem

Ashkelon

JUDAH

Dead
Sea

Gaza

PHILISTIA

Lachish

Hebron

MOAB

Ziklag

Beersheba

EDOM

0 5 10 15 20 25 Miles

0 10 20 30 40 50 Km

Introduction
to the
Old
Testament

The Old Testament is the surviving literature of ancient Israel. Most of it is written as a narrative, beginning in Genesis with the creation of the world and the rise of the nations of mankind, then focussing on the Patriarchs of Israel. The books from Exodus to Chronicles tell how the Israelites, under Moses's leadership, were saved from slavery in Egypt and led to the borders of the land promised to their forefathers; how they conquered it and overcame hostile neighbours until, in the tenth century BC, David and Solomon ruled an empire roughly covering present-day Israel, Jordan, eastern Lebanon and most of Syria. It tells how the united kingdom of Israel split into two mutually hostile kingdoms, north and south, and how the people were eventually conquered and deported by the great powers of Mesopotamia, sited in present-day Iraq. Israel's northern kingdom fell to the Assyrians in 722 BC and its southern kingdom (named Judah after its main tribe) to their successors, the Babylonians in 587 BC. The Books of Ezra and Nehemiah tell how, after the Babylonians in turn fell to the Persians, the Jews (i.e. the people of Judah) were allowed to return to their land and rebuild their Temple.

Not all of the Old Testament, however, is a narrative. Exodus and Deuteronomy include the Ten Commandments and the hundreds of other divine laws reportedly given to Moses—on family and civil life, on ethics and on worship. The Bible also records the utterances of a succession of prophets, from the eighth to the fifth centuries BC, who attacked social injustice and heathen worship in Israel. They often announced imminent punishment—which the Assyrian and Babylonian invasions largely fulfilled. Despite their many denunciations, they saw also a more distant future, when a messiah ('anointed one') would inaugurate an era of everlasting peace not only for Israel but for all mankind.

The prophets normally used a form of poetry which involved a rhyming not of syllables but of thought; each point in the message is expressed twice, in two parallel phrases. When their audience seemed more absorbed in the beauty of the poetry than in its message (Ezekiel 33:30—33), they resorted to prose sermons. Many other books of the Old Testament are also written in poetry. The book of Job is a debate, in the form of a drama, about the justice of a God who allows, or rather causes, a righteous man to suffer. The Psalms are outpourings of gratitude and cries for help, from anonymous individuals, from kings of Israel or Judah and from the whole community. The Proverbs contain hundreds of self-contained couplets on man's relations with his fellows and with God. Ecclesiastes is for the most part a work of cynicism, urging readers not to be too righteous (7:16) and complaining that righteous and wicked share the same fate (8:14); it ends, however, by declaring that man's sole purpose is to keep God's commandments. The Song of Songs is a drama of love, or a collection of love songs. Despite its erotic language, it was included in the Bible because it was interpreted allegorically, as describing God's love for Israel or, in Christian tradition, Christ's love for the Church.

Until the invention of typesetting (and printing) all documents were written by hand. In Old Testament times, trained scribes were the only people who were literate and the books of the Bible would have been copied out onto papyrus or vellum by scribes and stored as rolls, tied with ribbon or thread. The original language of most of the Old Testament is Hebrew. The Dead Sea scrolls, written down during the last two centuries BC provide the earliest known texts and include a complete copy of Isaiah and fragments of every other book except Esther. For most of the books, however, no complete copy of the Hebrew text exists earlier than the ninth or eleventh century AD because of the Jewish practice of burying scrolls when they became tattered. A translation into Greek, probably made between the third and first centuries BC, also survives; and there are later translations into Greek, and also into Syriac, Latin and Aramaic. The Jews have handed down a Hebrew text, called the Massoretic text, and Aramaic translations; other translations were preserved by the Church. When translations differ, as they often do, or if the meaning is not clear, it is often possible to reconstruct the original wording by translating back into Hebrew. The result is sometimes (though not always) clearer than the existing Massoretic Hebrew version. Choosing between different translations is a delicate task, requiring knowledge of the whole content of the passage and how it was used, an understanding of the various languages involved and familiarity with the problems of translation.

For some words, the meaning is still unknown. The best way to establish the meaning of a word is to examine how it is used in a series of different contexts but apart from a few brief inscriptions, nothing survives of the Hebrew spoken in the biblical period except the Old Testament itself. There are about 1000 words (not including names) that occur in the Old Testament just once and since they are unknown in modern Hebrew, we are heavily dependent on the ancient translations and on Jewish tradition to establish what they mean. Even these sources occasionally give no convincing sense, or disagree with one another. For example 2 Samuel 6:19 states that David at a feast gave every Israelite an *eshpar*. The ancient translations merely guess at its meaning (e.g. 'loaf' or 'piece of meat') and we are no wiser today.

Occasionally it is impossible to make satisfactory sense from any of the existing versions. There are two possible answers. Some, perhaps all of the puzzling words may have been errors made originally by a scribe who was copying the text, then repeated again and again as new copies were made. Sometimes it is obvious how such an error could have arisen and a word which makes sense is substituted. But in other cases it may be that the text is correct and we do not know enough biblical Hebrew to understand it. In this case, scholars search related languages such as Arabic or Ethiopic for a word which sounds the same and whose meaning would make sense in the biblical passage. If they find one, they assume that a similar word once existed in Hebrew. These methods have been used by different scholars in different ways and this accounts for many of the differences between English versions of the Old Testament. Most modern translations use a method to indicate a word has been substituted in this way to improve the sense of a passage.

The title 'Old Testament' is Christian. It originates in 2 Corinthians 3:14, which states that the 'old covenant' between God and Israel was annulled. 'Testament' is an ancient mistake which arose because *diatheke*, the word used in the Greek text, could mean not only 'covenant' but also 'will, testament'. Christians also arrange the text in chronological order: first histories (Genesis to Esther), then prayers and speculation about the present (Job to Song of Songs) and finally the prophecies, of which the New Testament, immediately following, is presented as the fulfilment. In Jewish tradition, the books (which for Jews are the whole Bible) are instead arranged in three divisions, in descending order of authority. First stand the Five Books of Moses; these constitute the Law, though teaching is a better translation of the Hebrew term (Torah). Next come the prophets (Isaiah to Malachi). The remaining books form the third division, simply termed the Writings.

The Roman Catholic or Latin Bible (the Vulgate) is a translation into Latin made by St Jerome in the fourth century.

It includes a number of additional books, known as 'The Apocrypha' which were written in the last two centuries BC and the first AD. Beginning with Martin Luther's translation into German in 1534, the Protestant Bible separated these from the main text and they are often now printed as a separate volume.

If they were written around the times of the events they describe, the books of the Old Testament would be dated between the time of Moses (perhaps 13th century BC) and Ezra (5th century BC). Modern scholars, however, date the 'Five Books of Moses' to a later period, partly because they refer to such things as a monarchy (Genesis 36:31) and a temple (Exodus 15:17), which were unknown in the thirteenth century. Most consider that the song of Deborah (Judges 5) was written about 1200 BC and that it is the oldest piece in the Old Testament. The latest parts were probably written in the second century BC, since Daniel 11 contains a detailed account of events which are known from independent sources to have taken place in 168 or 167 BC.

Close reading of the narratives of the Old Testament reveals many apparent inconsistencies and duplications. For example, were the followers of Korah, who mutinied against Moses, swallowed by an earthquake (Numbers 16:32) or burned to death (Numbers 16:35)? Did the Israelites leave Egypt in the middle of the night (Exodus 12:31, Deuteronomy 16:1) or in broad daylight (Numbers 33:3)? Was Jerusalem captured for Israel by Joshua (Joshua 12:10), by the tribesmen of Judah after Joshua's death (Judges 1:8) or by King David (2 Samuel 5:5—7)? How was Cain able to marry and have children when he and his family were apparently the only people alive at the time? Today, scholars believe that most of the Old Testament books were compiled from earlier sources, which were often contradictory, and that the editors who put them together did not make them fully consistent. They try to identify the historical traditions underlying these sources and to reconstruct history by taking what they consider the most reliable elements in the biblical account,

comparing them with contemporary records revealed by archaeology—and filling them out by their own ingenuity. As scholars continue to debate what the original sources were and therefore how reliable different parts of the Bible may be, such reconstructions vary a great deal.

Before any investigations can be made, however, the first step is to ask what the text of the Bible actually says; and that question is the main concern of this book. The following pages show what events, and what characters emerge from the text of the Old Testament as it stands today. The work of earlier scholars who treated the Old Testament as a unity is invaluable —particularly that of the medieval rabbis Rashi (born 1040) and Abraham Ibn Ezra (born 1089) who spent a lifetime studying its content. But it is not necessary to speculate on the prehistory of the Bible, nor to take a stand on every historical issue in order to appreciate the Bible as literature.

The Book of Genesis

The Book of Genesis deals with the origins of mankind. Beginning with the Creation and the story of the Flood, it traces the ancient history of the Hebrew nation from Abraham, the first Patriarch, to Joseph.

Recent archaeological research suggests that Abraham could have lived between 2000 and 1500 BC and this is partly confirmed by texts found at the ancient site of Mari, on the River Euphrates. These date from around 1800 BC and tell of waves of nomadic herdsmen, called Amorites, migrating from what is now southern Iraq northwards along the Euphrates. Both the route and their nomadic way of life seem similar to Abraham's.

Abraham was the first to receive God's promise that he and his descendants would possess the land of Canaan.

The beginning of the world

Adam was the first man and was created 'in the image of God' (Genesis 1:27). This may be meant literally, for prophets who saw God saw him in human form but it may simply mean that man was able to reason and had a conscience. Adam was the last creature to be physically formed, although his soul, the 'spirit of God' (Genesis 1:2), dated from the beginning of Creation. God made Adam from loose earth, and his name comes from the Hebrew word *adamah*, meaning earth.

God set Adam to tend the garden of Eden, and told him he could eat the fruit of every tree except the Tree of Knowledge of good and evil. On the day he ate this fruit, God warned him, he would die. There was also a Tree of Life which could confer immortality (3.22); it was not forbidden to Adam, but he never ate its fruit. There are two accounts of the creation in Genesis. According to Genesis 1, God created the animals before Adam, and man and woman were created together. In the second account, in Genesis 2, God made Adam first and then the animals in an attempt to find him a companion and helper. Adam's first achievement was to give the animals names. None proved to be an adequate companion for him, however, so God decided to make one for him. He put Adam to sleep, took a rib from his body, and from it made Eve.

Adam must have told Eve that they were not allowed to eat from the Tree of Knowledge but in spite of this, she was persuaded by the cunning serpent to try its tempting fruit. She also gave some to Adam, who strangely broke God's only commandment without protest. Now they had knowledge of good and evil. As this included sexual awareness, they became ashamed and covered their loins with fig leaves. When they heard God walking in the garden, they hid, and God called to Adam: 'Where are you?' Adam answered that he had hidden because he was ashamed of his nakedness. God accused him of eating from the forbidden tree, and Adam immediately blamed his wife. His punishment was to spend his life wearily tilling the earth, where thorns would now grow among the plants that were to be his only food. He was condemned to die and expelled from Eden to prevent him eating fruit from the Tree of Life. The entrance to the garden was barred by cherubs and a flaming ever-turning sword.

God had threatened that Adam would die on the *day* he ate the fruit from the Tree of Knowledge but instead set the maximum human lifespan at 1000 years, one day in God's reckoning (Psalm 90:4). Once humanity had discovered sex, every individual had to be mortal, for if no-one died, the world would be too small for all the people to live in. Only the species might now hope for immortality.

Adam and Eve soon had two sons, Cain and Abel. Their third son, Seth, was born 130 years later.

As a perfect creation, Adam lived for 930 years, not far short of the maximum of 1000 years; this meant he was able to meet his descendants seven generations on. As later generations became less perfect, further from God, so their life spans decreased (Genesis 5, 11). In Christian tradition, Jesus is the second Adam, bringing life where the first brought death. The new Tree of Life is the cross.

Eve was the first woman. According to Genesis 2, she was created from Adam's rib as a 'help adequate for him' (Genesis 2:18). To prevent Eve from eating from the Tree of Knowledge, Adam warned her that she would die if she even touched it but the serpent persuaded her that instead of bringing death, the fruit would give knowledge that would make her and Adam like gods. This promise, together with the beauty of the tree, drove her to eat. She also gave some fruit to Adam, perhaps using the same arguments that the serpent had used on her. When God found them out, Adam blamed Eve and Eve in turn blamed the serpent. Her punishment was the pain of childbirth, and vulnerability towards man; through her longing for him, he would rule her (3:16).

The name Eve (Hebrew *chavah*), which Adam chose for his wife, is explained in the Bible as 'mother of all that lives' (Hebrew *chay*), but this does not explain the *v*; instead there may be a connection between Eve's name and *chivya*, which in the closely related Aramaic language means 'serpent'. Eve beguiled Adam as the serpent had beguiled her.

Cain and **Abel** were the first sons of Adam and Eve. Cain was named through Eve's exclamation: 'I have acquired (Hebrew *kaniti*) a man with the Lord' (Genesis 4:1), meaning that in future, parents would be God's partners in the formation of children. 'Abel' means either 'breath' or 'emptiness'.

One day Cain and Abel each brought an offering to God but God accepted only Abel's. Abel, a herdsman, had brought the fat portions of the first-born of his sheep—the best he could offer, while Cain's offering is described simply as 'fruit of the soil'. Cain was angry at this rejection and God told him not to be angry but to bring better offerings. Instead, Cain killed his brother. When God asked where Abel was, Cain replied that he did not know: 'Am I my brother's keeper?' This is usually considered a brazen lie; it might just, however, be genuine, for no-one had ever died before, and Cain may have thought that Abel had merely gone to sleep and since woken and moved on.

God told Cain that Abel's blood was crying for revenge: as punishment, Cain would find the earth even less productive than Adam had, and would become a fugitive. When Cain cried that men would put him to death for his crime, God set a sign upon him—the 'mark of Cain'—to warn that if anyone killed him, his death would be avenged seven times over—upon the killer and his family.

Cain was the first inventor. He journeyed far from Eden—Adam had remained near its eastern border—to the land of Nod ('wandering'). There he built the first city, which he named after his son Enoch, who was born there. Cain's descendants are traced for six generations. The last is represented by three brothers, all innovators—Jabal, the first herdsman (replacing the murdered Abel); Jubal, the first musician; and Tubal-Cain, the inventor of bronze and iron tools. There was also a sister, Naamah.

The Bible does not name the mother of Cain's children, nor does it explain how by this time there were other people in the world. To account for Cain's wife, Jewish tradition tells that Cain had a twin sister whom he married. Other traditions suggest a wife was specially created for him by God. Most scholars accept this as one of the Bible's puzzling inconsistencies.

Seth, meaning '(God) has placed (new seed)' was Adam's third son, born after the death of Abel. Through him the line of descent is traced to Noah (Genesis 5). Most of the names of Seth's descendants are either identical or similar to those of Cain's line (4:17—22). Scholars deduce that the Bible preserves two alternative accounts of the earliest men: one traces them to Cain, the other to Seth, but both agree on most of the names. The version tracing the descendants of Seth originally went on to tell how the Flood destroyed everyone except Noah and his family, from whom the different nations gradually developed (Genesis 10). In the version tracing Cain's descendants, men invented crafts and lived together until God suddenly dispersed them as they tried to raise a tower (11:1—9) and nothing is said of a flood.

Enoch was the name both of Adam's grandson (the son of Cain) and of a descendant of Seth. Cain's son was born in the land of Nod and the first city was called after him. The Enoch descended from Seth represents the seventh generation of mankind, in the line leading to Noah. Though in general at that time each generation was more corrupt than the one before, Enoch walked with God. At the age of 365—comparatively young for that period—God took him (Enoch never died). His son was Methusaleh.

The age at which Enoch was taken, 365, suggests a knowledge of astronomy and a Book of Enoch, parts of which were written no later than the third century BC, tells how he was secretly taught the structure and destiny of the universe. The book is quoted in Jude (verses 14—15) but was later rejected by both the Church and the Synagogue. The complete text now survives only in an Ethiopian translation.

Methusaleh was the son of Enoch, Seth's descendant. In spite of the fact that lifespans were decreasing, he lived to the record age of 969, dying in the year of the Flood.

Lamech was the son of Methusaleh and father of Noah (Genesis 5:29). Another

Lamech, Cain's descendant five generations on, was the first man to take two wives. His third son, Tubal-Cain, invented metal weapons and Lamech boasted that he was now able to kill a man in retaliation for a mere wound; to avenge a single murder he would kill seventy-seven times (Genesis 4:23).

Noah was the son of Lamech and grandson of Methusaleh. He was a righteous man living at a time when people had become hopelessly wicked. God decided that only Noah and his family deserved to live and told him to build a boat (the Ark) so that he could escape a flood which would destroy the whole world. His contemporaries watched him building his boat for a hundred years, but they never repented. Noah brought to the Ark one male and female of every 'unclean' species and seven pairs of every 'clean' species. (The animals later permitted as food to the people of Israel were 'clean'.) Noah and his three sons entered the Ark together; their wives entered separately since while they were in the Ark they were to live apart.

The great Flood came, and it rained for forty days. Even high mountains were deep under water. The boundary established at creation between water and dry land was erased. The Ark drifted, and after more than six months afloat it eventually came to rest on top of a mountain. After several more months, Noah released a raven, which 'went to and fro until the waters were dried up from the earth' (8:7). Noah then sent out a dove—three times. The first time she found no land; the second she returned with an olive leaf; and the third she did not return.

Noah waited for God to tell him to leave the Ark, where he had spent just

ADAM AND EVE
The first man and woman were the last living things to be created when the world was made. Their home was Eden, a garden which contained everything they needed: rivers of clear water, trees and plants to give them food, and all the creatures of the world as their companions. Only one fruit was forbidden, the fruit of the tree which gave knowledge of good and evil.

over a year (7:11; 8:14). He offered up clean animals in thanksgiving and God, pleased by this, promised never to repeat the flood. As his pledge, God left the rainbow, showing his bow pointing away from the earth. God now explicitly forbade murder but allowed animals to be killed for meat.

The account of the Flood ends in God's blessing: 'Be fruitful and multiply and replenish the earth' (9:1).

Shem, Ham and **Japheth** were sons of Noah. They were saved with him in the Ark and from them the nations of the world were said to be descended. One day after the Flood, Noah, who had planted a vineyard, innocently became the first drunkard. He was lying sprawled naked on the ground when Ham found him and told his brothers. Shem and Japheth walked to him backwards with their faces turned away and covered him up. As soon as Noah awoke he 'knew what his youngest son had done to him' (9:24). Evidently Ham had done more than looked; Jewish tradition explains that he castrated Noah, to safeguard his own inheritance. Noah cursed Ham's fourth son with slavery (since he himself would never have a fourth son) but blessed the descendants of Shem and Japheth.

The descendants of Noah's three sons settled—speaking very broadly—as follows: Shem's descendants ('semitic') in the Middle East, Japheth's in Persia and Europe, and Ham's in Africa, Canaan and Western Arabia. The relative ages of the three are obscure; they are usually named in the order Shem, Ham, Japheth, but Genesis 10 gives the opposite order, and in 9:24 Ham is youngest.

Abraham and his family

Terah was Abraham's father and was born in Ur, just south of the River Euphrates, in what is now southern Iraq. Ur was a great centre of moon-worship, and this may explain why Terah's name is similar to one of the Hebrew words for 'moon' (*yareah*). In Jewish legend Terah is said to have been an idol-maker.

Terah had three sons, Abraham, the oldest, Nahor and Haran. Haran died as a young man and after his death, Terah set out for the land of Canaan. The Bible gives no reason for this; perhaps he simply thought it a more pleasant environment.

Instead of travelling straight across the desert, he followed the River Euphrates, but when he reached Syria he apparently changed his plans, for he continued northwards and settled in the trading city of Harran instead of turning south-west to Canaan. Perhaps the attraction of Harran was that, like Ur, it was a centre of moon-worship. Terah was aged 70 when Abraham was born and died aged 205 (Genesis 11:26, 32).

Abraham was the first of the Patriarchs, and was born in Ur. He was originally named Abram. According to legend, he was once left in charge of his father's workshop where he smashed all the idols except the largest. He placed the hammer in this great idol's hand and when Terah returned, told him it had broken the others. Terah protested that idols were powerless and Abram demanded to know why in that case anyone worshipped them. As punishment for this blasphemy, the local king threw Abram into a furnace (this is the meaning of 'Ur' in Hebrew although the name is not in fact Hebrew), but he emerged unharmed from the flames.

Abram married his wife Sarai in Ur, then travelled with his father to Harran. At the age of 75, he was commanded by God to continue to Canaan (his father's original destination). God's reason for choosing him is not given in the Bible but was apparently that only Abram acknowledged Him.

Abram took with him his nephew Lot, the son of his dead brother Haran. He had no children of his own and probably considered Lot as his heir but God now promised Abram that his own direct descendants would possess the land of Canaan. This must have seemed unlikely to Abram and became even more so when, soon after their arrival in Canaan, famine drove them on to Egypt and Sarai was abducted by Pharaoh. Abram was afraid that he would be

killed if Pharaoh discovered he was Sarai's husband, so he pretended to be her brother and Pharaoh showered him with gifts. Soon, however, Pharaoh and his household were stricken with 'great plagues'. Pharaoh realized that this was a punishment for some sin and he discovered that Sarai was actually Abram's wife. He summoned Abram and demanded an explanation. Receiving none, he expelled Abram and his household.

As if to erase this episode, Abram went right back to his starting point in Canaan, settling between Bethel and Ai. By this time both Abram and Lot owned enormous herds of cattle and sheep and they decided to separate. Lot left to settle in Sodom while Abram remained in Canaan.

Meanwhile God repeated to Abram his promise that his descendants would possess the land of Canaan. When Abram still seemed doubtful, God reassured him with a covenant. In Abram's time each party to a covenant used to dismember animals, stand between the pieces and ask to be treated in the same way if he broke the agreement (Jeremiah 34:18). On this occasion, Abram divided the animals and God was represented by a smoking brazier and a flaming torch passing between the pieces. The covenant was made but Abram was now told that his descendants would be enslaved in a foreign land for four generations before possessing Canaan.

So far, Abram is shown in the Bible as a tribal leader, powerful enough to be treated with respect by the Egyptian Pharaoh but living a peaceful nomadic life. Genesis 14, however, presents him as a warrior who could defeat the greatest armies of his day. The city of Sodom, where Lot now lived, was attacked by a coalition of four kings. They sacked Sodom and the neighbouring cities, capturing Lot. Abram came to the rescue, routing them with only 318 men, rescuing Lot and recovering all the spoil that had been looted. Historically, this account remains unproven, as there is so far no archaeological evidence that the four kings mentioned were ever friendly enough to undertake a joint campaign.

ABRAHAM

Abraham, the first of the Patriarchs, lived as a nomad, travelling from his birthplace in Mesopotamia through Canaan and, when famine struck, as far south as Egypt. A man of great integrity and faith, he was also a powerful leader with enormous herds of cattle and goats, and was evidently respected by the people through whose lands he passed. Nomadic people of the past have left few clues about their way of life but records from the ancient site of Mari shed some light on the customs and styles of Abraham's time.

Ten years after their arrival in Canaan, Abram and his wife Sarai were still childless and Sarai tried to remedy the situation by giving Abram her maidservant Hagar to bear his child in her name. When Abram was 86 his first son, Ishmael, was born to Hagar.

Thirteen years later, God told Abram that he would become father of many nations, and that his name Abram ('high father') would be lengthened to Abraham ('father of multitudes'). God added that the promise of the land would pass not to Ishmael but to a son of Sarai herself. Abraham and his descendants were to be circumcised. Accordingly, Abraham, now aged 99, underwent this, together with every male in his household. Soon afterwards, three angels—disguised as men—came to confirm the news that Sarah (as she was now known) and Abraham were indeed to have a child together.

The angels told Abraham that they had another mission to perform: they were to destroy the wicked city of Sodom. At this Abraham challenged God: 'Will you destroy the righteous together with the wicked?' God promised not to destroy Sodom if fifty righteous men could be discovered there, but although Abraham managed to bring the number needed down to ten, Lot seemed to be the only man worth saving in the whole city.

Abraham and his family next travelled southwards into the kingdom of Gerar and here Sarah was abducted again—this time by Abimelech, the Philistine king who ruled there. Once more Abraham said she was his sister. God, however, told the king in a dream that Sarah was married and Abimelech returned her immediately to Abraham. Like Pharaoh, Abimelech asked Abraham to explain himself, and Abraham replied firstly that he had feared for his life, and secondly that Sarah was indeed his own sister, but on his father's side only. Abimelech compensated Abraham ('your brother', as he pointedly called him to Sarah) generously and made a peace covenant with him.

At last Isaac, the son of Abraham and Sarah was born, and Abraham was overjoyed. A great feast was held when the child was weaned and soon Sarah

urged Abraham to banish his first son Ishmael. The family was living in Beersheba at the time and Abraham shrank from driving his son out into the surrounding desert. But God told him to listen to his wife and assured him that Ishmael would survive.

Now came Abraham's most difficult test—and the episode for which he is best-known: God ordered him to sacrifice Isaac as a burnt-offering. This command appeared to contradict the promise that Isaac's descendants would inherit the land, but in Abraham's eyes God's will overrode reason. Without protest, he took his remaining son on a three-day journey (in case he was accused of acting on impulse) to God's chosen spot on Mount Moriah, where the Temple would later stand. With no sign of emotion, he built the altar, arranged the wood, tied up Isaac, set him in place, and took the slaughtering-knife. At the last moment an angel called on him to stop: Abraham had proved that he would not withhold even his son from God. He was allowed to substitute a ram caught on the mountainside. Child sacrifice was common among Israel's neighbours, as we learn from the Bible itself and from archaeological finds. Here Abraham showed as much religious fervour as the pagan worshippers, but discovered that his God was satisfied with animal sacrifice.

When Sarah died, Abraham wanted to bury her in the cave of Machpelah in Hebron. The owner, Ephron the Hittite, not only offered him the cave, but also —against Abraham's wishes—the field where it lay. Abraham was embarrassed and offered to pay but Ephron replied: 'What is land worth 400 shekels, between you and me?' The price seems exorbitant; Jeremiah (32:9) bought a field for a mere 17 shekels. The man to whom the whole land of Canaan had been promised was humiliated over one small plot; yet his faith remained firm.

Realizing how close Isaac had been to death, Abraham now despatched his servant Eliezer to find his son a wife from the region of Harran, in Syria, where his father and his brother Nahor had settled. Eliezer's mission succeeded and he brought home Rebecca to be

Isaac's wife. Strangely, there is no mention of Abraham thanking him or approving the marriage, and Eliezer on his return described Isaac as 'my lord'—as if Abraham had died during his absence. Yet in the next chapter Abraham himself takes another wife and becomes the father of six more sons. Biblical scholars conclude that this chapter was originally part of a different version of Abraham's life story.

Abraham died at the age of 175 and was buried with Sarah. Later generations called him the 'friend of God'.

Nahor There are two people named Nahor in the Bible. One was Abraham's grandfather (Terah's father), the other Abraham's younger brother. Three female descendants of this younger Nahor married into Abraham's family: his granddaughter Rebecca married Isaac and his great-granddaughters Leah and Rachel married Jacob.

Lot was Abraham's nephew, the son of Abraham's youngest brother Haran, who died before the family left Ur. Lot went with Terah to Harran, and then travelled with Abraham to Canaan, to Egypt and back. Like Abraham, he acquired rich flocks and herds, but his shepherds fell out with those of his uncle. Tradition tells that Lot considered himself Abraham's heir and began to treat the promised land as if it were already his own, but perhaps it was simply that there was not enough grazing land for the animals of both men.

When Abraham suggested he should leave, Lot went to live in the city of Sodom. This city was notorious not for one sin alone but also for pride, materialism, idleness and indifference to the poor (Ezekiel 16:49). Lot was living in Sodom when it was attacked by the combined army of four kings and even after Abraham had defeated them and rescued him, he returned to the city. Later, two angels disguised as men arrived to destroy the city on God's orders and Lot was the only inhabitant to offer them lodging. He must have learned from Abraham the virtue of hospitality, but his stay in Sodom had blurred his sense of priorities. That night all the other citizens surrounded Lot's house, demanding his two guests 'in order that we may know them'; and Lot offered instead his two unmarried daughters.

Lot's offer failed to satisfy the angry Sodomites. Lot and his family were only saved when the angels struck the Sodomites blind leaving them groping for the door. The angels then told Lot to prepare to leave at dawn, when the city would be destroyed. Yet Lot hesitated, and the angels had to force him and his family to leave. They told the family to flee for their lives, without stopping or looking back, but as they fled, Lot's wife looked back and was turned into a pillar of salt as burning sulphur rained down upon Sodom. To Jesus (Luke 17:32) she symbolized those who look back longingly on an ignoble past, and prize their possessions above salvation.

Lot settled in a cave together with his daughters, who, believing that they and he were the only people left alive, made their father drunk and conceived through him. They brazenly named the children of these unions Moab (from the Hebrew *me-ab* 'from father') and Ben-Ammi ('son of my kindred'). Their descendants, the Moabites and Ammonites, lived in present-day Jordan. Their relations with the Israelites were stormy, and nobody from these peoples was permitted to 'enter the congregation of the Lord' (Deuteronomy 23:3). This ban did not, however, apply to women, for Ruth, the great-grandmother of King David, was a Moabitess.

SARAH
Sarah was a woman of quick emotions, capable both of generosity and spitefulness. For years she longed for a child of her own: Isaac, her only son, was born in her old age.

Sarah (or Sarai, as she was originally named) was Abraham's wife. Nothing is said of her ancestry but in Jewish tradition she is said to be the same person as Iscah, the daughter of Abraham's youngest brother Haran.

Sarai was so beautiful that she captured the heart of Pharaoh, King of Egypt, and Abimelech, King of the Philistines (surprising in view of her age: 65 on the first occasion, 89 on the second). Both kings carried her off to live with them since Abraham pretended that she was his sister, but both times she was eventually returned to Abraham when the truth emerged.

Sarai was beautiful, but she was childless. As the years passed, God's repeated promises that Abraham would father a great nation must have sounded more and more puzzling to the ageing couple. When Abraham reached the age of 85, Sarai decided that Providence needed help, and she offered her maidservant Hagar to Abraham to bear him a child. This was an act of great self-sacrifice, but when Hagar conceived and, predictably, treated her mistress disrespectfully, Sarai turned angrily (and illogically) upon Abraham. Then, no longer caring whether Abraham would ever see his child, she treated Hagar so

harshly that she ran away. Sarai can have taken little pleasure in the fulfilment of her original plan when Hagar returned to bear Abraham his first son, Ishmael.

Thirteen years later, God announced to Abraham that the promise of the land would not pass to Ishmael after all, but to a child of Sarai, then aged 89. Her name would be changed to Sarah. In Hebrew, *sara(h)* means 'princess' and the ending *-i* means 'my'; hitherto, she had been only 'my (that is, Abraham's) princess' but now she would produce descendants through whom she would be acknowledged as 'princess' by many

HAGAR

Hagar, an Egyptian, worked as Sarah's maidservant and at Sarah's own suggestion bore Abraham's first child. A document dating from around 1400 BC from Nuzi (now in Iraq) shows that this was not unusual. It describes how a woman who had no child agreed to provide her husband with a second wife from a foreign land. However, according to the same document, the original wife could not then banish the child of the second—as Sarah proceeded to do. Abandoned in the desert with only a single bottle of water, Hagar and her son, Ishmael, were saved by an angel. In both Jewish and Arab tradition Ishmael's descendants are the Arabs.

nations. She first learned the news when three angels visited Abraham. Eavesdropping outside the tent, she laughed in disbelief thinking both herself and Abraham too old. When the angels asked Abraham why Sarah had laughed (they tactfully omitted to say that she had thought *him* too old), she tried to deny it. Abraham too had laughed on first hearing the news, but God did not rebuke him; his was apparently a laugh of sheer joy.

Disbelief turned to delight when Isaac was born. But in spite of the fact that she now had a son of her own, she still saw Abraham's first son Ishmael as a threat. The two boys played together, but Sarah made Abraham banish Ishmael and his mother, the maidservant Hagar to the desert. No more is heard of Sarah until her death, at the age of 127, reported immediately after the binding of Isaac. She was buried in the cave of Machpelah.

Melchisedek ('King of righteousness') was king of Salem (i.e. Jerusalem) and a priest of El Elyon ('God the Highest') in Abraham's time. As Abraham returned from his victory over the four great kings who had attacked Sodom, Melchisedek refreshed him with bread and wine and blessed him in the name of El Elyon. Abraham recognized that El Elyon was the God he himself worshipped and therefore gave Melchisedek a tenth of all his spoil.

Melchisedek tried to refuse this, but Abraham insisted that he take it.

Melchisedek reappears in Psalm 110:4, where a king of all Israel or of Judah is promised: 'You are a priest for ever, in the succession of Melchisedek.' For Christians, Melchisedek, who in Genesis has 'no beginning and no end', prefigures Christ.

Hagar was Sarah's maidservant. She came from Egypt, and apparently joined Abraham's household during his stay there. Sarah and Abraham were childless, so ten years after their arrival in Canaan, Sarah offered Hagar to Abraham as a substitute wife, to bear children on her behalf. This seems to have been accepted practice. Hagar soon conceived, and came to despise Sarah, who proceeded to 'afflict' her (perhaps by overworking her) until she fled towards her native Egypt. An angel met her by a spring, told her that her descendants would be too many to be counted, and urged her to return and put up with Sarah's harsh treatment. And so her son, Ishmael, was born at Abraham's home.

Later, Sarah herself bore a son, and she persuaded the reluctant Abraham to expel Hagar. He sent Hagar out into the desert, carrying Ishmael and with only one bottle of water. Rather than watch her son die of thirst, she laid him down under a bush and sat weeping nearby. Again an angel spoke to her, but this time he did not tell her to return; instead he showed her a well, so that she and her son could survive without Abraham. The wife she later chose for Ishmael was an Egyptian, like herself.

Ishmael was Abraham's oldest son. His mother was Hagar, Sarah's maidservant. Hagar, pregnant with Ishmael, ran away from her mistress. In the wilderness she was visited by an angel. The angel told her to call the baby Ishmael, which means 'God listens'. The angel said that God had listened to her cries of suffering and added that her son would be a 'wild ass of a man', at odds with everyone—a reference to the fierce independence of the desert tribes that would be descended from him.

Abraham was 86 years old when Ishmael was born, and it seemed certain that this would be his only child. However, when Ishmael was 13, God announced to Abraham that Sarah would also bear him a son, who would clearly be his heir instead of Ishmael. It was at this time that Abraham and the males of his household, including Ishmael, were circumcised.

Soon after Ishmael's new brother Isaac was weaned, Sarah saw Ishmael laughing at him (so reads the traditional Hebrew text) and asked Abraham to expel him. According to the old Greek translation, however, which may be more accurate, Ishmael was not laughing at Isaac but playing with him, and Sarah's complaint was that Ishmael was behaving as her son's equal. So Ishmael was carried away, on his mother's shoulder—surprising for a boy of about 16. In this account Ishmael appears as a child hardly older than Isaac; the passages in the Bible which refer to a thirteen-year gap between the two boys perhaps belong to a version written by a different author.

Ishmael settled in the wilderness of Paran (between the Negev and the Sinai peninsula) and became an archer. His mother found him an Egyptian wife. Long afterwards he attended the funeral of the father who had banished him.

Like Jacob, Ishmael had twelve sons, each the ancestor of a tribe. His descendants were nomads, spread over a wide area between Arabia and Egypt (Joseph was carried from Canaan to Egypt by Ishmaelite traders). Their relations with Israel were not always friendly (Psalms 83). In Jewish and Islamic tradition, Ishmael is the ancestor of the Arabs.

Isaac was the son of Abraham and Sarah. His name, meaning 'he laughs', is linked in the Bible with the laughter of his aged parents at being told by an angel that they were to have a son, though it may mean 'May he (i.e. God) smile' (upon the child). When Isaac was weaned, perhaps at the age of 3, Abraham held a great feast to celebrate. After Ishmael's banishment Isaac enjoyed his father's complete attention.

Isaac's father Abraham was a righteous, God-fearing man.

Nonetheless God decided to test his obedience. He did this by ordering Abraham to take his only son to Mount Moriah and there sacrifice him as a burnt-offering. It was three-day journey, but only when they were walking towards the mountain, with Abraham holding the knife and the fire and Isaac carrying the wood, did the boy notice that they had not brought any animal and ask what they were going to use as a sacrifice. Abraham replied that God would provide a lamb, and Isaac asked no further questions. On the mountain Abraham built an altar and bound Isaac alive to it. The old man took up the knife, and was just about to slit his son's throat, when an angel intervened and stopped the sacrifice.

What we make of Isaac's attitude to this event depends on his age. As the next chapter of Genesis opens with Sarah's death at the age of 127, and as Sarah gave birth at the age of 90, it seems he was 37. If so, he must have co-operated in being tied up, fully prepared to die, a willing martyr. However, the fact that he suspected nothing until almost the last moment and accepted Abraham's unconvincing reply, hardly suggest a grown man. On the other hand, he was old enough to undertake a three-day journey and to carry the wood up the mountain.

At the age of 40, Isaac married Rebecca, his cousin's daughter. Abraham had not wished him to marry a Canaanite woman and had sent his servant to his family in Syria to find a suitable wife. In this, too, Isaac had no say, but he loved Rebecca, finding comfort for the loss of his mother.

For 20 years the couple were childless, until his twin sons Esau and Jacob were born. God then confirmed to Isaac in a vision that he had inherited the promises made to Abraham: he would have many descendants and would inherit the land of Canaan. Like Abraham, Isaac lived a nomadic life, travelling around Canaan with his household and animals. Also like Abraham, he spent some time among the Philistines. Fearing that King Abimelech would desire his beautiful wife and kill him, he introduced her as his sister but Abimelech discovered

ISAAC
Isaac, the son of Abraham and Sarah,
continued their nomadic lifestyle but remained
in Canaan. Apparently unambitious, he seems
to have been a gentle, kindly man. In his old age
he went blind, perhaps from cataracts, and was
tricked into blessing Jacob instead of Esau.

their true relationship when he saw Isaac caressing her. He rebuked Isaac for lying to him but allowed him to stay.

Abraham had dug wells to water his animals during his stay in King Abimelech's land. Now, seeing Isaac's flocks and herds becoming bigger and bigger, the Philistines were envious and stopped up the wells to prevent Isaac from using them. Isaac reopened them, restoring the names Abraham had given them. The Philistines may have acted for religious reasons as well as out of envy. Place names such as 'the Lord sees' (Genesis 22:14) suggest religious lessons which the Philistines wanted to suppress. Eventually Isaac moved on south-eastwards to Beersheba.

When Isaac was old and blind, he wanted to bless his favourite son Esau, the hunter, and asked him to prepare a tasty meal of fresh venison for the occasion. Rebecca overheard, and persuaded Jacob, Esau's twin, to put on his brother's clothes and impersonate him before Esau returned from the hunt. Jacob took the food to his father and Isaac suspiciously asked who he was. 'Esau your first-born', came the reply. Isaac, unconvinced asked how his son had found the game so quickly. 'Because the Lord your God granted me success,' lied Jacob. The old man recognized Jacob's voice, yet the hands, which Rebecca had covered in goatskin, felt like the rough, hairy hands of Esau. Isaac ate the meal, not realizing that it was goat's meat cooked by Rebecca. Then he kissed Jacob and, reassured by the scent of Esau's clothes, finally blessed him. Just after Jacob left, Esau himself entered. Isaac, discovering the deception, trembled with shock and bewilderment. Yet, despite Esau's pleas, the blessing could not be taken back or repeated.

This episode can hardly have made Isaac any more fond of Jacob, but Rebecca reminded him that Esau had taken local heathen wives, and recommended that Jacob should be encouraged to marry within the family. Isaac agreed and, warming to Jacob, also gave him a further blessing which had not been included in the earlier one intended for Esau: Jacob was to inherit the land of Canaan.

REBECCA
The beautiful Rebecca was brought from Syria to marry her cousin Isaac, to prevent him from marrying out of the tribe. She was chosen when she innocently showed charity to a stranger at the well, but later proved that she was capable of scheming to achieve her own ends.

Isaac died aged 180, and was buried by Esau and Jacob. Unlike both his father Abraham and his son Jacob, he never left the promised land. Although his life was less adventurous than theirs, he was the vital link between them.

Rebecca was the beautiful daughter of Bethuel (the son of Abraham's younger brother Nahor) and looked after her father's sheep. One day when she was fetching water at the spring, she offered some to a stranger, and even drew water for all his camels. The stranger at once gave her golden ornaments. When the stranger explained to her parents and to her brother Laban that he was Abraham's servant Eliezer, and wanted her as Isaac's bride, the family decided for her: 'Take her and go!' The only question put to Rebecca herself was whether she was willing to leave immediately. She consented and left with her nurse Deborah and several maidservants.

For twenty years Rebecca was childless, and when she eventually did conceive, her pregnancy was so painful that she went to ask God the reason. She learned that she was carrying the ancestors of two nations already at war even before they were born.

While Isaac loved the elder son Esau, Rebecca's favourite was Jacob, the younger boy, who kept her company at home. It was she who persuaded Jacob to impersonate his brother and obtain Isaac's blessing—as if to make up for her parents' earlier interference in her own life. After the deception had succeeded, she won Isaac round to Jacob by reminding him that Esau had taken heathen wives. At the same time she advised Jacob to flee to her brother Laban in Syria, to escape Esau's murderous wrath. She told Jacob that he need stay there only 'a few days'; in fact she was never to see him again.

The Bible records the death of Rebecca's nurse, Deborah, but not Rebecca's own.

Eliezer was Abraham's chief steward. He is named only at Genesis 15:2, where Abraham complains that, despite God's promises, this stranger, apparently from Damascus, is his prospective heir. No doubt he was the 'servant' whom Abraham sent to Syria to find Isaac a wife. Reaching Nahor's city, he stood by the spring, and decided that any girl who offered water from her pitcher not only to him but also to his camels would be a good wife for Isaac. A charitable girl, he seems to have reasoned, would not imagine that he was lazy, but disabled, and would understand that he could not water his camels without help.

When the first girl who came to the spring fulfilled the requirements exactly, he gave her golden bracelets and a golden nose-ring, and then asked her name. She told him that she was Rebecca, a granddaughter of Nahor. At her parent's house he recounted the story, tactfully saying that he had asked her name before giving her ornaments. The family approved the marriage but wanted her to remain with them a while longer before leaving. Eliezer, however, rather than risk any change of heart, brought her immediately to Isaac.

Laban was Rebecca's brother. (The name has been associated with *lebana*, 'moon'.) His sister returned from the spring one day wearing gold ornaments which had been given to her, by a stranger (see *Rebecca; Eliezer*). Laban ran and invited the man to his home. The man turned out to be Eliezer, Abraham's servant, and he asked if she would marry Abraham's son Isaac. Laban approved the match at once, butting in before their father.

Laban had two daughters: the dull-eyed Leah and the beautiful Rachel. When Jacob came to Harran to find a wife from among his own people (see *Jacob*), he offered to tend Laban's flocks for seven years to win 'Rachel thy younger daughter'. The careful description sounds as if he half expected to be cheated. Laban replied: 'It is better that I should give her to you than to anyone else'—not committing himself, but coming so close to a promise that Jacob could not press him further without seeming rude. At the end of the seven years, Laban made the wedding feast, but secretly substituted Leah for Rachel. When in the morning Jacob reproached him (understandably after seven years!), Laban explained that in his country the younger daughter could not marry before the elder. His justification was, perhaps, that no one would want to marry Leah, and so he had done his best for Jacob by letting him marry her himself. It was permissible, however, for a man to take a second wife and Jacob was able to marry Rachel as soon as the festive week was over.

Part of the bargain, however, was that Jacob had to work seven more years for Laban. Jacob stayed on to work for Laban when the seven years were over. Laban told Jacob to name his wages and Jacob asked for all the black lambs and the speckled and spotted sheep and goats, from Laban's flocks. Laban agreed, but then removed all the animals of this description and gave them to his sons to look after. But he had not reckoned with Jacob's tricks for making sheep and goats produce speckled and spotted young (see *Jacob*): within six years Jacob had grown rich at Laban's expense, even though Laban had varied the agreement ten times.

Eventually Laban, who now had sons of his own, became so hostile that Jacob and his family ran away secretly. Laban set out in pursuit, not least because Rachel (without Jacob's knowledge) had stolen Laban's household gods.

When Laban caught up with the runaways he demanded these back, complaining loudly at Jacob's deception. Jacob allowed Laban to search his camp, but Rachel had hidden the gods in her camel's howdah, on which she remained seated. She prevented Laban from searching the howdah by telling her father: 'The common condition of woman is upon me.' So Laban found nothing. Jacob reproached him bitterly and, at Laban's suggestion, they agreed to set up a heap of stones, called Galed, as a boundary between them.

Esau was the elder of the twins born to Isaac and Rebecca. At birth he was 'ruddy and hairy all over like a hair cloak'. He grew up to be an 'expert hunter', and became his father Isaac's favourite. One day Esau returned exhausted from his hunting, and asked his brother Jacob for some lentil broth.

Jacob demanded in exchange Esau's rights as first-born, and Esau agreed, saying: 'I am on the point of death; what use is the birthright to me?' It seems strange, on the face of it, that Esau should be hungry enough to sell his birthright for broth. On the other hand we can only guess at just what the birthright entailed since it is not said to have carried any advantages, either material or spiritual.

Esau was devoted to Isaac. When attending upon him he would wear his finest clothes. Although he once offended him when, at the age of 40, he married local wives, he nevertheless remained Isaac's favourite son; and, to please his father, he even took an additional wife, from his own family.

When Jacob stole his blessing (see *Jacob*), Esau broke down in tears. Isaac blessed him as best he could: his land would be fertile, but he would live by the sword; he would serve Jacob, but free himself in the end. Esau so hated Jacob that he looked forward to Isaac's death, when he planned to kill his brother—who wisely fled, on his mother's advice.

Esau later moved from Canaan to the hill country of Seir, south (and south-east) of the Dead Sea. According to Genesis 36:7, his reason was that Canaan was too small for his own and Jacob's flocks; yet he had already settled in Seir while Jacob was away (Genesis 32:3), perhaps disgusted by the way his family had treated him.

Twenty years later Esau heard that Jacob was on his way back, and set out to meet him. Soon he met Jacob's messengers, bringing gifts of flocks and herds. Perhaps he had long forgiven his brother; perhaps the gifts won him over—we do not know; but when they finally met, Esau ran and embraced Jacob, kissing him and weeping with him—the most emotional greeting in the

ESAU
Esau was a skilled hunter and his father Isaac's favourite. He seems to have been a straightforward and impetuous man, capable both of quick anger and of generosity. When Jacob cheated him out of his inheritance, he first wept, then planned to kill him. Yet when the two met years later, Esau ran to embrace Jacob in the most emotional greeting of the Bible. Esau's descendants became the Edomites, one of Israel's powerful neighbours in Canaan.

whole Bible. Addressing Jacob naturally as 'my brother' (while Jacob less sincerely called him 'my lord'), he first declined the gifts, but was persuaded to accept them. He invited Jacob to travel on with him. Jacob replied that he could not travel as fast and would join his brother in Seir; but he never did, and Esau was probably not surprised. They met again only at Isaac's funeral.

Jacob was the younger twin born to Isaac and Rebecca. His name comes from the Hebrew *akeb*, 'heel', because at birth he was holding Esau's heel, as if to prevent his being born first. Unlike Esau the hunter, Jacob stayed at home, and became his mother's favourite. The Bible calls him a plain, straightforward man but Esau might have disagreed. The bargain struck by Jacob—lentil broth in exchange for Esau's birthright—suggests that he was in fact quite calculating.

When his mother ordered him to impersonate Esau and steal his blessing (see *Isaac*), Jacob first objected that Isaac might feel his skin. Once his mother had dressed him, however, he impersonated Esau convincingly, replying, when Isaac asked how he could have returned so quickly with the food, that God had helped him. Isaac blessed him with dew from heaven, richness of the earth, corn and wine in plenty, and mastery over his brothers (including, apparently, all Abraham's descendants). Then Jacob rushed out without a word. Esau bitterly reinterpreted Jacob's name as 'he that supplants' (*yaakob*). Soon Rebecca had to warn Jacob to flee to her brother Laban, for Esau was 'panting' to kill him. Isaac, too, advised Jacob to visit Laban, in order to take a wife from his own people. He also blessed him again, so that God would give him numerous descendants and pass to him the blessing of Abraham, including the Promised Land.

On the first night of his journey, Jacob dreamed of a ladder (or stairway) reaching up to heaven, with angels going up and down. In the dream God made a promise which confirmed Isaac's blessing: the land on which Jacob lay would belong to his descendants, who would be as numerous as the dust

JACOB
Although the Bible calls Jacob a plain or guileless man, this is not always borne out by his actions. He seems to have been both easily led and easily deceived, becoming successful through cunning as much as through hard work. He was given the name Israel by God and the twelve tribes of Israel were descended from his children.

of the earth, and God would guard him and ultimately bring him back to Canaan. In awe, Jacob called the place Bethel 'house of God'. He vowed to worship God there on his return, and to offer him a tenth of his produce.

When he arrived in Harran, the shepherds at the well pointed out Laban's daughter Rachel, on her way to water her sheep. The well was stopped with a great stone which could be removed only by all the shepherds

together; this may mean not that the stone was heavy but that the well was common property. As soon as Jacob saw the beautiful Rachel, however, he rolled the stone away, watered her sheep, and then, before she knew who he was, kissed her. She ran to tell her father Laban, who invited him to stay.

Jacob offered to work seven years to win Rachel and loved her so much that the time passed like a few days. At the end he asked Laban, again rather directly: 'Give me my wife...that I may go in unto her' (Genesis 29:21). The day after the wedding, however, he discovered that his veiled bride was Rachel's elder sister, Leah. When he protested, Laban replied that in his country the younger daughter could not be married before the elder—whatever tricks Jacob had played in his own home to supplant his brother. When the week's festivities were over, Jacob finally married Rachel, but had to work seven more years in payment.

Jacob still loved only Rachel, even though she was barren. Meanwhile Leah bore him six sons and a daughter, and both wives gave him their handmaids as concubines. The handmaids each bore him two sons. Finally, at the end of Jacob's second seven-year term, Rachel's first child, Joseph, was born. Jacob now told Laban that he wished to leave, but Laban's flocks had thrived so well in Jacob's care that Laban pressed Jacob to work on. Jacob asked as wages all the speckled and spotted goats, as well as the black lambs. Laban agreed but made sure that in future Jacob only had white animals to look after. Jacob, however, took some sticks and peeled their bark off in stripes. He then placed them near the watering-troughs, where the animals mated. By some magic, this made the flocks produce striped or spotted young. Jacob did not put out the striped sticks when the weaker animals mated; these he left for Laban. (Genesis 31:10—12 gives a different version: although Laban left Jacob white animals only, the females were miraculously mounted by speckled and spotted males.) Jacob's deceiver thus got his deserts.

After six years Laban had become so hostile that Jacob left secretly with his household for Canaan. Laban overtook him in Gilead, east of the Jordan, complained that Jacob had not given him a chance to take leave of his daughters, and accused Jacob of stealing his household gods. These had in fact been stolen by Rachel, unknown to Jacob, who challenged his father-in-law to search the camp. Rachel successfully hid them in her howdah (see *Rachel*) and Jacob took Laban to task for rummaging through his property. He

pointed out, too, that he had kept his departure secret because he believed that even after twenty years of hard, honest work Laban could very well send him away empty-handed. In the end they set up a heap of stones, each agreeing to keep to his own side, and Jacob left Laban with a promise never to ill-treat his daughters.

As he approached Canaan, Jacob hoped to make peace with Esau, and sent messengers to his new home in Seir, south of the Dead Sea. They reported back that Esau was on his way to meet him with 400 followers, and the terrified Jacob sent ahead droves of animals as gifts. That night an angel attacked Jacob. They wrestled until dawn, and Jacob suffered an injured thigh. He won eventually and refused to release the angel unless he blessed him. The angel agreed to this, and also renamed him Israel—'he that strove with God'. No reason is given for the attack; the angel seems to have served as Jacob's sparring partner, allowing him to win in order to boost his morale for the encounter with Esau. At daybreak, Esau appeared and Jacob went forward, bowing seven times. When Esau ran and embraced him, Jacob wept with relief; he had not dared hope for such good luck. It was 'like seeing the face of God'. But when Esau invited Jacob to join him in Seir, Jacob replied that with his young children and new-born lambs he preferred to follow at his own slow pace. As soon as Esau left, Jacob took the opposite direction. Esau does nothing in this episode to justify Jacob's terror and distrust; but then his feelings are hardly surprising in view of what he had done to his older brother in the past.

As Jacob's children grew, new problems beset him. He settled near Shechem, where his only daughter, Dinah, was raped and imprisoned by the local prince's son. His sons Simeon and Levi massacred all the Shechemites in revenge, and Jacob hastily travelled southwards. Near Bethlehem, Rachel died giving birth to his youngest son, Benjamin. Then his eldest son, Reuben, slept with Jacob's concubine, Bilhah. Jacob's greatest sorrow, however, came through his favouritism towards Joseph,

for whom he made a royal robe. One day Joseph told Jacob and all the brothers how he had seen in a dream the sun, the moon and eleven stars bow down to him. Jacob told him not to be arrogant, and played down the dream by remarking that the moon symbolized Joseph's mother, who was already dead. Nevertheless the episode remained in his mind.

One day Jacob sent Joseph to Shechem to see how his other sons and their flocks were faring. That evening the brothers returned without Joseph, but carrying his cloak, soaked in blood. Jacob did not know that Joseph had been sold as a slave, and that his brothers had dipped his coveted cloak in the blood of a goat. It was a fitting punishment for the man who had made use of a goat to deceive his own father (see *Isaac*). Jacob, certain that Joseph had been killed by some wild animal, could not forgive himself for sending him on that fateful journey and he went into permanent mourning.

For the next twenty years Jacob clung to Benjamin, the sole survivor of Rachel's family. Then a terrible famine drove his ten eldest sons to Egypt to buy grain. They returned with the news that the Egyptian vizier had interrogated them as spies, and on hearing that they had a younger brother, had demanded to see him before he would sell them any grain. Jacob refused to let Benjamin go; but when the grain was exhausted and he saw his little grandchildren starving, he agreed to entrust Benjamin to Judah. He gave his sons some Canaanite delicacies to win favour with the vizier and reluctantly said goodbye to them.

Sooner than he had expected, they returned to inform him that Joseph was alive, and was in fact none other than the vizier of Egypt. Jacob could only believe the news when he saw the wagons sent by Joseph to carry him to safety in Egypt. On this journey, too, God appeared to him by night, promising that he would be the founder of a great nation in Egypt, and that his descendants would one day return to Canaan. But his years of mourning had taken their toll. When Joseph rode out to greet him, the old man's first words were: 'Now I am ready to die.' He was soon presented to Pharaoh, who politely asked his age; Jacob answered that his 135 years had been 'few and evil'.

Despite his words to Joseph, Jacob lived another seventeen years. On his deathbed, he made Joseph swear to bury him in the cave of Machpelah. He then assigned Joseph's sons, Ephraim and Manasseh, equal rank with Jacob's own sons in the division of the land; Joseph would thus receive a double portion, as if he were the first born. Finally he summoned all his sons to be blessed (though in fact he denounced his three eldest sons, Reuben, Simeon and Levi), and then passed away. The Egyptians embalmed him, and mourned him for seventy days; as a further honour, all Pharaoh's courtiers accompanied the long funeral procession to Canaan.

Leah was Jacob's first wife, the elder daughter of Laban. She had dull eyes, unlike her beautiful sister Rachel and Jacob did not love her. To make up for it, God made her fertile. She longed to be loved by her husband and this is reflected in the names of her first three sons. To her, Reuben meant that God had 'looked upon my humiliation' (*ra-a be-onyi*); Simeon was so called because God 'heard (*shama*) that I am unloved'; Levi's name expressed her hope that 'now my husband shall be joined (*yilave*) to me'. She also bore Judah, Issachar and Zebulun (on whose birth she said: 'This time my husband will honour me—*yizbeleni*—for I have borne him six sons'), as well as Jacob's only daughter, Dinah—all within seven years. She gave Jacob her maidservant Zilpah as an additional wife, perhaps because she sensed that Jacob had to have as many children as possible in order to fulfil God's promise that within a few generations his descendants would possess the land. Zilpah bore Gad ('fortune') and Asher ('happy'). Yet, to the end, when Jacob said 'my wife', he meant only Rachel (Genesis 44:27). When Rachel once asked Leah for some mandrakes (aphrodisiac plants) that Reuben had gathered, Leah voiced her resentment: 'Is it not enough to have

LEAH
Leah was Jacob's first wife but not his first choice. In fact Jacob thought he had married her beautiful sister and only discovered the truth when the marriage was completed; presumably the bride was heavily veiled during the ceremony. She is described as having dull or weak eyes.

taken away my husband?'(Genesis 30:15). Rachel may have been the favourite wife, but Leah's descendants played a far greater part in Israel's history. They included Moses, Aaron and the priests, as well as David and the kings. She died before Jacob, who was later buried beside her in the cave of Machpeleh—away from Rachel at last.

Rachel was Jacob's first love and second wife, the younger daughter of Laban.

He met her as soon as he arrived in Harran, by the well where she was tending her father's sheep. (Her name means 'ewe', whereas her sister Leah's name may have meant 'cow'). She was graceful and beautiful and Jacob was outraged when, after working seven years for her hand, he found himself married instead to Leah. He married Rachel a week later. Jacob loved only Rachel, yet she was childless, and demanded: 'Give me children, or I shall

34

die'(Genesis 30:1). Jacob reacted angrily, partly at her implication that motherhood was a woman's sole purpose. She gave Jacob her handmaid Bilhah as a substitute wife. Bilhah gave birth to Dan ('vindicator') and Naphtali ('cunning'). Rachel once asked Leah for some mandrakes, which were believed to promote fertility, in exchange for her turn to spend the night with Jacob; but Leah conceived her sixth son on her extra night while Rachel remained barren until long afterwards, when Jacob's other wives had already presented him with ten children. Then she finally bore Joseph, saying that God had removed (*asaph*) her shame, and praying that he would add (*yoseph*) another son.

When Jacob escaped from Laban, Rachel stole Laban's household gods (see *Laban*), perhaps retaining some belief in their power. Alternatively, she may have wanted to make sure that her father's wealth would be inherited by Jacob, rather than by one of the sons who had been born after Jacob had married Laban's daughters. When there were rival claimants, possession of the household gods marked the lawful heir. Jacob promptly buried Laban's gods when he discovered the theft. Rachel was granted a second son, but died in childbirth and was buried in Bethlehem. She had named the child Ben-oni, 'son of my travail' but his father renamed him Benjamin, 'son of the right hand'.

The twelve tribes

Reuben ('Look! A son!') was Jacob's eldest son, born to the unloved Leah. As first-born he had most to lose when Jacob showed his preference for Reuben's half-brother Joseph (such rejection of the first-born son was later forbidden in Deuteronomy 21:17). Yet, when the other brothers wanted to kill Joseph and throw his body into a pit, it was Reuben who warned them not to harm him, and suggested that they throw him into the pit alive. Reuben intended to rescue him later, and was distraught when he found he had disappeared. He once slept with Bilhah, Jacob's concubine, probably not out of lust but to demonstrate his right of

RACHEL
Jacob's love for Rachel is one of the most moving stories in the Old Testament. The first seven years he worked for her father seemed 'but a few days for the love he had for her' and the fact that she had no children made no difference to him. For years Rachel watched bitterly as her sister Leah, and their two handmaids all bore Jacob's children. Behind the brief details of the births it is easy to see her increasing despair. At last, however, she had a son of her own, Joseph.

In Egypt, Joseph kept Simeon hostage while the other brothers went home to fetch Benjamin; Jacob cared so little for Simeon that he delayed their return to Egypt as long as he could. On his deathbed Jacob declared that Simeon and Levi would be 'scattered in Israel'; the tribe descended from Simeon became the smallest during the wilderness wanderings (Numbers 26:14), and is not even mentioned in Moses' last blessing (Deuteronomy 33).

Levi was the third son of Jacob and Leah. He is mentioned (outside genealogies) only in the Shechem incident (see *Simeon*). His tribe was 'scattered in Israel', but in a different sense from Simeon's; his descendants, the Levites, served as priests and teachers throughout the country.

Judah was the fourth son of Jacob and Leah. His name comes from the Hebrew *odeh*, 'praise', because when he was born his mother praised God. He was the natural leader among the brothers, even though Reuben was the first-born and Joseph the father's favourite. When Joseph was in the pit (see *Joseph*), Judah suggested that he should not be left to die but sold to a passing caravan. Later, during a great famine, the Egyptian vizier (they did not yet know he was Joseph) had refused to sell corn to the brothers without seeing Benjamin. Jacob refused to let him go, and it was Judah who changed Jacob's mind by pointing out that their children would otherwise starve, and by offering to take personal responsibility for Benjamin.

In Egypt, Joseph trapped Benjamin and proposed to keep him as a slave (see *Joseph*), and again Judah was the spokesman, offering himself in Benjamin's place. It was Judah's plea that finally moved Joseph to reveal his identity.

Genesis 38 relates an earlier episode, soon after Joseph's sale. Judah parted from his brothers and married a Canaanite wife, who bore him three sons. The first (Er) was wicked, and was struck down by God, so that the younger son (Onan) was obliged by custom to marry his widow, Tamar, and

JUDAH
Although he was not Jacob's eldest son, Judah was the natural leader of the brothers and acted as their spokesman and decision maker. Jacob accurately prophesied on his deathbed that Judah's descendants would become the major tribe of Israel. When the Israelites divided the land of Canaan among the tribes, Judah's tribe drew the first lot and Israel's greatest kings were among his descendants.

succession. Reuben went with his brothers to Egypt during the famine and returned with the vizier's request to see Benjamin. When Jacob would not allow Benjamin to go, Reuben offered to guarantee his safe return, saying that Jacob could kill both Reuben's own sons if he failed. Jacob did not bother to reply. On his deathbed Jacob called him, very appropriately, 'unstable as water', and told him he would suffer for sleeping with Bilhah (Genesis 49:4).

Simeon was the second son of Jacob and Leah. With his brother Levi, he avenged the rape of his sister Dinah. Her brothers agreed to let her marry her attacker on one condition: that he and his people be circumcised. But then Simeon and Levi, apparently acting alone, slaughtered them all on the third, most painful day after the circumcision. Jacob condemned them both for their cruel treachery, as well as for putting the family in danger of revenge attacks.

JOSEPH

The longed-for son of Rachel grew up talented, handsome and spoiled by his loving parents. He annoyed his brothers by boasting of dreams which seemed to show he was their superior and eventually they sent him into slavery. In Egypt he proved himself an able administrator and rose to a high position in Pharaoh's court. When he died, Joseph asked for his bones to be returned to Canaan. Many years later, the returning Israelites carried out his wish.

raise children in his brother's name. Onan married her, but prevented conception artificially, rather than father children for his dead brother. For this sin he, too, died. Judah told Tamar to wait until his third son Shela reached manhood. However, he did not want to risk this son's life, too, so the marriage was postponed. Determined to raise a child from Judah's house, Tamar went to Timnath, where Judah was due to shear his sheep. She disguised herself as a prostitute and seduced him. He

offered her a kid from his flock in payment for her services. She agreed, but asked for his seal and its cord as a pledge and then disappeared.

Three months later, Judah heard that Tamar was pregnant, and ordered her to be burned. When she produced his seal and cord, however, he admitted his guilt in keeping Shela from her. She bore Judah twin sons, Perez and Zerah, and when Jacob's household joined Joseph in Egypt, Perez already had two sons of his own.

Joseph was the first born of Jacob's favourite wife Rachel and inherited her good looks. When he was 17, he looked after Jacob's sheep along with the sons of Bilhah and Zilpah. The young Joseph made himself unpopular by slandering his brothers to his father. They liked him even less when Jacob made him a coat of many colours (or possibly a long-sleeved coat) marking him for leadership: the only other person whose garment is described by the same Hebrew phrase was a princess

(2 Samuel 13:18). The brothers' hatred and jealousy deepened when Joseph dreamed that he and they were binding sheaves, and that their sheaves suddenly bowed down to his. When he reported it, they retorted: 'Do you think you will reign over us?' Later he told them another dream in which the sun, moon and eleven stars bowed down before him. Clearly not a master of tact, the insufferable lad told this dream again, this time in the presence of Jacob (Genesis 37:9, 10) who rebuked him: 'Shall I and your mother and brothers bow down before you?'

One day his brothers went to Shechem to feed the sheep and Jacob sent Joseph to see if all was well. When he arrived, the brothers tore off his coat and threw him into a pit without any water to drink. While they were away eating, however, he was rescued by some passing merchants. They sold him to other merchants, who in turn sold him to a third group, who brought him to Egypt.

In Egypt Joseph was sold to Potiphar, captain of the guard. Potiphar found Joseph so efficient in his work that he put him in charge of all his household. Joseph did a good job, taking care of everything for his master, so that all Potiphar had to worry about was 'the food which he ate'. But all was not to go smoothly for long. Joseph was a handsome man and Potiphar's wife was attracted to him. One day she invited him to sleep with her. Joseph refused, not wanting to betray his master or offend God.

Day after day Potiphar's wife tried to sway Joseph, but without success. One day he came in to do his work when the men of the house all happened to be out (Genesis 39:11). She grabbed his coat and asked him again to sleep with her. Joseph fled, leaving the coat in her hand. She raised the alarm and told her servants, and later her husband, that Joseph had attacked her but fled when she shouted, leaving his coat behind. Potiphar threw Joseph into the royal prison. Joseph was now again in a pit—as he described the prison (Genesis 40:15)—but his ability soon placed him in charge of all the prisoners. These included the chief cup-bearer and the

chief baker. One day they told Joseph that they had had disturbing dreams the previous night and Joseph offered to interpret them. The cup-bearer had seen a three-branched vine; from the grapes he squeezed wine into a cup that he handed to Pharaoh. This meant, Joseph told him, that in three days Pharaoh would 'lift up his head' and restore him to his post. The baker had seen himself carrying three baskets on his head; the top basket was full of bread and cakes, which the birds were eating. Joseph's interpretation was that in three days Pharaoh would 'lift up his head' too—literally, and hang him. The interpretations differed because in the dreams the cup-bearer was doing his job, while the baker was being prevented. Three days later, Pharaoh celebrated his birthday and treated both men as Joseph had predicted.

Joseph had asked the cup-bearer to speak to Pharaoh on his behalf, but the ungrateful man forgot him. Two years later Pharaoh dreamed of seven fat cows that were swallowed by seven lean cows and then similarly of seven full and seven thin ears of corn. Pharaoh's counsellors could not offer any interpretation; and then the cup-bearer remembered the 'young Hebrew slave' (as he unflatteringly described Joseph) who had correctly interpreted his dream in prison. Joseph, now aged 30, was hastily brought out of the dungeon, heard the dreams and worked out their meaning step by step. The two dreams were identical (Genesis 41:25). Each cow or ear of corn symbolized a year; the lean cows and the thin ears, a rarity in Egypt, must indicate famine; both dreams then meant that seven years of plenty would be followed by seven years of famine. Joseph was too enterprising to stop there; he politely advised Pharaoh to appoint a wise man to store the surplus of the fat years. Pharaoh immediately accepted Joseph's interpretation—as if deep down he had known the meaning all along—and appointed him vizier, second to himself alone. So at the age of 30 Joseph found himself wielding power over all of Egypt. He was now dressed in fine linen, and a golden collar, and he rode in the viceroy's chariot. Asenath, an

Egyptian priest's daughter, became his wife.

During the seven years of plenty, Joseph bought up the surplus grain for Pharaoh and set up huge stores. In this period, he had two sons: Manasseh, meaning 'causing to forget (my sufferings and my father's house)', and Ephraim, 'fruitfulness'. The famine that followed was not confined to Egypt, and 'all the world' came to buy grain from Joseph (Genesis 41:57). Among the prospective buyers he recognized his ten brothers; only Benjamin had remained at home. Joseph did not reveal his identity and accused them of being spies. They answered that they were all sons of one father—who would hardly have risked ten sons as spies—and that their youngest brother was at home while a twelfth brother 'is not' (Genesis 42:13). He imprisoned them for three days, and then released all except Simeon, warning that although he would sell them corn this time, he would not see them again unless they proved their story by producing their youngest brother. Before they left he replaced their money in their corn sacks, to bewilder them all the more.

About a year later the brothers returned with Benjamin. Joseph told his steward to invite them to his home, and then appeared, asked after their father, blessed Benjamin, and invited them to eat. They were astounded when he placed them in order of age: his ten elder brothers had been born within just seven years, so this would not have been easy. They drank and became merry, and then Joseph ordered his steward to fill their sacks with corn and again to replace their money (perhaps to show that they were guests). He also ordered the steward to hide his divining cup in Benjamin's sack. Soon after the brothers left, the steward arrested them and duly found the cup. The brothers offered themselves to Joseph as slaves, but he only wanted the thief: the other brothers he released to return 'in peace' to their father (Genesis 44:17).

Why did Joseph put his brothers—and his father—through such torment? Perhaps he wanted to give them a chance to repent of their sin in selling him. Repentance is clear only when the sinner faces the same temptation to which he once succumbed, and overcomes it. Joseph had set up a situation where the brothers could with every excuse abandon their father's favourite son. But this time they did not. Judah told Joseph that without Benjamin their father would die.

Joseph had wept secretly before (42:24, 43:30), but now he broke down and told his astonished brothers: 'I am Joseph.' He forgave them for selling him; it was God's plan, he said, to prevent world starvation. He instructed them to return home and to bring the whole family to Egypt, for five years of famine were still to come. He could not resist adding that they should tell their father of all his glory, and not quarrel on the way (45:13, 24).

Joseph settled his family in Goshen, in the north-eastern corner of Egypt, and continued to sell corn to the starving Egyptians. When they had exhausted their money and also their cattle, they sold themselves and their fields to Pharaoh. Joseph allowed them seed corn but only on condition that they gave one-fifth of the produce to Pharaoh.

Joseph supported his family in Egypt to the end of his life, even though his brothers feared he might finally take revenge on them when Jacob died. He died at what by patriarchal standards was the early age of 110. His body was embalmed and placed in the coffin and his brothers promised that their descendants would one day carry it back to Canaan. It was in fact carried by Moses himself (Exodus 13:19) and laid to rest in a plot that Jacob had bought near Shechem (Joshua 24:32).

Dinah ('judgement') was Jacob's only daughter, born to Leah. One day she ventured out of Jacob's camp (then pitched near Shechem) to meet other girls, but the local prince's son, also called Shechem, found her and raped her. It seems, however, that his intentions became honourable for he came to Jacob with his father Hamor to discuss marriage. Hamor proposed that Jacob's family should intermarry freely with his own citizens, and receive full

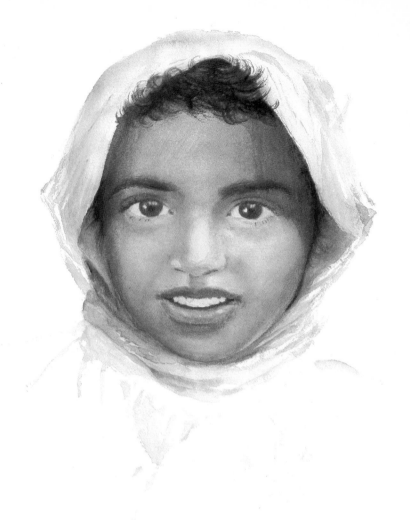

BENJAMIN
Benjamin was Jacob's youngest son. His mother, Rachel, died when he was born, and Jacob kept Benjamin at home, the favourite of his old age.

citizens' rights; Shechem added that he would pay any sum to marry Dinah. Jacob's sons agreed, on condition that all males in Shechem underwent circumcision. Jacob himself was present but was apparently too disgusted to speak.

Three days after the circumcision, when the Shechemites were at their weakest, Simeon and Levi slaughtered every male and plundered the city. Jacob condemned their act but they were unrepentant: 'Should he treat our sister as a harlot?' The Bible says no more of her.

Benjamin was Jacob's youngest son, born of Jacob's favourite wife, Rachel, who died when he was born. After Joseph disappeared, Jacob had only Benjamin left of his beloved wife's family and his father kept him at home. But Jacob was forced to let him go with his brothers to Egypt to prevent the family from starving (see *Joseph*). Benjamin's usual image is that of an overprotected child, but he was a father of ten when Jacob's family came down to Egypt (Genesis 46:21), and is called by his father a 'ravening wolf' (Genesis 49:27).

POTIPHAR
The captain of the guard at Pharaoh's palace bought Joseph from traders and trusted him sufficiently to put him in control of all his household affairs.

Manasseh and **Ephraim** were Joseph's sons. When the aged Jacob blessed them, Joseph positioned them so that Jacob would place his right hand on the head of Manasseh, the elder. Jacob, however, crossed his hands, laying his right hand on Ephraim. When Joseph tried to correct him, he explained that Ephraim would be the greater. The blessing was that Israelite fathers would bless their own sons that they should grow up like Ephraim and Manasseh. Just what they would admire in Ephraim and Manasseh is not stated; perhaps it was their uncompromising loyalty both to their ancestral faith and to the gentile society in which they lived.

Potiphar was captain of the guard in Egypt at the time Joseph was sold into slavery. His name means 'he whom the Ra (sun god) gave'. Many translations call him a eunuch but the Hebrew word may mean only 'courtier'. Potiphar bought Joseph from the traders and put him in charge of his household. Joseph worked well but Potiphar's wife attempted to seduce him and when he refused, complained to her husband that she had been attacked. Potiphar threw Joseph into prison—a surprisingly lenient punishment. Perhaps he did not believe his wife's story.

The Book of Exodus

The Book of Exodus and the Book of Numbers tell the history of the Israelites on their journey from Egypt to the land of Canaan, the land which God had promised long ago to the descendants of Abraham, Isaac and Jacob. By around the thirteenth century BC, the Israelites who had settled in Egypt during the famine years, had increased so greatly that the Pharaoh felt threatened by them. Unsure of their loyalty to Egypt, he took steps to keep them under control and reduce their numbers. First he made them into slaves, and when, even under these conditions, they continued to multiply, he ordered that all male babies should be killed. Still the Israelites continued to grow in numbers and the exasperated Pharaoh issued a new decree: all male babies born to Israelite women were to be thrown into the Nile. It was into these conditions that Moses was born.

Moses and his family

Miriam was Moses's sister. She is first mentioned after his birth (Exodus 2), even though she was older. When his mother hid Moses among the rushes of the Nile, to save him from Pharaoh's command that all Israelite boys be slain, Miriam waited and watched. As soon as Pharaoh's daughter found him, recognized that he was an Israelite child and took pity on him, Miriam ran over

MIRIAM
Miriam was the older sister of Moses and seems to have shared his strength of character. When Moses was born, Miriam helped to save his life and after the crossing of the Red Sea she led the women of Israel in a dance of triumph.

41

and offered to find an Israelite
wet-nurse to look after him until he was
weaned. Pharaoh's daughter gratefully
agreed and Miriam produced her own
mother. Miriam is next mentioned at
the Red Sea, after the Israelites had
crossed safely and their Egyptian
pursuers had been drowned (see *Moses*).
Moses and all Israel celebrated in song
(Exodus 15) and Miriam took her drum
and led out all the women to dance and
to 'sing unto the Lord, for he is indeed
exalted; horse and rider he has cast into
the sea.' In that passage she is called a
prophetess.

During the wilderness wanderings
(Numbers 12) she became envious of
Moses's superior prophetic powers, and
complained about him to her brother
Aaron. For reasons never stated, they
resented Moses's marriage to an
Ethiopian woman. Their reported words
show that jealousy was their real motive:
'Did the Lord speak through Moses

MOSES

*Moses was brought up as a prince at the
Egyptian court and, somewhat reluctantly,
became the Israelites' spokesman, demanding
their release from slavery. His task did not end
when the Israelites were freed. Before they could
hope to conquer the Promised Land, they had to
be fully prepared both physically and spiritually.*

*Moses, the intermediary between God and the
discontented Israelites, explained the new laws
of belief and behaviour which were to
distinguish them from their pagan neighbours.
Usually steadfast, patient and faithful, a
moment of anger and doubt deprived him of the
right to enter the Promised Land.*

alone? Did he not also speak through us?' God summoned them to the tabernacle and told them that there was no other prophet to whom he spoke to so directly ('face to face') as to Moses. He infected Miriam with leprosy for seven days, for which time the people halted their journey. Apparently she never married. Like her brothers, she died just before the entry to the Promised Land.

Moses was the youngest child of the Levite Amram and his aunt Jochebed (Exodus 6:20). He had a brother, Aaron and a sister, Miriam. His father apparently never saw him and his mother, having hidden him for three months, obeyed the letter of the law which required all male babies born to Israelite women to be thrown into the Nile. She placed the baby in the Nile—but in a watertight reed chest—in the rushes by the bank. His sister stayed to watch from a distance to see what would become of the boy. She was still there when Pharaoh's daughter came down to the river to bathe. Pharaoh's daughter took pity on the crying child and accepted his sister's offer to find him a wet-nurse. Unknown to the Egyptian princess, the wet-nurse was the boy's own mother.

Pharaoh's daughter named the boy Moses (Hebrew *moshe*), which, according to Exodus 2:10, is Hebrew and means 'pulled' (from the Nile). However, it probably comes from the Egyptian *mose*—'is born'. She saw to it that he was brought up in the royal palace. Separated from the Israelite community, he had no experience of the degrading effects of slavery and no chance to become familiar to his countrymen. Both these facts no doubt helped to make him a better leader.

When he grew up, he visited the Israelites, and killed an Egyptian whom he saw killing an Israelite slave. Moses had checked that there was no witness, and hid the body in the sand. The next day, however, he intervened in a dispute between two Israelites and it became clear that news of the killing had leaked out for one of them asked angrily if Moses was going to kill him as he had killed the Egyptian. When Pharaoh

found out about the killing, Moses fled to Midian (in the east of the Sinai peninsula), where he met his future wife Zipporah, and was employed as shepherd by her father Jethro.

One day, while he was guarding Jethro's sheep at Mount Sinai, he saw a bush that burned but was not consumed. As he approached, God called him and told him to return to Egypt to free his people. Moses was 80 years old—having apparently been Jethro's shepherd all his adult life.

Moses objected that he was not eloquent enough to persuade Pharaoh and God angrily told him to take his brother Aaron as spokesman. By performing miracles with God's aid—making his hand white, and turning his staff into a snake and water into blood—Moses won the Israelites' confidence. But he soon lost it again when Pharaoh answered Moses's demands by adding to their burdens. 'The Israelites have not heeded me,' he cried. 'How will Pharaoh heed me?' (Exodus 6:12). Yet Moses confronted Pharaoh and demanded Israel's release. When Pharaoh repeatedly refused, God inflicted ten plagues upon the Egyptians. The first turned all the water in the Nile into blood, so that the fish died and the Egyptians were unable to drink the water. The second plague filled the land with frogs. As God promised, they invaded houses, even people's beds, ovens and kneading bowls. There were so many that when they died they were gathered together in heaps 'and the land stank' (8:14). The third plague turned the dust of the land into lice (or gnats); the Egyptians told Pharaoh that it was indeed the work of God. But Pharaoh 'hardened his heart', still refusing to let the Israelites go. Further plagues followed—of flies (or wild beasts), cattle disease, boils, hail, locusts, darkness and finally the death of the first-born, 'both man and beast'. Moses acted throughout as God's messenger to Pharaoh and God protected the Israelites from these ever-worsening plagues, punishing only the Egyptians.

Moses was, throughout, always courteous towards Pharaoh. Although his aim was for the Israelites to be free

to leave the country, all he asked for was three days freedom so that they could sacrifice in the desert. At one point Pharaoh actually agreed (10:24) and Moses increased his demands: now, he insisted, the Israelites should be allowed to take all their cattle with them and Pharaoh himself should contribute to the sacrifice.

Before the coming of the tenth and most terrible plague, God told Moses and Aaron to instruct the Israelites to prepare for a journey, and to mark their doors with lamb's blood. God would recognize their households and pass over them without harming them when the first-born were killed—giving rise to the 'Feast of the Passover'. The Egyptians were appalled at the results of this last plague, and Pharaoh at once summoned Moses and Aaron and told them to leave, with all the Israelites.

Almost immediately, Pharaoh regretted his decision and sent his army after them. Believing they were trapped, the ungrateful Israelites turned on Moses, saying they would have preferred to live in servitude than die in the wilderness. But God, through Moses, parted the Red Sea, allowing the Israelites to escape across dry land and then drowning the pursuing Egyptians.

Moses was called the greatest of the prophets (Deuteronomy 34:10). The Hebrew word literally means 'spokesman' (Exodus 7:1), and Moses's greatness lay less in his predictions of Israel's destiny (Deuteronomy 32—3) than in his revelations of God's will. On Mount Sinai, he gave Israel the Ten Commandments (or rather all but the first two, which God himself spoke in the first person), and many other laws, on ethics ('love thy neighbour as thyself'—Leviticus 19:18), family and civil life, festivals, diet, sacrifices, ritual purity and much else. He delivered God's command to build a portable sanctuary, and served as its first priest, before consecrating Aaron to take his place. A prophet is also his people's intercessor before God, and here too Moses excelled. Yet even Moses could not see God's face, but only his back (or 'afterglow')—Exodus 33:23.

Moses found that freeing the Israelites' minds was even harder than freeing them physically from slavery in Egypt. They remembered the abundant fish, meat, bread and vegetables (though not the slavery) of Egypt, and clamoured to return whenever they were short of food or water, or merely bored at their diet of manna. Before the Red Sea divided, they cowered before an Egyptian army which they out-numbered a thousand to one (Exodus 12:37, 14:7), and blamed Moses for their plight. When spies reported that the Canaanites, who occupied the Promised Land, were strong and warlike people, the Israelites tried to appoint a new leader to take them back to Egypt, and God sentenced them to wander forty years in the desert until all those who had known slavery—i.e. the adults aged 20 and upwards—had died (Numbers 13—14).

Moses, a meek man (12:3), found it difficult to cope with all this opposition, despite the miracles God performed through him. In a crisis, if God did not intervene immediately, Moses might fall on his face (14:5, 16:4) or simply weep (25:6). Occasionally he lost his temper: when he came down from Mount Sinai to find the Israelites worshipping a golden calf, he smashed the tablets which God himself had inscribed with commandments and entrusted to him. On another occasion God told Moses to produce water for the Israelites by speaking to a rock. Moses, however, angrily struck the rock. Because of this one lapse, he was condemned to die in the desert along with his contemporaries (20:12). He later blamed the people for this (Deuteronomy 3:26), called even the new generation rebellious, and predicted that they would deteriorate further after his death (31:27). Yet in spite of his occasional weakness, he faithfully guided Israel's journeys, down to Eilat and then north-eastwards. Under his leadership they captured the territory east of the Jordan, from which the attack on Canaan itself would be launched. Age never dimmed his eyes, nor diminished his strength (34:7). He died, 120 years old, on Mount Nebo, east of the Dead Sea, where he could see the whole Promised Land. God buried him in a nearby valley, which is unnamed, to prevent people from worshipping at his grave.

Moses had two sons, Gershom and Eliezer, but very little is known of them, nor of their mother Zipporah. He probably had little time for them, though a second wife, from Ethiopia, is mentioned once (Numbers 12:1). Gershom's son became priest at the illicit sanctuary of Dan (Judges 18:30).

Aaron was Moses's brother, older by three years. We know nothing of his early life and he first appears in the Bible when God commanded Moses to tell the Israelite slaves that they would soon be freed from Egypt. Moses protested that he lacked eloquence, and so God told him to make Aaron his spokesman. Together the two succeeded in convincing the people. But they had yet to convince the Egyptian Pharaoh. In the repeated confrontations with Pharaoh that followed, Aaron sometimes accompanied Moses. Despite the reference to Aaron's gifts as a speaker, he never spoke alone; indeed it was sometimes Moses who alone addressed Pharaoh (Exodus 8:9, 26: 11:4—8). Aaron's main contribution came from the supernatural power of his rod. By striking this against the Nile or the Egyptian soil, he started the first three plagues, of blood, frogs, and lice (see *Moses*).

Usually Aaron appears as passive, even weak. He was left in command when Moses went up Mount Sinai for forty days and nights to be with God. Moses was late back, however, and the people, thinking he would never return, demanded a new god to worship. Aaron had to do something to satisfy them. He asked for the golden earrings of the men, women and children. Perhaps he thought that they would never agree, but when they promptly stripped the ornaments off, he had no choice but to make the gold into the image of a new god, a golden calf.

When Moses returned and saw the calf he demanded an explanation. Aaron answered like a schoolboy: 'Let my lord not be angry . . . I said to them: who has gold? They stripped it off themselves and gave it to me, and I threw it into the fire, and this calf *came out*' (Exodus 32:22—4). On a later occasion their sister Miriam complained to Aaron about Moses, and though Aaron did no more than listen he was rebuked. When Korah rebelled against the secular and religious authority of Moses and Aaron, Moses's defence of Aaron was all too apt: 'And what is Aaron, that you complain against him?' (Numbers 16:11).

It was again no direct action of his own that condemned Aaron to die without reaching the Promised Land. The people had become thirsty in the desert, and God commanded Moses and Aaron to assemble them all together, then to speak to a certain rock. The rock would then miraculously produce water. Moses, however, angrily struck the rock with his rod, and although he acted alone, both brothers were condemned to die in the wilderness. Evidently Aaron was held responsible for what he condoned, as well as what he did.

Aaron's main role is as the first High Priest, which is surprising since he was appointed after the episode of the golden calf. He had four sons who were also consecrated as priests. Somehow, the ceremony went wrong. At one point the two elder sons, Nadab and Abihu, offered 'strange fire' (perhaps 'fire at the wrong time') and were immediately burned to death. Moses rebuked Aaron, who was, as usual, silent. Later on in the ceremony, Aaron and his two surviving sons, Eleazar and Ithamar, should have eaten a 'goat of the sin-offering'. Moses discovered that they had failed to do so, and grew angry again. At this, Aaron finally protested that he had suffered enough for one day, and Moses relented.

At Aaron's consecration he wore an ephod (shoulder-cape) of gold, of violet and purple and scarlet yarn, and of linen. Attached to each shoulder was an onyx stone, inscribed with the names of six of the twelve tribes of Israel. He also wore a breast-plate of the same materials. Inset in four rows were twelve different gems, each bearing the name of one tribe. Gold chains held the two garments together. At the same time he wore a violet mantle, with pomegranates (of violet and other material) and golden

AARON
Aaron shared with Moses the responsibility of persuading Pharaoh to release the Israelites and acted as Moses's deputy during the desert wanderings. Although he seems to have been less steadfast than his brother, he was appointed the first High Priest. The description of his priestly garments in Exodus 28 and 39 is often thought to be an idealized picture, dating from many centuries after the Exodus; but the clothes of priests and high priests were based on it until the destruction of the Temple in AD 70.

bells round the hem, a chequered linen tunic, a sash of embroidered linen, and linen trousers. On his head was a linen turban, with a golden rosette inscribed: Holy to the Lord' (Exodus 28).

These remained the consecration garments of the High Priest in every generation; the office passed after Aaron's death to his son Eleazar, and then to Phinehas and generally to 'the priest that is greater than his brothers'. All Aaron's descendants were priests, but those other than the High Priest only wore the tunic, trousers, turban and sash at their consecration. On other occasions a priest would wear simply a linen robe and linen trousers, which were more practical for such duties as slaughtering sacrificial animals, removing their ashes from the altar, and diagnosing leprosy. Another important duty was to bless the people.

The priests were not given any land in Israel but instead were granted certain privileges (Numbers 18). These included the flesh of animals offered for sacrifices, the first-fruits of the harvest, the first fleece of the sheep, and the first-born of animals (to be sacrificed, if they belonged to 'clean' species) and of men (to be ransomed by money). They also suffered restrictions; for example, they could not marry divorcees.

Jewish tradition transformed Aaron's weakness to a virtue which seemed closest to it: they saw him as a 'lover of peace'. If ever two of Aaron's acquaintances quarrelled, Aaron would tell each one that the other was full of regret, and when the two next met they were fully reconciled.

Eleazar was the third son of Aaron. His two elder brothers, Nadab and Abihu, were killed when they made a mistake in the ritual intended to consecrate them as priests. Eleazar and his younger brother Ithamar were spared.

Eleazar succeeded Aaron as High Priest; he often appeared as Moses's assistant and helped him count the Israelites. When Joshua was appointed Moses's successor, he still needed Eleazar to communicate God's will (Numbers 27:21); and Eleazar later helped him distribute the land (Joshua 14:1). His son was the fiery Phinehas.

Phinehas (an Egyptian name) was the son of Eleazar, the high priest and grandson of Aaron. He rose to prominence when the Israelites, about to enter Canaan, were camped east of the Jordan. They were worshipping idols and sleeping with the local Moabite and Midianite women, and as punishment were dying of plague. One day Phinehas saw an Israelite prince take a Midianite princess to his tent. Phinehas thrust a spear through them both. The plague immediately ceased and God gave him a 'covenant of peace', perhaps to cool his violence, promising that his descendants would always be priests (Numbers 25:12).

After Canaan had been conquered, he accused the tribes that had settled east of the Jordan of returning to idol worship. They had set up their own altar, but they assured him that it was symbolic and that they would never sacrifice outside the central sanctuary (Joshua 22:28, 29). In the time of the Judges, he was still pronouncing oracles in God's name (Judges 20:28). His death is not recorded; in Jewish tradition he is the same person as the immortal Elijah, for both are called 'zealous for the Lord' (Numbers 25:13, 1 Kings 19:10).

Korah was a great-grandson of Levi, and a first cousin of Moses and Aaron. During the wilderness wanderings he led a revolt against the two leaders (Numbers 16). He was supported by Dathan and Abiram, by a certain 'On, son of Pelet' and by a company of 250 men. Dathan, Abiram and On all belonged to the tribe of Reuben, the eldest of Jacob's twelve sons; no doubt they resented being governed by descendants of his younger brother Levi. They declared that *all* the congregation of Israel were holy and that Moses and Aaron had no special right to either secular or religious authority. Moreover, they complained that Moses and Aaron had brought them not to the Promised Land flowing with milk and honey, but instead to a wilderness.

Moses challenged Korah and his 250 men to offer incense in the tabernacle and thereby test whether God approved of them. The 250 rebels accepted the

challenge; as they stood at the entrance of the tabernacle, holding their incense-pans, they were consumed by fire. Meanwhile the ringleaders Korah, Dathan and Abiram were swallowed by an earthquake. 'On, son of Pelet' had apparently left the revolt. Korah's sons must have disowned their father at the last moment, for they also survived. Their descendants became prominent temple singers, and composed many of the Psalms. It was perhaps in order to spare their feelings that when the rebellion is mentioned in later biblical books, no reference is made to Korah.

Jethro, chief priest of Midian, became Moses's father-in-law. Moses fled to Midian to avoid being arrested for the murder of an Egyptian. When he arrived there, his first act was to help Jethro's daughters draw water from a well. Jethro invited him to stay, and gave him his daughter Zipporah (Exodus 2). Moses remained in Midian until God called him to return to Egypt. After the Israelites had left Egypt, Jethro recognized the Lord as the greatest God (though not the only one) and joined Moses in Sinai (18:11). There he found Moses overwhelmed by the innumerable disputes he was expected to settle, and advised him to form a hierarchy of officials, from men of strong character who were God-fearing, truthful and incorruptible. Finding that combination rare, Moses settled for men of strong character (18:25). (The system later broke down; in Numbers 11:16 Moses was again governing unaided and seventy assistants were appointed.)

Jethro's sons settled in Canaan alongside Israel (Judges 1:16, 4:11) but Jethro himself returned to Midian. Moses was sorry to see him go, not least because Jethro was familiar with the desert (Numbers 10:31). Strangely Jethro's departure is related twice, once before Moses received the Ten Commandments, once afterwards (Exodus 18:27; Numbers 10:30).

Zipporah ('bird') was the daughter of the Midianite Jethro and was Moses's wife. On their way to Egypt, God unexpectedly tried to kill Moses and

Zipporah saved him by cutting off her son's foreskin, which 'she touched against his (Moses's) feet' (Exodus 4:25). Moses later decided to complete the journey to Egypt alone, and Zipporah rejoined him—with two sons—after the Israelites had been freed. She is not mentioned again, although Moses's 'Ethiopian wife' is mentioned (Numbers 12:1). This might possibly refer to Zipporah, for the Midianites were dark-skinned and 'Ethiopian' may be a general term for dark-skinned people.

Bezalel was the craftsman who, during the desert wanderings, made Israel's Tabernacle or portable sanctuary, the Ark and other sacred furniture, and the priestly garments. He was a genius ('filled with God's spirit'—Exodus 35:31) in craftsmanship of all kinds, working metals, cutting precious stones and carving wood. He was aided by Aholiab, an inventive craftsman and expert embroiderer (38:23). Together they trained assistants for other necessary tasks (such as constructing the framework). Moses received the command to make the sacred furniture first, but Bezalel insisted on making it last, so that he would have somewhere to put it as soon as it was completed.

Rulers

Pharaoh The Pharaoh under whom Moses was born had seen Jacob's family grow into the Israelite nation. He felt threatened by their numbers and unsure of their loyalty, so he enslaved them. When they nevertheless continued to multiply, he told the Israelite midwives to kill all boys at birth. The midwives did not do so. When challenged, they explained to Pharaoh that Israelite women were too vigorous to need midwives (Exodus 1:19). Pharaoh then ordered 'all his people' to throw all new-born boys (presumably Israelite only) into the Nile. His own daughter saved the infant Moses and raised him in the palace. In spite of this, when Moses killed an Egyptian slavemaster Pharaoh sought his life. The Pharaoh had hardly treated the Israelites kindly, yet they regretted his death—for the next was harsher still. (See also *Moses*.)

The Pharaoh of the Exodus is often identified as Ramesses II, who reigned from 1290—1224 BC. He was determined to keep the Israelites in slavery. When Moses demanded their release, he replied: 'Who is the Lord, that I should

47

in some of the later plagues, God hardened it for him (9:12; 10:20, 27).

On the night that the final plague killed all Egyptian first-born, including Pharaoh's own son, Pharaoh summoned Moses and allowed the Israelites to leave to sacrifice in the desert—which was all that Moses had ever asked for. He hoped that this would be the end of their demands, and even asked them to add prayers for him (Exodus 12:32). They failed to return (they had in fact already offered their sacrifice in Egypt—12:28), and Pharaoh and his army pursued them into the Red Sea. It seemed that the Israelites were now doomed, but the water miraculously parted before them, then descended to engulf the Egyptians—drowning those who had once ordered the drowning of Israelite children.

Sihon was king of an area that extended about 25 miles east of the Jordan, lying between its tributaries the Arnon (which runs into the middle of the Dead Sea) and the Jabbok (some 50 miles further north). When Moses asked him to allow the Israelites to pass peacefully through to Canaan, Sihon attacked them—and was conquered (Numbers 21:24). According to Deuteronomy 2:30 God had hardened his heart, as he had done Pharaoh's. Farther north lay the kingdom of Og, a giant whose bed was 13 feet (4m) long; he, too, attacked the Israelites. They defeated him and extended their conquests as far north as Lake Galilee.

Balak was King of Moab, east of the Dead Sea. He had seen the Israelites conquer the territory of his northern neighbours (Numbers 21:21—35) on their way to the Promised Land, and tried to protect his own kingdom by hiring a Syrian prophet to curse them. The prophet Balaam warned that he could speak only 'the word that God places in my mouth' (22:38). Balak took him to a spot where he could see only some of the Israelites—apparently hoping that these might be the least worthy and that Balaam could condemn the whole people on their account. Then he offered rich sacrifices. The king offered sacrifices three times, and

PHARAOH RAMESSES II
The Pharaoh of Moses's time may have been Ramesses II, who ruled Egypt for 66 years from 1290 to 1224 BC. He is best known for his spectacular building programme, which included the temple of Abu Simbel, on which the Israelites may have worked. In the Bible he appears as a harsh ruler, determined to keep the Israelites in slavery, and to make their working conditions as difficult as possible. His mummified body is now in the Cairo Museum.

heed his voice?' (Exodus 5:2). Instead of freeing them, he made their lives even more difficult. One of their tasks was to produce bricks (possibly for Ramesses' ambitious building programme). Now he decreed that they must produce as many bricks as before while also gathering their own straw. His harshness resulted in the Ten Plagues (see *Moses*). As each plague struck, Pharaoh promised he would let the Israelites go if only the plague ceased; but when it did, he 'hardened his heart', or rather, each time Balaam ended up blessing Israel instead of cursing them. Balak grew angry (23:11), then distraught (23:25—'neither curse them nor bless them!'), and finally dismissed Balaam (24:11). He could only listen helplessly, however, while Balaam concluded his prophecies, foretelling Moab's conquest by a 'star from Jacob' (i.e. David), and cursing every other nation in sight.

Balaam was a Syrian prophet who believed in Israel's God. His blessings and curses were thought never to fail (Numbers 22:6), and he himself claimed to 'share the knowledge of the Most High' (24:16). Balak, King of Moab, sent messages to Syria, offering to pay Balaam if he would curse the Israelites and thus prevent them from conquering Moab. Balaam consulted God, who in a dream forbade him either to go to Moab or to curse Israel. Balak was persistent, however, and Balaam asked God again. God now said he could go, but only if he spoke as God commanded. Balaam agreed, hoping to curse the Israelites against God's will. In anger, God placed an angel in his path, visible to his she-ass but invisible to the prophet himself. The ass moved aside and when Balaam struck her for leaving the road, asked him why he did so. Balaam, with no sign of surprise at hearing her speak, replied: 'You are making a fool of me.' Only then was he able to see the angel, who repeated God's warning. When Balaam arrived in Moab, he ordered Balak to build seven altars and sacrifice seven bullocks and rams. Then he would speak the curse. The preparations were repeated three times but the curses he intended to make (Deuteronomy 23:5) always came out as blessings: 'How goodly are thy tents, O Jacob !' (Numbers 24:5). Eventually Balak sent him home unpaid.

Balaam was killed by the Israelites during a war of revenge fought against another of their enemies, the Midianites.

In 1967, Dutch archaeologists discovered fragments of a sheet of plaster at Deir Alla (called Succoth in the Bible) on the east bank of the Jordan, north-west of Amman. The writing on it dates from around 700 BC and mentions Balaam by name, calling him 'seer of the gods'. It also lists various curses. In spite of its poor condition, the inscription shows that Balaam's reputation as a prophet was known beyond the Bible.

BALAAM
Balaam was a Syrian prophet, famous for the power of his curses and apparently vain enough to believe he could outwit God. Against God's orders, he tried three times to curse the Israelites—but the words came out as blessings instead.

The Book of Joshua

The Book of Joshua continues the history of the Israelites' struggle to occupy the Promised Land of Canaan, after the death of Moses. The original inhabitants of Canaan resisted strongly. Their cities, each under its own king, were well fortified and some may have been captured and recaptured before finally submitting. Joshua succeeded Moses as leader and under his guidance, the land was divided among the twelve tribes. Some scholars consider, however, that the account of the campaign has been telescoped in retelling into a shorter period of time than it actually took; the victories credited to Joshua may have been won by a number of leaders over a long period of slow, sporadic occupation.

The conquest

Joshua ('the Lord delivers') led Israel's fight for Canaan, the Promised Land, after the long years of wandering in the wilderness. He had, however, already distinguished himself before this. Shortly after the Israelites left Egypt (see *Moses*), they were attacked by the Amalekites (Exodus 17:8). Moses called on Joshua to choose men and beat back the attackers. 'And Joshua mowed down Amalek and his people with the edge of the sword' (17:13). He became Moses's assistant, waiting on the lower slopes for Moses to come down from Mount Sinai (24:13), and guarding his temporary shrine (33:11). He was jealous for Moses when two men began to prophesy (Numbers 11:28) since he felt that only Moses and men with whom Moses had shared his prophetic spirit had the right to do this.

As the Israelites neared Canaan, Moses sent one noble from each tribe to spy out the Promised Land and Joshua went as representative of the tribe of Ephraim. The spies reported that the Canaanites were strong and most of the Israelites felt they could never conquer them. Joshua and Caleb alone insisted that they could (14:9). Later, when God told Moses to prepare to die, Joshua was his obvious successor, and it was on Joshua's head that Moses laid his hands to transfer the spirit of wisdom (27:18).

After Moses died, God promised to be with Joshua in the campaign, and spoke to him before every major battle. He once sent an angel, disguised as an armed man. Joshua bluntly asked which side the angel was on. The offended angel gave no straight answer and never returned (Joshua 5:14).

Before invading the Promised Land, Joshua first sent two spies secretly into Jericho, their first target: the men reported that all the Canaanites were terrified. Encouraged by this, Joshua led Israel across the Jordan, which, like the Red Sea, miraculously divided to let them across, confirming Joshua's authority in the eyes of his followers. At God's command, the Israelites circled Jericho in silence once a day for six days; on the seventh day, after seven circuits, the priests blew horns, the people shouted and the walls fell down. The Israelites destroyed everyone and everything, as God commanded them to do throughout the conquest.

Further west, Joshua captured Ai (see *Achan*), by the trick of attacking and then pretending to retreat; when the citizens rushed out in pursuit, a hidden Israelite detachment burned the city, while the main force under Joshua suddenly turned and slaughtered the inhabitants.

Soon after these successes, Joshua was duped by the inhabitants of Gibeon (5 miles to the south-west); a delegation of Gibeonite men with worn garments and mouldering food convinced him that they came from a distant land. Joshua believed them and felt there was nothing to be lost by making a peace treaty with them. Three days later, however, he discovered that the men had been lying. Their land was being attacked by a coalition of kings from the southern cities and they had tricked Joshua into promising support. Joshua felt honour-bound to keep the treaty he had made with them and went to fight in their defence. Joshua's victory over the southerners was no ordinary one: hailstones miraculously descended upon the enemy and the sun stood still until they were all slaughtered or routed.

The feeble resistance remaining in the south of Canaan was soon overcome, but now the northern kings gathered a huge army to the waters of Meron (about 15 miles north-west of Lake Galilee). Joshua defeated them by a sudden attack and went on to burn their chief city Hazor and occupy the rest.

In his last campaign Joshua killed the giants of the hill country, who had terrified his fellow spies in Moses's day. All the land from the River Jordan to the Mediterranean (apart from the southern coastal strip, retained by the Philistines) had been conquered within five years.

God promised that Israel would one day vanquish the Philistines and other neighbours. At God's command, therefore, Joshua divided all the territory, whether conquered or not (13:6), by lot among the tribes. He showed no favouritism to his own tribe of Ephraim which shared territory with Manasseh. When they complained that their territory was too small, he told them to cut down its forests to make more room.

Joshua's leadership was religious as well as military. Before starting the conquest, he used flint knives to perform circumcision (which had been neglected during the harsh desert wanderings) on all the Israelites males. Devotedly he carried out Moses's last commands: he proclaimed the law before all Israel and set down a copy written on stone; he ensured that daughters as well as sons received their due inheritance (17:4), he assigned cities

JOSHUA

Of the adults who set out from Egypt, only two survived to enter the Promised Land of Canaan 40 years later. One of these was Joshua, a strong and experienced warrior who knew the importance of psychological warfare as well as the use of strength. The Israelites who fought under his inspired leadership were outnumbered by the Canaanites and had inferior weapons. Yet in five years they conquered the whole of the Promised Land. Joshua's religious leadership was equally important: he carried out Moses's last commands devotedly and proclaimed the law before all Israel.

to the Levites (who, as priests, had no specific area of land) and set up cities of refuge for any who killed by error. In his last speeches he warned Israel that they would lose the land if they neglected God's commandments and declared that, even if Israel chose other gods, 'I and my household will serve the Lord' (24:15). He died aged 110, and was buried in his own small city of Timnath-Serah, in Ephraim's territory. According to 1 Chronicles 7:27 he left no male heir.

Caleb was a prince of the tribe of Judah. At the age of 40, Moses sent him as a representative of his tribe to reconnoitre Canaan. Most of the Israelites believed the Canaanites could never be conquered: Caleb was the first to contradict them publicly (Numbers 13:30). Joshua later joined him and both just escaped being stoned by the rest of the Israelites. They were the only two of their generation who lived to enter Canaan.

At the age of 85, Caleb was as strong as ever (Joshua 14:11) and he asked Joshua to grant him the land of Hebron. At the time this was inhabited by giants, but Caleb expelled them. He offered his daughter's hand to whoever conquered Debir (about 5 miles to the south-west). She was won by his younger brother Othniel, and she persuaded Caleb to give her also the neighbouring pools—a valuable dowry in a land where water was scarce (15:19).

Rahab was a harlot who lived in a house built into the wall of Jericho. Two spies sent by Joshua chose her house as a place from which to observe the citizens' morale (see *Joshua*). When the king's baliffs came to arrest them, she hid them on her roof and said that they had left. She told the spies that she had helped them because she had heard of the Lord's miracles in the wilderness and recognized him as the only God. She added the vital information that the Canaanites were in terror of the Israelites. The grateful spies promised to spare her and her family when they took the city, provided that she hung a scarlet cord from her window to identify the house. She then helped them to

51

RAHAB
Rahab, a prostitute, lived in a house built into the city walls of Jericho. When Joshua sent spies to discover the morale of the people inside the besieged city, Rahab hid them, explaining that she believed in God. In return, the Israelites spared her family when they attacked.

escape through the window. In Jewish tradition she married Joshua and her descendants included Jeremiah and Baruch. Matthew 1:5, however, makes her the wife of Boaz's father Salmon and an ancestress of David and Jesus.

Achan was an Israelite who fought at the battle of Jericho. God had commanded the Israelites to destroy the treasures captured from the city but after the battle, Achan took silver, gold and a Babylonian embroidered cloak from the spoil; as a punishment, Israel was defeated in the next battle, at Ai, and thirty-six Israelite soldiers lost their lives. Joshua learned from God that someone had hoarded the spoil and called an assembly of all the tribes at which Achan was identified by lot. He then confessed, and the spoil was found in his tent. It and all his property was burned and he and his family were stoned to death (Joshua 7).

The Book of Judges

In the years after the Israelites entered the Promised Land, they continued to fight with the local inhabitants for possession. Each tribe had been allotted its own territory (except for the priestly tribe of Levi, which was granted cities) and there was no single, strong leader to unite them. The Judges seem to have been more or less local leaders whose careers overlapped. They probably lived between 1250 and 1050 BC.

Judges of Israel

Othniel was the first of the Judges of Israel. He was the younger brother of Caleb and married Caleb's daughter Achsah as a reward for capturing the city of Debir, south of Jerusalem. Possessed by the spirit of God, he later delivered Israel from Syrian oppression (Judges 3:11).

Ehud was from the tribe of Benjamin and was instrumental in expelling the Moabites from the city of Jericho, which they had taken from the Israelites. The Israelites were forced to pay tribute to the Moabite king Eglon and on one occasion, Ehud led the delegation. The king's guards did not notice that Ehud was carrying a sword, for he was left-handed and therefore carried the weapon on his right side. After leaving, he returned to Eglon, as if he had forgotten something, and announced that he had a secret message. Eglon dismissed his servants and Ehud said that the message came from God. As Eglon, an exceedingly fat man, struggled to his feet out of respect, Ehud plunged the sword into his belly, locked the doors and escaped before Eglon's guards dared open them. In the hill country of Ephraim, he rallied the Israelites, who chased and killed the Moabite invaders.

Jabin was the Canaanite King of Hazor and oppressed the Israelites for twenty years. An earlier Jabin of Hazor had been slain by Joshua (Joshua 11:1, 10).

Deborah ('bee') was a Judge who held assizes about 8 miles north of Jerusalem. She was also a prophetess and when the Canaanites attacked the Israelites with an army and 900 iron chariots, she told the Israelite commander, Barak, how to overcome them. Barak was to rally the northern tribes to Mount Tabor, where God would lure the Canaanites to battle. Deborah accompanied Barak and saw her prophecy fulfilled: a downpour (Judges 5:21) left the chariots stuck fast in the mud on the mountainside and the Canaanites were routed. Deborah praised God in a magnificent poem (Judges 5), calling herself 'a mother in Israel', blessing the tribes who contributed to the victory and taunting those that stood aloof.

Barak, the Israelite commander who, with Deborah, led the Israelites against a great Canaanite army, lived about 15 miles north of Lake Galilee. This was a long way from Deborah's assizes, but he may in fact have been her husband. (His name is also given as Lapidoth and in Hebrew both names mean the same thing: 'lightning'.) When Deborah told him to fight the Canaanites, he insisted that she accompany him. Deborah agreed, but warned that if she did so, the glory of victory would be hers. At Deborah's prompting (Judges 4:14) he led his 10,000 troops into the attack, routed the Canaanites and slaughtered them all except their commander, Sisera. When Barak caught up with him, Sisera had already been killed.

Sisera was the commander of the Canaanite army which, with its 900 iron chariots, was confident of overpowering the Israelite forces. Instead, his army was completely routed. He escaped and took refuge with Jael, an Israelite who had married a foreigner. Thinking he was safe, he accepted her hospitality but while he slept, she hammered a tent-peg through his temples and killed him.

Jael was married to a non-Israelite friendly with the Canaanites. When Sisera's army was routed, he fled to her tent. She gave him milk and he fell asleep. Jael, loyal to her Israelite origins, then killed him.

Gideon, the fifth Judge of Israel, was from Ophrah, perhaps 20 miles south-west of Lake Galilee. The Israelites were still fighting to keep the land they had conquered and now the Midianites, who lived to the south-east, were raiding their territory. God commanded Gideon to expel them. At first Gideon did not believe it possible: when an angel first announced to him 'the Lord is with thee' he asked why, in that case Israel was suffering so much (Judges 6:13). Before fighting the Midianites, he demanded signs both from the angel (who had to remain until Gideon prepared a hasty sacrifice) and from God himself. One night Gideon asked that a fleece left outside be wet in the morning and the ground dry; the next night he left the fleece out again but requested the opposite (6:36-40). God patiently did as he asked.

Convinced at last, Gideon gathered an army of 32,000 men. God, however, told him to reduce it, in case the Israelites should think they had won without the help of God. After dismissing all the men who were afraid, he selected the rest by bringing them all to a spring and telling them to drink. He retained only the 300 who stayed alert while they drank, standing up and raising water in cupped hands.

The next night he crept into the Midianite camp and eavesdropped: one Midianite had dreamed that the camp was flattened by a rolling barley loaf, and his companion interpreted this as meaning that Gideon would soon defeat them. Knowing that their morale was low, Gideon equipped each of his soldiers with a horn and a torch covered by a pitcher. He led them to the Midianite camp, telling them to blow the horns, break the pitchers and shout. The Midianites were terrified, and began to kill each other in their confusion. Many of the people who tried to escape, including the princes Oreb and Zeeb, were intercepted and killed by the Ephraimites to the south. The kings Zebah and Zalmunna, however, escaped across the Jordan.

Gideon's victory did not win him the support of all Israel, however. As he pursued the Midianite kings, he passed through Succoth and Penuel, east of Jordan, and the people there refused to give bread to his weary soldiers. When he had captured Zebah and Zalmunna—whom he would have spared if they had not killed his brothers (8:19)—he thrashed the elders of Succoth with thorns, slaughtered the people and destroyed the tower of Penuel. To the Ephraimites who had helped him by killing the escaping princes, he showed a different side of his character. When they reproached him for not calling them earlier, he meekly replied that his exploits were dwarfed by theirs.

At this time, some Israelites were still worshipping the pagan god Baal and shortly before Gideon's victory over the Midianites, God ordered him to strike a blow against this practice. He obeyed, although out of fear he acted at night. He destroyed Baal's altar in Ophrah, and burned two bullocks his father had dedicated to Baal on a new altar to God. He used Baal's sacred wooden pole as firewood. The Baal-worshippers demanded his death, but Gideon's father persuaded them to let Baal fight his own battles. After this, Gideon was nicknamed Jerubbaal 'let Baal contend!' (6:32). In spite of his action against Baal-worship, he later made the gold he captured from the Midianites into an ephod—here, a garment used for an idol—after which 'all Israel went astray'.

After the victory, his people offered to make him king but he refused the throne. He lived to old age, with many wives and seventy sons.

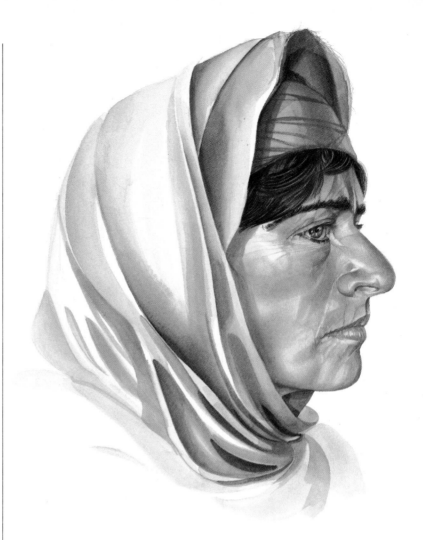

DEBORAH
When the Israelites first settled in Canaan, each local area was ruled by its own warrior chief. In peacetime they acted as judges, responsible for law and order and for making sure that the settlers did not adopt a pagan religion. Deborah, the only woman judge recorded, was both a prophetess and a warrior, who herself led a victorious army against the Canaanites.

Abimelech was Gideon's son by a Canaanite concubine (Judges 8:31) and persuaded the largely Canaanite citizens of Shechem to make him their king. In Ophrah (his father's home) he executed all Gideon's seventy other sons (born to Israelite wives (9:5)) except Jotham, the youngest. Jotham warned the Shechemites that no-one capable of useful work would want to be a king and that Abimelech would soon prove a disaster.

Over the next three years Abimelech extended his territory and resided in nearby Arumah (9:31, 41). In Shechem itself, he became unpopular, and Gaal, apparently a Canaanite from another city, led a revolt against him. Abimelech successfully ambushed Gaal's army and retook Shechem, burning the tower where the citizens had sheltered. He then attacked the neighbouring city of Thebez, besieging its tower. A woman inside the city threw a millstone at him and broke his skull. Before he died, he ordered his armour-bearer to run him through with his sword so that it could not be said he died by a woman's hand (9:54).

Jephthah was born in Gilead, east of the Jordan. His father's name was also Gilead; his mother was a harlot and because of this his brothers banished him. In nearby Tob he became leader of an outlaw band. He must have made himself a reputation as a warrior, because after a time he was invited back to Gilead as ruler, to fight off Ammonite invasions from the east. Jephthah grudgingly agreed but first tried to negotiate with the invaders. They told him that Gilead was originally theirs and he replied with a lecture on Israel's desert wanderings (Judges 11:15—27): Israel, he said, had captured Gilead not from the Ammonites, but from the Amorites, who had attacked Israel and been defeated. The Ammonites were unmoved. Jephthah next appealed to the tribesmen of Ephraim without success. Now he had no choice but to go to war.

Jephthah vowed that if he returned victorious, he would sacrifice as a burned offering the first creature to come out of the doors of his house (11:31). He defeated the Ammonites but on returning home was greeted by his only child, a daughter. When he cried that he had 'opened his mouth to God' (11:35), she understood, and asked only to be spared for two months to mourn her virginity (i.e. childless death); and then Jephthah fulfilled his vow.

The Ephraimites so resented Jephthah's winning the battle without their help that they crossed the River Jordan and threatened to burn his house. In a similar situation, Gideon had appeased them (see *Gideon*) but Jephthah fought. His soldiers captured the fords of the Jordan, and slaughtered any Ephraimite trying to return west. (Capturing the fords was especially appropriate since Ephraimites were recognized by a peculiarity of speech which made them unable to pronounce the 'sh' sound in the Hebrew word *shibboleth* 'stream'—12:6). Jephthah died after six years' office, and was buried in 'the cities of Gilead'.

JEPHTHAH
Jephthah made a bargain with God that if he won a certain battle, he would sacrifice the first creature who came out of his house on his return. Tragically, this was his own daughter and, to keep his side of the bargain, she was killed.

Manoah was the father of Samson. His wife was childless until an angel announced to her the birth of a son who would deliver Israel from the Philistines; the boy would be a Nazirite (Numbers 6), forbidden to drink alcohol or cut his hair. She told Manoah about the child and how he should be brought up, but said nothing of the Philistines (Judges 13:7). The news had to be kept from them, and she did not trust her husband to keep a secret. Manoah himself later saw the angel, who confirmed his wife's report. When Manoah offered a sacrifice, the angel disappeared and Manoah feared that he would now die. His wife, however, patiently explained that this would defeat God's purpose, since she had not yet conceived a child.

Samson was the immensely strong Israelite hero destined to deliver Israel from the Philistines. The Philistines occupied the coastal area of Israel

and were continually fighting the Israelites. Samson was born in Zorah, close to the border with the Philistine lands. Before his birth an angel told his mother that he would be Israel's saviour. He was endowed with superhuman strength, once tearing a lion apart with his bare hands (Judges 14:6). He was brought up as a Nazirite, forbidden to drink alcohol or to cut his hair.

The lifelong vows of abstinence had been made on his behalf before his birth, but this did not prevent him from pursuing Philistine women and it was through them that he had the opportunities to harass their menfolk. His only bride (unnamed) came from the Philistine city of Timnah. At the marriage feast, he set the Philistines a riddle, wagering thirty men's clothing that they could not solve it within seven days. When his bride discovered the answer and told them, he settled his bet by killing thirty Philistines in Ashkelon and taking their clothes. When her father promised her to another man, Samson tied the tails of 300 foxes together, fastened torches into the knots, and let them loose in the Philistine fields.

Later, Samson visited a harlot in Gaza, a city inside the Philistines' land and the Philistines waited to trap him at the city gate; Samson, however, carried away the whole gate on his shoulder. Far from being supported by his people, he was once handed over to the Philistines by the tribesmen of Judah; he broke his bonds and slew 1000 Philistines with the first weapon to hand, the jawbone of an ass.

Mighty as he was, Samson could not withstand women's nagging. His Philistine bride had persuaded him to explain the riddle by weeping throughout the week of the wedding feast. Later, Delilah (who is not called his wife) prised from him the secret of his strength—his long hair. Betrayed to the Philistines, he was captured and blinded. They set him to grind corn in prison, but later paraded him at a festive assembly. There he asked the attendant to guide him to the pillars supporting the temple and prayed God to grant him strength once more. His strength

SAMSON

Samson was famous more for his strength than for his intelligence. He fought a one-man war against the Philistines at a time when they were a strong, well organized power, then later courted a Philistine woman and allowed her to wheedle from him the secret of his strength. Later, blinded and mocked by his captors, he recovered his powers for a last, heroic act, and brought the temple of the Philistines crashing down to destroy both his enemies and himself.

DELILAH
Delilah, a Philistine woman, was responsible for betraying Samson, the man who had killed countless numbers of her countrymen. Complaining that she would never believe he loved her unless he trusted her with the secret of his strength, she nagged him until he told her his strength lay in his hair. While he slept with his head in her lap, she shaved his head and handed him over to the Philistines.

returned and, content to die with the Philistines, he pulled down the pillars and the whole building collapsed, killing more Philistines than he had ever killed while he lived.

Delilah was the last Philistine woman that Samson pursued. Five Philistine nobles promised her nearly thirty pounds of silver if she could discover the secret of Samson's strength. She moaned to him continually that unless he told her, she would not believe he loved her. Twice he lied to her about it. First he said that his strength would leave him if he were bound in fresh bow strings, then if he were bound in ropes. Each time she told the Philistines and they acted on her information. And each time he easily shook himself free from his bonds—but not from her. The third time, he admitted that his strength lay in his long hair, but added that it would fail if the locks of his hair were

woven together. Again, the Philistines acted on Delilah's information and, as before, he shook them off. At last, however, he grew so tired of her complaining that he told her the truth. She made him lie down with his head on her knees, shaved off his hair while he was asleep and sent him out to fight. Samson, unaware that he had lost his great strength, was captured and Delilah collected her reward.

Shamgar and other Judges are briefly referred to. Shamgar killed 600 Philistines with an ox goad (3:31). Tola, Jair (10:1—3), Ibzan, Elon and Abdon (12:8—13) were strictly judges not warriors. Jair, Ibzan and Abdon were noted for their many children (at least thirty each); Jair and Abdon at least must have grown rich for Jair's sons and Abdon's sons and grandsons each rode on his own ass.

Micah came from the hill country of Ephraim and it was through him that an illicit shrine came to be established in Dan, a hundred miles to the north. He had stolen nearly thirty pounds of silver from his mother and when he confessed, she dedicated it to the Lord. However, overlooking the Second Commandment that no graven images should be made, she had some of it made into idols (Judges 17:3). Micah consecrated his son as priest to the idols but later engaged a wandering Levite and trusted that God would now bless him.

After a time, the shrine was visited by spies from the tribe of Dan, who lived uncomfortably close to the Philistine border and were looking for a safer area in which to settle. When they consulted the Levite, he assured them in God's name that they would be successful. The spies returned to their companions and when the tribe passed by again on their way to their new home they carried the priest and his idols away with them.

Micah and his neighbours went after them but the Danites were too strong for them. They continued on their way and established the shrine in their new territory, in a city named Dan, after the tribe.

The Book of Ruth

RUTH
Ruth was a Moabitess from an area east of the Dead Sea. Moabites were traditional enemies of Israel but when Ruth's husband died, Ruth's love for Naomi led her to accept the traditions and religion of her adopted people, and she returned to Bethlehem with her. The Book of Ruth shows her to have been a loyal and determined woman.

The Book of Ruth is set during the time of the Judges (between 1250 and 1050 BC). It gives an insight into the lives of ordinary people of the time, people who were not directly involved in the struggle to secure the land. It also provides a family history for King David, who was descended from Ruth.

Ruth ('friendship') was a Moabitess, living at the time of the Judges. Moab was Israel's neighbour to the east of the Dead Sea. Moabites were descended from Lot and his elder daughter and had been enemies of Israel while the tribes were in the wilderness. Israelites were usually forbidden to marry them but Ruth married Chilion, an Israelite visitor who had come to escape famine in his own country. He died young, leaving her childless. Ruth refused to abandon her widowed mother-in-law Naomi and returned with her to Israel. 'Thy God is mine,' she declared, 'death alone can part us' (1:16-17). In Bethlehem, Naomi's town, Ruth visited a field to pick up the odd ears of corn the owner's reapers had left, as the poor were entitled to do. To her surprise, the owner blessed her, offered her water and bread, and instructed his reapers to let her take whatever she wished. Naomi later explained that the man was Boaz, a kinsman of her late husband. Since both Naomi's sons had died, and Ruth was childless, there was no male heir to the

husband's estate. As a kinsman Boaz was obliged to buy the estate (Leviticus 25:25) and marry Ruth to provide an heir. In fact marriage was a moral obligation only; the law required only the *brother* of the deceased to marry the widow—Deuteronomy 25:5. On Naomi's advice, Ruth crept that night into his threshing floor, where he slept, lay at his feet and asked his intentions. She was not trying to compromise him but to show she was willing to be his wife:

when he pointed out that there was a kinsman closer than himself, she stole out before dawn. The next day, Boaz obtained the closer relative's consent and married Ruth. They had a son, Obed. David was her great-grandson.

Naomi ('pleasant') was Ruth's mother-in-law. She lost her husband Elimelech and both sons—Mahlon ('sickness') and Chilion ('wasting') in Moab, where she went to escape famine.

BOAZ

Boaz was a prosperous landowner, a leading citizen of Bethlehem and a relative of Ruth's first husband. If a man died with no heir, it was the custom for his brother to marry the widow so that the family name could be preserved. Although Boaz was not obliged to marry Ruth, he willingly did so, taking on all the responsibilities of the family.

Her grief was made worse by guilt; she felt that it was her responsibility to provide her daughters-in-law with new husbands (Ruth 1:13). Although she persuaded Mahlon's widow, Orpah, to start a new life in her native Moab, Chilion's widow, Ruth, refused to leave her. Together they returned to Naomi's native village, where she asked the shocked women to rename her Mara ('bitter'). Her spirits revived when she heard that Boaz had behaved kindly towards Ruth, and she counselled Ruth to go to Boaz that night. Later she nursed Ruth's son Obed and loved him like the sons she had lost (4:14—17).

Boaz was an ageing landowner in Bethlehem, related to Naomi's husband. He had heard of Ruth's devotion to Naomi, and treated her generously when she visited his field to glean. He was startled to find her on his threshing floor one night, but gratified that she had not preferred a younger man (Ruth 3:10). There was a nearer kinsman who had the right to marry Ruth and buy her deceased husband's estate if he wanted to. Boaz therefore summoned him before the elders of the city next day, but the kinsman declined. Boaz was not *required* to marry Ruth, but gladly went beyond the letter of the law. Their descendant, Solomon, named one of the two pillars at the temple entrance after Boaz (1 Kings 7:21).

The Books of Samuel

The two Books of Samuel begin the history of the kings of Israel, around 1002 BC. A strong leader was needed to fight against the Philistines, a people who occupied the coastal area of Israel. The Philistines had superior iron weapons and were well organized and united. They continually harassed the disunited tribes of Israel. The Books of Samuel record the dramatic events of the reigns of Saul and David, who successfully united the tribes, fought off the Philistine threat and established an extensive empire of their own.

Samuel and his time

Samuel was priest, prophet and judge of Israel during the eleventh century BC. He was the son of Hannah and Elkanah. Before his birth, his mother had consecrated him to the service of God. As soon as he was weaned, she gave him to the priests at Shiloh. The chief priest was called Eli. He was a weak man, unable to control his corrupt sons, but for the time being he was Samuel's master. One night Samuel, still a child, was lying asleep in the Temple when he was visited by an angel. The angel announced that Eli's dynasty was doomed. Samuel told Eli in the morning, and the old man answered: 'It is the Lord; let Him do what seems good to Him' (1 Samuel 3:18).

In time Samuel became famous both as priest and also as the first great prophet since the time of Moses. When Eli died on hearing that his sons had been killed in battle, Samuel inherited his position and became the national leader. All Israel listened and obeyed when he appealed to them to get rid of their heathen gods (1 Samuel 7:3). He also defeated their old enemies, the Philistines by calling down God's thunder. The Philistines were so terrified that the Israelites then easily routed them (7:8—13).

Samuel was also a judge, making an annual circuit of central Israel while his sons assisted him in the south.

Israel, however, needed a king with continuing authority over all the tribes, a king who would enable them to act together against their common enemy the Philistines. One day a man named Saul visited Ramah, Samuel's home town, and Samuel learned from God that Saul was to be king (9:17). Samuel anointed him privately, then had Saul acclaimed by all Israel.

Saul proved to be a capable military leader and won several victories over Israel's enemies but Samuel soon regretted his appointment and proceeded to undermine his power. On one occasion Saul had called on the Israelites to fight back a Philistine invasion; Samuel promised to make a sacrifice to ask God's help but for seven days, he did not appear. More and more men were deserting, and eventually Saul offered the sacrifice himself. At that moment Samuel arrived and announced that Saul's rule would soon come to an end (13:14). Later Samuel told Saul to exterminate another enemy, the Amalekites—men, women, children and animals. Saul spared Agag, their king, as well as the best livestock, and the uncompromising Samuel had Agag brought before him. Claiming that Saul had been rejected by God, he hacked Agag to pieces (15:33).

God told Samuel that Israel's new king would be found among the sons of Jesse in Bethlehem; to prevent Saul from becoming suspicious, he was to take a heifer to sacrifice there (16:2). Following God's instructions, Samuel rejected the first seven of Jesse's sons but when Jesse presented his youngest son, David, Samuel immediately anointed him. He then returned home and—apart from briefly sheltering David from Saul (19:18)—lived out the remainder of his life quietly there. In appointing David (a king whose dynasty would endure) he had completed his task. His death (no age is mentioned) was mourned by all Israel.

It is difficult to assess Samuel because of inconsistencies in the Bible account of his life. In the story of his first meeting with Saul, he appears as the local seer of Ramah, someone who might be expected to trace lost asses for a quarter shekel's fee (9:8); this hardly sounds like the leader of all Israel found in chapters 7 to 8. Again, in 9:16 he accepts that God ordained the monarchy in order to save Israel from the Philistines; but elsewhere he speaks against it, seeing it as a vote of no confidence in himself (12:3). A king, he warned, would enslave the people and seize their property (8:11—17); their only rightful king was God (12:12).

Hannah ('grace') was Samuel's mother. For many years she had been barren and suffered bitterly because her husband Elkanah had another wife, Peninah, who bore many children. Peninah regularly reduced her to tears, although Elkanah made a clumsy attempt to comfort her: 'Am I not better for you than ten children?' (1 Samuel 1:8). The family went on an annual pilgrimage to Shiloh where the Temple then stood and there one day she prayed. She vowed that if God gave her a son, she would in turn give him to God, to serve in the Temple. Her prayer was granted, and she called her son Samuel, interpreting the name as 'asked from God' (*shaul me-el*). As soon as he was weaned she left him in Shiloh. Each year when she returned there on the annual pilgrimage she would visit him and give him a new coat. She later bore Elkanah three more sons and two daughters (2:21).

Hannah's song of triumph (2:1—10) is more like the celebration of a military victory ('my mouth opens wide against my enemies...the bows of the mighty are broken') than the birth of a child; it was probably inserted later.

Eli was the priest at Shiloh in Hannah's day. When he saw her praying with her lips moving but no sound coming out he thought she was drunk. This was not impossible, for Israelite festivals were, after all, celebrated in wine and strong drink (Deuteronomy 14:26). Tactlessly, he rebuked her but when she explained what she was doing, he promised her prayer would be granted. Her son, Samuel, was born as a result and was given into Eli's care.

Eli had two sons of his own, Hophni and Phinehas. They were unruly and Eli was too weak to control them. They used to seize the parts of animal offerings which were intended to be consumed by the sacrificer or burned on the altar. They also slept with the female Temple attendants. They paid no attention to Eli's protests 'because God wanted to kill them' (1 Samuel 2:25); in other words, their behaviour was unforgivable. God's verdict was announced first by an unnamed prophet (2:27—36) and then by Samuel: his sons would die on a single day, most of his descendants would be massacred and the office of High Priest would be transferred to a different family. Eli's descendants would have to serve under them. (This was fulfilled when Saul slaughtered the priests of Nob and when Solomon replaced Abiathar, Eli's great-great-grandson, by Zadok.)

Eli accepted it without protest. Eli died at the age of 98, after Israel fought a disastrous battle against the Philistines at Aphek, a few miles east of modern Tel Aviv. His sons had indeed died together; Israel had been defeated; and the Ark, which had been taken from Shiloh to the battlefield, had been captured. When he heard this news, Eli fell backwards from his stool by the Temple gate, breaking his neck.

SAMUEL

The last great judge of Israel was a proud, pious man who reluctantly chose Saul when the people demanded a king who would unite them. Samuel was a traditionalist who disliked the new order and prophesied that a king would bring ruin to Israel. He was pitiless towards his enemies (he personally hacked a captive king to death) and openly despised Saul for what he considered to be weakness.

HANNAH
Hannah, the mother of Samuel, was her husband's favourite wife, but for many years remained childless. At last, worn down by the mocking of her husband's more fertile second wife, she pleaded for a child in the Temple of Shiloh and vowed to offer it to the service of God. Her son, Samuel, was brought up by the priests.

Saul and his reign

Saul became the first king of Israel in about 1002 BC. Under constant threat from such enemies as the Philistines, Israel needed to be unified by a strong king. Saul seemed to fill that need. He was from the small tribe of Benjamin, so his choice would not cause as much tribal rivalry as the choice of a king from one of the more powerful tribes would have done. And his appearance gave him natural authority: a handsome man, he was a head taller than any of his countrymen.

Saul was anointed king by the priest and prophet Samuel. He had been searching for some stray asses when he came near the city of Ramah (about 5 miles north of Jerusalem) and his servant suggested that they should consult the seer who lived there. It was Samuel. Saul was amazed when Samuel invited him to a feast and privately anointed him (1 Samuel 9). A different story appears in 10:17—24. Saul assembled all the Israelites, and Saul was chosen as king by lot. Any opposition to him was soon silenced when Saul led an Israelite army of 330,000 to victory against the Ammonites. In his time as king, he fought many successful battles against the neighbouring states who still coveted Israel's land. He defeated the Amalekites in the south-west, expelled the Philistines from the centre of his realm with victories at Geba and Michmas (both largely due to the courage of his son Jonathan) and the valley of Elah (where David slew Goliath), and secured his eastern borders (14:47). When the Philistines attacked again in the north, however, Israel was routed and Saul, who had withdrawn to Mount Gilboa, fell upon his own sword. Three of his four sons died with him. The victorious Philistines found his body next day. After cutting off his head and stripping him of his armour, they carried the bodies of Saul and his sons away in triumph and fastened them to the walls of their city, Beth-shean. His armour was exhibited in the temple of their goddess Ashtaroth. Later, however, men from Israel came to rescue the bodies.

According to the existing Hebrew text of 1 Samuel 13:1 Saul had reigned just two years. However, in Hebrew the first half of this verse states that Saul was only one year old when he became king and it seems certain that a figure here has been omitted. Because of this doubt about the beginning of the verse, scholars feel that the second figure of two years may also be incorrect. Many people estimate that Saul's reign lasted not 2 but 20 years.

Saul was a modest, even diffident man. When Samuel first offered him the kingship, he protested that his was the lowest family of the smallest tribe. When his uncle asked him what Samuel had said, Saul did not even mention that he had been anointed king. Samuel predicted that a king would come to exploit and enslave the people but this prophecy was never fulfilled in Saul, but rather in David and—especially—in Solomon. Saul spared Agag, King of the Amalekites, against Samuel's wishes. And although he had sons and daughters, he was not ruthless enough to establish his own dynasty.

Another weakness was his mental instability. He repeatedly 'raved' (or 'prophesied'; the same word is used for both in Hebrew), invaded by a spirit from God: once after being anointed (10:10), again after hearing the Israelite women praise David above him (18:10), and after his daughter Michal, David's wife, foiled his attempt on David's life (19:24). His relationship with David was also unpredictable. The young shepherd (and future king) David was brought to court to soothe the troubled Saul with the harp. But when David killed the Philistine Goliath (see *Goliath*), Saul did not recognize him (17:55), even though by then David had become his armour bearer (16:21.) Later he gave David his daughter Michal in marriage but when David's fame grew, the insecure Saul tried several times to kill him. He even gave Michal to another husband. He had outbursts of generosity towards David (19:6, 24:19) but on one occasion slaughtered all the priests of the city of Nob for unwittingly helping him (22). In spite of his suspicions of David, he was thwarted largely by his own children— Jonathan (David's friend) and Michal

SAUL
Israel's first king was a strong, devout warrior who managed to unite the quarrelsome tribes under his leadership and ably defended the kingdom against its powerful enemies. Yet he felt insecure throughout his reign and was troubled by bouts of depression, almost paranoid suspicion and violent madness.

(David's wife), and by his inconsistency.

Religious passion once led him to sentence his own son Jonathan to death. Saul's army was pursuing a Philistine army when the priest told Saul that God would not let him continue the pursuit all night. Assuming that this was because one of his men had committed some sin, Saul declared that the sinner responsible would die. The priest discovered that it was Jonathan who had sinned: he had eaten wild honey in

breach of Saul's order to fast. Only the people's outcry (14:45) saved his life. On another occasion he threw his spear at Jonathan, angry at his son's support for David.

Samuel, who had anointed Saul king in the first place, apparently regretted his choice. He twice declared that God had rejected Saul, for offering sacrifice himself before the battle of Michmas instead of waiting for Samuel, and for sparing Agag. Saul's sanity was undermined by these pronouncements: he had always owed his authority to Samuel, and depended on his guidance so greatly that he even tried to reach him in the realm of the dead (28:11). On the eve of the battle of Gilboa, terrified of the Philistines, he received no divine message, and felt so isolated that he asked a witch to summon the spirit of the recently departed Samuel. The spirit predicted Saul's imminent defeat and death. Beaten in battle by the Philistines, Saul committed suicide rather than fall into enemy hands. Three of his sons, Jonathan, Abinadab and Malchishua, died with him. He left a fourth son, Ish-bosheth, and two daughters, Merab and Michal.

Jonathan was Saul's son and played a crucial part in the battles with the Philistines. Once Saul put him in charge of a thousand troops, with whom he destroyed the Philistine garrison at Geba (1 Samuel 13:3). One day when the Philistine army was encamped at Michmas, Jonathan and his armour-bearer crept alone across the ravine that separated the two armies and inflicted heavy casualties. After this Saul was able to lead the Israelites through to victory (14:1—23).

Jonathan was devoted to Saul, even though on the very day of this victory Saul sentenced him to death for eating wild honey when Saul had ordered the army to fast. This devotion later conflicted with his love for David. By this time Saul considered David a threat and he could not understand Jonathan's selfless love for a man who seemed likely to take his future throne. Saul wanted to kill David and called Jonathan's failure to fight for the throne an affront to his mother's virtue, meaning that Jonathan was behaving as if Saul were not his true father (20:30). Yet Jonathan tried hard to reconcile his father and his friend; sometimes he seemed to succeed (19:6, 20:2), but when Saul one day threw his spear at Jonathan himself, he was forced to accept at last that David would have to flee (20:33). At shooting practice Jonathan shouted out a warning, apparently to his servant but really intended for David: 'You are within

JONATHAN
A heroic warrior yet also a peacemaker, Jonathan was devoted both to his father Saul and to David. His lack of personal ambition outraged Saul: he could not understand why Jonathan loved and protected David, a man who seemed certain to deprive him of his claim to the throne of Israel.

range of the arrow! Run!' (20:37—8).
Even while David was living as an outlaw, Jonathan remained loyal to their friendship. He once went to David and assured him that he would become king; Jonathan wished only to be his deputy (23:17).
Jonathan died with Saul on Mount Gilboa, defeated by the Philistines. David mourned him in an emotional lament: 'How are the mighty fallen!' (2 Samuel 1:25) and later buried him. He left a five-year-old son, Mephibosheth.

Mephibosheth was Jonathan's son. His name, originally Meribbaal ('Baal strives'), was deliberately distorted to conceal the name of a heathen god (see *Ish-bosheth*). He was only 5 when Jonathan was killed, and as his nurse fled from the victorious Philistines, she dropped and crippled him (2 Samuel 4:4). When David had established his kingdom, he invited Mephibosheth to eat at his table, out of loyalty to Jonathan, and gave him Saul's former estate in Gibeah. The estate was worked by a former servant of Saul, named Ziba (9:10).

Later, when David's son Absalom attacked Jerusalem and David fled, Ziba met David with supplies of food and drink. He said that Mephibosheth had remained in Jerusalem and expected to be made king (16:3). David promptly gave Ziba Mephibosheth's estate. After the rebellion, Mephibosheth told David that Ziba had lied; he had asked Ziba to take him to David, but Ziba had instead gone alone. Mephibosheth's tokens of mourning—he neither trimmed his beard nor washed his clothes throughout David's flight from Jerusalem—confirmed his version, but David divided the estate between them (19:29). Later, when the Gibeonites demanded the execution of seven of Saul's descendants (see *David*), David spared Mephibosheth—perhaps because he was no threat.

Ish-bosheth, Saul's fourth son, was originally named Eshbaal (1 Chronicles 8:33) 'man of Baal'. Baal was the name of the Canaanites' principal heathen god and Jewish tradition replaced his name with the Hebrew *bosheth*, 'shame'. When Saul and his three other sons died, Saul's general, Abner, proclaimed Ish-bosheth king over the northern tribes, while David ruled Judah.

Ish-bosheth lost Abner's support when he accused Abner of taking Saul's concubine, Rizpah. Soon afterwards his two remaining captains murdered him at home during his afternoon sleep and brought David his severed head.

Michal was the younger daughter of Saul. When Saul's army was fighting the Philistines, Saul offered to marry his daughter to whoever killed the giant Goliath (1 Samuel 17:25). David succeeded. Saul first promised David his elder daughter Merab, but married her to someone else at the last moment (18:19). He then offered him Michal at the price of a hundred Philistine foreskins. Saul hoped that David would be killed in the attempt to capture them (18:25), but David brought twice the required number, and so married Michal, who loved him dearly. When Saul had become suspicious of David

MICHAL
Saul's daughter, Michal, fell in love with David and became his first wife. She was a resourceful and independent woman and her quick thinking saved David's life when Saul tried to kill him. Later, however, she appears as a proud, almost arrogant character, despising her husband for his abandoned dancing before the Ark of the Covenant.

and sent agents to kill him at his home, she let him out by the window, placed a life-size idol in his bed, and told them that he was sick. The deception was not discovered until David was safely away. Saul was furious and Michal diplomatically explained that David had threatened to kill her.

While David was hiding in the Judean desert, Saul gave her to another husband, Palti. After Saul's death, however, when his commander Abner wanted to join David's side, David

insisted that Michal should return with him. Palti accompanied her almost as far as Jerusalem, weeping all the way (2 Samuel 3:16). Her regal upbringing led her to scoff at David's abandoned dancing when he installed the Ark in Jerusalem (6:20). It seems that David never again cohabited with her and she never bore a child. According to 21:8, David slew 'five sons of Michal, Saul's daughter, whom she bore to Adriel'; but Adriel's wife was Merab and her name should be read here not Michal's.

Abner was Saul's cousin and was appointed his chief of staff. On one occasion David, while living as an outlaw, stole into Saul's camp by night and took Saul's spear and water flask. He then taunted Abner for neglecting the king (1 Samuel 26:15). In fact, however, Abner was so loyal that, after Saul's death, he set up Saul's only surviving son Ish-bosheth as a rival king to David. In the war that followed between David and Ish-bosheth, David's army, under Joab, was more effective and penetrated to Gibeon (2 Samuel 2: 12—32), in the heart of Ish-bosheth's territory. Abner suggested a tournament between twelve soldiers from either side. Each soldier caught an opponent by the head and thrust a sword through him, so that all fell simultaneously. In the battle that followed, Abner killed David's nephew, Asahel, in self-defence. He avoided defeat only by reminding Joab of the bitterness of civil war, appealing to him: 'shall the sword devour for ever?' The two armies withdrew—for the time.

Abner continued to support Ish-bosheth, abandoning him only when the king reproached him for taking Saul's concubine. After serving Saul's house so well, he thought he did not deserve such criticism and he travelled to David's court in Hebron.

He was welcomed there and sent on a mission to win over Ish-bosheth's subjects in the north. However, the brothers of Asahel, the man he had killed in self-defence, lured him back and murdered him in revenge.

Rizpah was Saul's concubine. After Saul's death, his general, Abner, took her into his household, possibly as a claim to succession (compare 2 Samuel 16:21). Her two sons perished as two of the seven descendants of Saul hanged by David to end a drought. (The drought was sent as punishment for Saul's attacks upon the Gibeonites, whom Israel had promised never to harm—2 Samuel 21.) Rizpah covered the bodies of all seven with sackcloth, and throughout the summer prevented any bird or animal from settling on them—a lone symbol of decency amid the implacability of God and man alike.

GOLIATH
Goliath stood over 9ft (2.7m) tall and was the Philistines' champion warrior. Once when the Israelite and Philistine army found themselves in a military stalemate, he daily issued a scornful challenge, but no-one believed that he could be overcome. At last David, armed only with a sling, accepted the challenge and by a skilful shot, knocked him off balance, then killed him. His defeat demoralized the Philistines, and the Israelites won a crushing victory.

When David heard of her vigil he brought their bones to be buried in the grave of Saul's father.

Goliath was a Philistine champion from the city of Gath who lived during the reign of King Saul. To decide the outcome of a confrontation between the Israelite and Philistine armies about 15 miles west of Jerusalem (1 Samuel 17) he challenged the Israelites to offer an opponent to meet him in single combat.

Goliath was over 9 feet (3 metres) tall, with heavy armour, including an iron spear weighing more than 14 pounds (6 kilograms). David (Saul's armour bearer at the time) accepted the challenge, and, before the contemptuous Goliath could come close, knocked him unconscious with a stone shot from his catapult to the forehead. He then used Goliath's own sword to cut off his head. According to 2 Samuel 21:19, however, a certain El-hanan slew 'Goliath from

Gath, the staff of whose spear was like a weaver's beam', almost exactly as in David's story (1 Samuel 17:7). Some say there were two giants called Goliath, or consider El-hanan another name of David; cynics suggest that the exploit was El-hanan's but was later attached to David's name. 1 Chronicles 20:5 states that El-hanan slew Goliath's *brother*.

Ahimelech, a grandson of Eli, was priest at Nob (just north of Jerusalem). After the Philistines had destroyed Shiloh and its Temple, Nob became the central shrine. When David fled from Saul, he went to Nob and persuaded Ahimelech that Saul had sent him on a secret mission. Ahimelech gave him holy bread and Goliath's sword (1 Samuel 21:2–10). The incident was witnessed by Saul's chief herdsman, Doeg the Edomite and he informed Saul of what he had seen. Saul accused Ahimelech of treachery but the priest answered by praising David's patriotism. He and all his clan were condemned to death. Of all Saul's followers, only Doeg was prepared to slay the priests. Eighty-five died, fulfilling Samuel's prophecy that Eli's descendants would die young (2:32); only Abiathar, a son of Ahimelech, survived (22:20).

Achish was King of the Philistine city of Gath. David fled to him to escape Saul. Achish's courtiers, however, had not forgotten David's exploits against the Philistines—he had, for example, killed their champion Goliath. Afraid that they would now kill him in revenge, David pretended to be mad. Achish was convinced, rebuked his servants for ever admitting David to court ('am I short of mad men?') and sent him away unharmed (1 Samuel 21:11–15). When David had acquired 600 followers, however, he returned to Gath. It must have been embarrassing for David to have to explain away his earlier performance but the credulous Achish received him favourably. Seeing the opportunity to divide and rule the Israelites, he granted David's request for a city of his own and gave him Ziklag, about 25 miles south-west of Gath and 15 miles north-west of Beersheba.

For more than a year David managed to persuade Achish that he was raiding Judah (to the south-east), when in fact he was fighting the Amalekites and other enemies of Israel to the south-west (1 Samuel 27). Achish intended David to fight for the Philistines in the decisive battle against Saul at Gilboa, but when the other Philistine nobles suspected David's loyalty, Achish reluctantly dismissed him. Achish must have felt foolish when David became king of Israel and routed all of the Philistines (2 Samuel 5:17–25). However, David did not destroy the kingdom of Gath, which still had a king called Achish in Solomon's day (1 Kings 2:39).

David and his family

David (c.1030–960BC), was the youngest of eight sons of Jesse. He was born in Bethlehem, of the tribe of Judah. He was handsome, with a red complexion and fine eyes. While he was looking after his father's sheep one day, he was summoned home to meet Samuel. The prophet anointed him king, though Saul remained on the throne (1 Samuel 16:12).

David was first invited to court as a harpist, to relieve Saul's bouts of depression, and became his armour bearer. Soon afterwards, he killed the Philistine giant Goliath in single combat, and was rewarded with the hand of Michal, Saul's daughter. He also became a close friend of Saul's son, Jonathan. David evidently became a popular hero and when the Israelite women began to sing: 'Saul has smitten thousands, but David tens of thousands', Saul saw him as a rival for the throne and tried to kill him. David eventually fled for his life. He went to live as an outlaw, building up an army of outlaws and malcontents who roamed the wilderness of Judah, occasionally exacting 'protection' from wealthy citizens. Saul, however, pursued him relentlessly and he became a vassal of Achish, King of the Philistines. David convinced Achish that he was raiding Israel, while he was in fact fighting Israel's enemies. Meanwhile the Philistines were preparing for an onslaught on Israel at Mount Gilboa, and Achish intended David to fight on the Philistine side. The other Philistine leaders mistrusted David and sent him away and David, despite his show of protest, must have been relieved. It was during this battle that Saul and three of his sons, including Jonathan, were killed.

After Saul's death, David, now aged 30, was anointed king by the tribe of Judah in Hebron. Saul's surviving son, Ish-bosheth, was made king of the northern tribes and a struggle began for supremacy. Ish-bosheth's untrained army, drafted from the tribes, was no match for David's professionals, and when Ish-bosheth died, the remaining tribes swore allegiance to David in Hebron. David was married to Saul's daughter Michal, and this reinforced his claims to kingship. His army now entered Jerusalem through its water shaft and captured it from the Jebusites (2 Samuel 5:8), establishing an impregnable capital which he made the focus of Israel's religious traditions by installing there the ancient Ark. He was no less successful against foreign nations. As soon as he became King of all Israel, the Philistines twice attacked near Jerusalem, hoping to cut him off from the northern tribes, but were each time utterly routed. He then conquered in turn Moab (executing two out of every three Moabite soldiers), most of Syria, and Ammon (after more than a year's siege). He placed his own garrisons in Edom, south of the Dead Sea. He must also have pacified the last Canaanite enclaves in Israel's territory (Judges 1:27–33). Most of David's empire had never belonged to any of the twelve tribes, and their ancient organization now became submerged.

David was a successful leader who inspired utter loyalty in his soldiers. He was also a skilful politician, for he managed to avoid dishonour not only while in exile among the Philistines, but also by his behaviour as rivals to the throne were eliminated after Saul's death. A messenger who falsely claimed to have killed Saul at Gilboa (2 Samuel 1:15) was executed, as were the two captains who brought him the severed head of their lord Ish-bosheth. When Saul's former general, Abner, was murdered, David composed an elegy and gave him a state funeral (2 Samuel

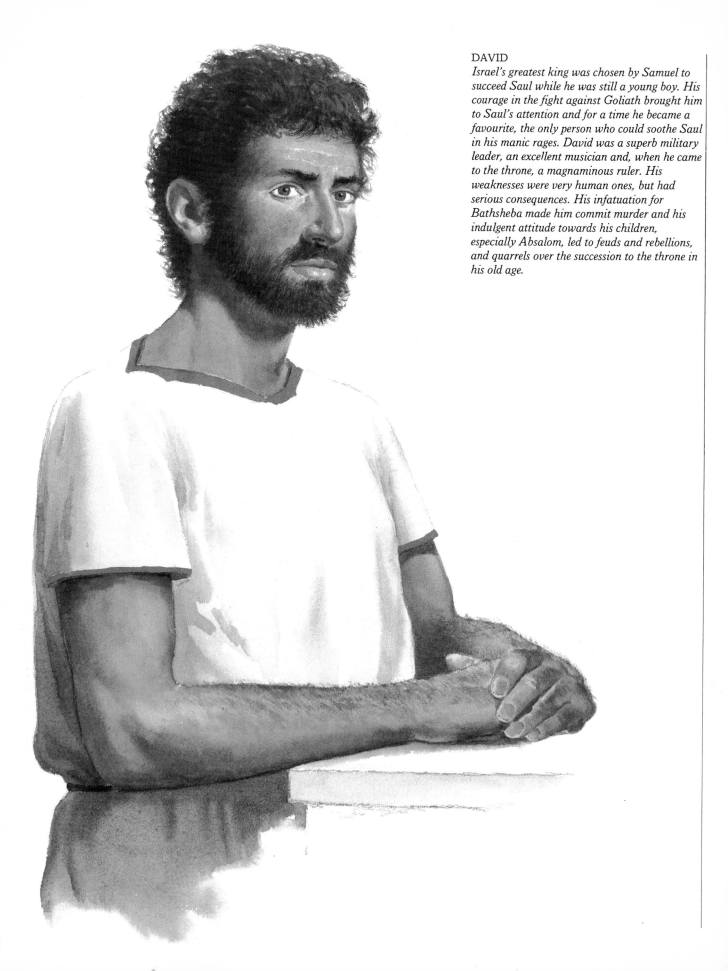

DAVID

Israel's greatest king was chosen by Samuel to succeed Saul while he was still a young boy. His courage in the fight against Goliath brought him to Saul's attention and for a time he became a favourite, the only person who could soothe Saul in his manic rages. David was a superb military leader, an excellent musician and, when he came to the throne, a magnaminous ruler. His weaknesses were very human ones, but had serious consequences. His infatuation for Bathsheba made him commit murder and his indulgent attitude towards his children, especially Absalom, led to feuds and rebellions, and quarrels over the succession to the throne in his old age.

3:33). Seven more sons and grandsons of Saul were killed on his orders—but only to end a three-year famine which God had told him was a punishment for Saul's attacks on the Gibeonites. (Israel had sworn never to harm them.) Later, David swore to spare the life of Saul's relative Shimei, who had cursed him; instead, he asked Solomon to kill him.

His private life, however, was turbulent. As was normal for the time, he had several wives and concubines. His fourth (and apparently last) wife was Bathsheba, the wife of one of his generals. He seduced her, then sent her husband to his death in battle so that he could marry her. His indulgence as a father allowed his eldest son, Amnon to seduce his own half-sister Tamar and another son, Absalom, who killed Amnon in revenge, rebelled against him and claimed the throne. The rebellion cost tens of thousands of lives, including Absalom's own. Further revolts broke out until David, close to death, named his son Solomon as his successor. Dynasties had never been known in Israel; leaders had simply emerged.

In his last year, at the age of 70, he felt cold, however many garments were laid on him, until the beautiful virgin, Abishag, was placed in his bed. David 'knew her not' (1 Kings 1:4); he must have been weak indeed.

In the middle of all the turmoil of his life, he was resilient and pragmatic. When his illegitimate son by Bathsheba fell sick, he fasted for a week, but when the child died David ate again, saying: 'I shall go to him, but he will not return to me' (2 Samuel 12:23). Similarly, after Absalom's death, he soon resumed his royal duties. The faith that sustained him appears in many of the psalms ascribed to him.

The Book of Chronicles idealizes David's life, omitting his years of hiding from Saul and his court scandals, and instead recounting his detailed plans for the construction and personnel of the Temple (1 Chronicles 22–9). His reign was remembered as a time of success and prosperity. Hence when Israel fell under foreign domination, the hope grew that a messiah ('anointed') of David's line would one day restore that glorious age.

ABIGAIL
David met his second wife, Abigail, while he was living as an outlaw, a fugitive from Saul. She was married at the time to a prosperous farmer and saved his life by herself paying off David's band of outlaws. Attracted by her beauty and strength of character, David married her as soon as he heard her husband had died.

Abigail (which may mean 'my father is joy') was a beautiful and wise woman, who became David's second wife. Abigail's first husband was Nabal ('churl'), a rich farmer in part of the Judean desert, where David and his soldiers hid from Saul. David and his band of outlaws demanded protection money from Nabal for not harming his shepherds or flocks. Nabal refused, describing David's army disparagingly as 'men that break away each from his master' (1 Samuel 25:10). David resolved to wipe out Nabal's family, but when Abigail heard that he was approaching with his men, she rode out with asses laden with bread, wine, mutton, corn and dried fruit. These she presented to David, apologizing for her 'churlish' husband. The next day she told Nabal what had happened. 'His heart died within him, and became as a stone'; he died ten days later, apparently of a stroke. At this news David blessed the Lord and proposed marriage to Abigail, who humbly accepted. At the same time he took another wife, Ahinoam, who bore his first son, Amnon. Both wives were captured in an Amalekite raid on David's city Ziklag, but were soon recovered. Abigail bore David's second son, called either Chileab (2 Samuel 3:3) or Daniel (1 Chronicles 3:1). David also had a sister called Abigail, the mother of the warrior Amasa.

Bathsheba was the beautiful wife of Uriah. She may have been the granddaughter of the wise Ahitophel; his son and her father bear the same unusual name, Eliam.

While her husband was away fighting against the Ammonite capital Rabbah (see *David*), David saw Bathsheba bathing (2 Samuel 11:2), from his palace roof; perhaps she intended to catch his eye. He had her brought to him and soon afterwards she sent the message that she was pregnant. David summoned Uriah back from the war and sent him home with a gift of food, hoping that he would sleep with his wife and later think the child was his. Uriah, however, slept at the palace door, protesting that he could not indulge in home comforts while there was a war on; he may in reality have known the truth from David's servants. David told him to stay another night and made him drunk—but he still refused to go home. Uriah was then sent back to the battlefield, carrying a message for the commander, Joab. Although Uriah did not know it, the message instructed Joab to put him in the front line and then retire, leaving him to be killed. Joab obeyed but less blatantly sent several soldiers, including Uriah, right up to the city wall, where they were shot by the Ammonite archers.

Bathsheba married David immediately after her week's mourning, and though the son she bore died, she later gave David a second son, Solomon. When David grew old and his oldest surviving son, Adonijah, claimed the throne, Bathsheba made sure that Solomon would be king by reminding David that he had secretly promised her this (1 Kings 1:17).

BATHSHEBA
Bathsheba was, unintentionally, the cause of David's greatest crime: he arranged for her husband to be killed so that he could marry her and acknowledge her child as his own.

Abishag was brought as a young girl to David's court when, in his old age, he suffered from a condition which made him always cold. His servants suggested that a young virgin would keep him warm. Abishag, from the city of Shunem in northern Israel, was selected. Although she shared David's bed, he 'knew her not' (1 Kings 1:4). After David's death, his son Adonijah asked Solomon's permission to marry her. Marrying a concubine of a previous king sometimes constituted a claim to the throne and Solomon refused to allow it. Nothing more is known of her.

Amnon was David's eldest son. He fell in love with his beautiful half-sister Tamar (2 Samuel 13) and, despairing of ever approaching her, he pined away. His cousin Jonadab asked what was troubling him and on Jonadab's advice, Amnon took to his bed. He then asked his anxious father whether Tamar could bake him some cakes. David readily indulged his sick son's whim. Tamar duly arrived but Amnon refused to eat until the two were left alone. He asked Tamar to feed him and then attacked her. She pleaded with him not to rape her but instead to ask David's permission to marry her. (David would have refused, for Amnon knew all too well that incest was forbidden—Leviticus 18:9; Tamar was simply trying to shake him off.) After the rape, Amnon felt disgusted and told Tamar to leave and although she cried that this wrong exceeded the first, he made his servant lock her out. Tamar never recovered. Like a mourner, she tore her royal cloak, put ashes on her head, and went about moaning, until her full brother Absalom brought her to his house. There she remained, desolate. Two years later, Absalom invited Amnon to sheep-shearing festivities, plied him with drink and had him slain. It was this act of revenge and its punishment by David that led ultimately to Absalom's revolt.

Absalom was David's third son. He was the handsomest man in Israel. His hair, which he cut annually, weighed about five pounds.

When Absalom's full sister Tamar was raped by their half-brother Amnon he took her into his household and then concealed his feelings for two years before taking revenge (2 Samuel 13:23). After killing Amnon he fled to Geshur, east of Lake Galilee, where he remained for three years until David recalled him to Jerusalem. For two years, however, David kept him under house arrest and refused to see him. Frustrated by this treatment, Absalom set Joab's crops on fire to gain his attention (14:30), and through him obtained an audience and reconciliation with his father.

The resentment caused by years of exile and confinement drove Absalom, now David's eldest surviving son, to claim the throne. David's rule had become less popular: he had neglected the daily administration of justice and had imposed forced labour (2 Samuel 20:24). Absalom won popularity by calling for reform. He also courted the elders (2 Samuel 17:4), whose traditional power David had apparently abolished.

Four years later he proclaimed himself king in Hebron, as David himself had once done (15:10). Support for Absalom was massive, so much so that David, afraid of being trapped inside Jerusalem, fled across the Jordan. He took refuge in Mahanaim, whose inhabitants, vulnerable to raids from the east, could evidently be relied on to support the reigning king. Absalom occupied

ABISHAG
The young girl from Shunem who was chosen to comfort David in his old age was famous for her beauty. After David's death his son, Adonijah, asked permission to marry her. This was interpreted as a claim to his late father's throne—and Adonijah was killed by the new king, Solomon.

ABSALOM
Absalom was handsome, popular and, apparently, vain. His life, both personal and public, was full of drama and tragedy. He killed his own half-brother to avenge the rape of his sister; lived for years in exile, then led a popular but unsuccessful uprising against his father, David.

Jerusalem but realized too late that the real key to victory would have been David's death. In the hope of achieving this, he marched into unfamiliar country across the Jordan. But here David's professional army inflicted 20,000 casualties on his untrained forces. The revolt collapsed when Absalom caught his head in a tree and was impaled by Joab's darts.

Absalom's personal life was no less tragic; his three sons (14:27) died before him. Seeing that he would have no son to carry on his name, he set up a pillar near Jerusalem to commemorate his name instead (18:18).

Adonijah was David's fourth son. He claimed the throne in David's old age at which time he was apparently the eldest surviving (2 Samuel 3:4). He was spoilt (his father had never rebuked him—1 Kings 1:6) and very handsome and began to act as if he were already king—preparing chariots and outrunners, and a feast of accession for his supporters, who included the general Joab and the priest Abiathar. He was out-manoeuvred by the prophet Nathan and David's wife Bathsheba, who together persuaded David to declare Solomon as his successor (see *Nathan*). Adonijah's feast was interrupted by the news that Solomon had been publicly anointed and acclaimed. Adonijah fled to the altar (presumably in Gibeon, then the main sanctuary—1 Kings 3:4) but was pursued, captured and brought before Solomon. Solomon sent him home. Later, Adonijah asked through Bathsheba for permission to marry Abishag—the girl who had been placed in the ageing David's bed in an attempt to warm him up. Solomon answered that his request amounted to a claim to the throne, and had him killed. Relations with a predecessor's concubine could indeed constitute a claim to succession (Genesis 35:22); but Abishag had never been intimate with David (1 Kings 1:4). Perhaps Bathsheba anticipated this outcome when she agreed to speak on Adonijah's behalf.

David's warriors

Joab was David's nephew, the eldest of three warrior sons of his sister Zeruiah. He became David's chief of staff, and was indispensable in all his wars, both internal and foreign. He was utterly loyal to David: he obeyed David's order to have his captain Uriah killed in battle (so that David could marry Uriah's wife Bathsheba) and when the city they were besieging was about to fall he asked David to come and complete the conquest, so that the city should bear David's name.

JOAB
David's nephew and commander-in-chief was intensely loyal to David but ruthless to everyone else. His bravery, military skill and sheer ferocity were invaluable in extending Israel's borders yet Joab treacherously murdered several rivals and even slew David's rebellious son Absalom against the king's explicit order.

David's grief over Absalom's death overwhelmed him but Joab did not shrink from taking him to task; he roused David to resume his royal duties by complaining that David was behaving as if he would rather have seen Absalom alive than his own supporters (2 Samuel 19:6; compare 24:3).

To his enemies, Joab usually showed excessive violence. On one occasion, in an early battle against Ish-bosheth's forces, he agreed to stop the fighting even though he was in a winning position but in general he was ruthless. In the last battle against Absalom, David ordered him to 'deal gently for me with young Absalom' (2 Samuel 18:5); instead he killed him with three darts. David seems never to have discovered Joab's part in Absalom's death. Perhaps he was so grieved by the loss of his son that he wanted no details.

On two occasions when David welcomed to his side an enemy general, Joab promptly murdered his potential rival: Abner, commander to Ish-bosheth and Amasa, commander to Absalom. Yet David relied on him so greatly (2 Samuel 3:39) that he remained unpunished.

Eventually, however, his punishment came. In David's old age, Joab backed Adonijah's claim to the throne against Solomon's. Solomon promptly had him killed, even though he had taken sanctuary at the altar.

Abishai was Joab's brother, Zeruiah's second son. He played a major role, in David's battles, though always under the command of his elder brother Joab and was ranked just below David's three finest warriors (2 Samuel 23:19). He fought against Abner (2:24), against a coalition of Syrians and Ammonites (10:10), against Absalom (18:5) and against Sheba (20:6). Abishai had the opportunity to kill two other enemies of David: Saul himself, whom he and David once found asleep in his camp (1 Samuel 26:7); and Shimei, who had cursed David (2 Samuel 16:9). Both these killings would have brought discredit to David, who wisely ordered the men to be spared. Abishai once rescued an aged David from a Philistine giant but the escape was such a narrow

A major crisis in David's life came when his son Absalom murdered another of his sons. David banished him but after a time, found himself torn between his desire to recall Absalom and reluctance to lose face. Seeing this, Joab brought before David a woman who pretended to be a widow. She told David that one of her two sons had killed the other. Although it was the custom to avenge one death with another, she implored David not to

allow the family to kill the murderer, as this would leave her childless. When David agreed to spare him, she admitted her story was a parable: if he had agreed to spare her son, why did he not spare Absalom? David understood that Joab had sent her, but that he was right. Absalom was recalled, but eventually, embittered by years of exile and then house arrest, he rose against his father—only to be killed in the ensuing civil war.

one that David's followers swore he should never risk his life in battle again—though he continued to do so (2 Samuel 21:16—17).

Asahel was Zeruiah's youngest son, the brother of Joab and Abishai. He is described as being 'swift as a gazelle' (2 Samuel 2:18). He died in Gibeon attempting to kill Ish-bosheth's commander, Abner. Abner was unwilling to start a vendetta with a member of David's family (Asahel was David's nephew) and advised him to attack a less important soldier. When Asahel persisted, Abner killed him. Abner was later killed in revenge by Asahel's eldest brother, Joab.

Uriah was a Hittite (at this time a general term for foreigners from the north). His name (Hebrew: 'my light is the Lord') suggests that his family had adopted Israel's faith. He was one of David's elite corps of thirty warriors (2 Samuel 23:39) and was married to Bathsheba. David ordered him to be killed so that he could marry Bathsheba.

Ittai the Gittite, (that is, from Gath), was a soldier who must have joined David during his stay in Ziklag (see *David*). He remained loyal during Absalom's rebellion, and must have been a much-prized warrior, for David put him in charge of one-third of the army.

Amasa was one of David's nephews, a son of his sister Abigail (2 Samuel 17:25). Absalom made him commander of his rebel forces, and after the revolt David tried to win back Absalom's sympathizers by appointing Amasa commander in place of Joab. His first task was to raise an army from Judah in three days to march against the new rebel, Sheba. He failed. Later, during the campaign, Joab treacherously murdered him. Taking Amasa's beard with his right hand as if to kiss him in a gesture of friendship, Joab plunged a sword into his groin with his left.

Benaiah, son of a Chief Priest (1 Chronicles 27:5), was put in charge of the (apparently foreign) soldiers of David's bodyguard (2 Samuel 8:18). He killed a lion single-handed, and slew two Moabite warriors as well as killing an Egyptian assailant with the Egyptian's own spear (2 Samuel 23:21). During Adonijah's rebellion he remained loyal to David, who chose him to represent the army at Solomon's coronation (1 Kings 1:32). After the coronation, Solomon ordered him to execute Adonijah (a threat to Solomon's throne), Joab (at the altar) and Shimei (as David's dying order). He was rewarded with Joab's post as Chief of Staff.

Religious leaders

Uzzah was a son of Abinadab, from the city of Kiriath-jearim. Throughout Saul's reign, the Ark was kept in his house (1 Samuel 7:1). When David decided to bring the Ark to Jerusalem, Uzzah accompanied the procession. Suddenly, however, the oxen drawing the cart stumbled, and when Uzzah steadied the Ark with his hand, he was struck dead. David left the Ark in the house of a man named Obed-edom and waited three months before completing the procession to Jerusalem. In 2 Samuel 6:10, Obed-edom is called a Gittite (i.e. from Gath), perhaps implying that if Israel's Ark was violated in some way, a non-Israelite would not be affected. But 1 Chronicles 15:18 says he belonged to the priestly tribe of Levi.

Gad was a prophet, known as 'David's seer' (2 Samuel 24:11). During Saul's reign he advised David not to flee abroad from Saul's fury but to remain in Judah (1 Samuel 22:5). During David's reign, Gad rebuked him for counting the Israelites (God had promised the patriarchs that they would be too many to count—Genesis 13:16, 32:12), and let him choose his punishment: seven years famine, three months flight from enemies or three days plague. David chose the last, saying: 'let us fall into the hand of God, not of man (i.e. corn merchants or soldiers)' (2 Samuel 24:14). When the plague ceased, an angel appeared by the threshing floor of a man named Araunah in Jerusalem and Gad told David to buy the site for the Temple.

Nathan was a prophet consulted by David, after he had brought the Ark to Jerusalem. David proposed building a house for the Lord, where the Ark could be permanently kept. Nathan at first approved (2 Samuel 7:3) but that night God told him that, instead, he would build a house for David, that is, establish his dynasty for ever. The Temple would be built not by David but by his son. According to 1 Chronicles 22:8, Nathan added that David had 'shed much blood', but 1 Kings 5:3 more charitably explains that David was not secure from his enemies.

Later on in his reign, David made Bathsheba pregnant and sent her husband Uriah to his death (see *Bathsheba*). Nathan did not shrink from delivering an unwelcome message. He pretended to report the case of a rich herdsman who had stolen his poor neighbour's only lamb. 'That man shall die!' was David's indignant verdict. 'Thou art the man!', Nathan replied. He added that David would be punished: his own wives would be dishonoured (by Absalom, as it turned out) and Bathsheba's child would die. Yet Nathan blessed Bathsheba's second child Solomon (2 Samuel 12:25), and ensured that he would succeed David.

In David's old age, his eldest surviving son Adonijah claimed the throne. Nathan advised Bathsheba to remind David that he had promised her that Solomon would succeed him. (This is the first reference to such a promise; cynics wonder whether David ever made it, or whether Nathan and Bathsheba conspired to persuade the confused old man that he had.) As soon as Bathsheba left David, Nathan told him that Adonijah was at that moment feasting to celebrate his accession. David was enraged. He commanded Nathan and Zadok the priest to anoint Solomon immediately and have him acclaimed king.

Abiathar was the sole survivor of Saul's massacre of the priests of Nob (1 Samuel 22:18—20). He joined David in hiding from Saul, and was able to consult God for him, using an ephod. In some passages the ephod was a priestly girdle (e.g. 2 Samuel 6:14), but

Abiathar's ephod seems to have been a device that could give either an affirmative answer (e.g. 1 Samuel 30:8) or none at all (14:37). By means of the ephod, Abiathar warned David that Saul was about to attack Keilah, where the two had fled (23:11), and later assured him of victory over some Amalekite raiders who had captured the wives and children of David's followers.

Abiathar continued to serve David after he had come to the throne. When Absalom and his supporters occupied Jerusalem in revolt against David, Abiathar and his brother Zadok helped to undermine the occupation by secretly passing information through their sons to David. (This 'brother' Zadok seems to contradict 1 Samuel 22:19—20, according to which no relative of Abiathar survived. Some scholars suggest he may have been the priest serving in Jerusalem when David captured the city.) David apparently promoted Zadok above Abiathar (Zadok is always mentioned first); this, together with the nagging thought that David had brought about the massacre of his clan in the first place, may explain why Abiathar later supported Adonijah's unsuccessful revolt against David (1 Kings 1:7). When Solomon, David's named successor, ascended the throne, Zadok was appointed priest, while Abiathar was banished to the priestly city of Anathoth.

Supporters and enemies

Ahitophel and **Hushai** lived in Jerusalem during David's reign. Ahitophel was a wise man whose advice was said to be like the word of God (2 Samuel 16:23). He left David's court to support Absalom's rebellion (see *Absalom*). When David fled from Jerusalem, Ahitophel advised Absalom to show defiance by sleeping with David's concubines. He also offered to lead 12,000 men immediately to find and kill David. Hushai also seemed to support Absalom but was secretly loyal to David. He told Absalom that the defeat of David and his followers required a far larger army, of 'all Israel', which Absalom himself should lead (17:11). The vain Absalom took Hushai's

advice. Ahitophel went home and suffocated himself, perhaps because he knew that the revolt was doomed and that he would fall into David's hands. Meanwhile, Hushai kept David informed through the priests of Jerusalem.

Ahimaaz was the son of Zadok the priest and served as a spy for David when Absalom occupied Jerusalem. David told Ahimaaz to remain behind with the Ark (2 Samuel 15:36) and send him information. He and a fellow priest slipped out to David's hiding place in Bahurim, just south of Jerusalem, to warn him that Absalom would soon set out to find him. The two priest spies were seen leaving Jerusalem and Absalom's agents at Bahurim tried to find them; fortunately for them, they were hidden by a sympathizer. When Absalom was eventually killed, Ahimaaz wanted to give David the news himself. The bearer of bad news was often unwelcome and David's commander Joab knew that David would be grieved by Absalom's death. He therefore sent an Ethiopian servant, but Ahimaaz insisted on going too. Running through the Jordan valley, he was able to announce the victory before the Ethiopian, who had presumably taken the direct but hilly route. When David asked after Absalom, however, Ahimaaz pretended not to know. He left the Ethiopian to announce the bad news—that Absalom was dead (18:22—33).

Barzillai was a wealthy citizen who brought furniture and food for David and his followers when they fled to Mahanaim before the rebel forces of Absalom (2 Samuel 17:27). After the revolt David invited him to stay in Jerusalem, but he declined, saying he was aged 80—too old even to taste his food (19:35). He asked David to take Chimham (presumably his son) instead. On his death-bed David charged his son Solomon to support the children of Barzillai (1 Kings 2:7).

Jonadab was David's nephew, the son of his brother Shimeah. He was the first to notice that David's son Amnon was

lovesick. He won Amnon's confidence and worked out the detailed plan enabling Amnon to seduce his own half-sister, Tamar. When Tamar's full brother Absalom killed Amnon, it was rumoured that Absalom had also killed all Amnon's brothers; only Jonadab knew the truth. He was also able to tell David that Absalom had planned the murder since the day of the outrage. He evidently had a gift for extracting confidential information.

Shimei was a relative of Saul. He supported Absalom's rebellion (see *Absalom*) out of spite for David. He lived in Bahurim, the village to which David first fled from Jerusalem and there he cursed him and pelted him with stones (2 Samuel 16:5). When David returned victorious Shimei abjectly begged forgiveness. At that time David swore to spare his life but with his dying breath, charged Solomon to kill him (1 Kings 2:8). Solomon ordered Shimei never to leave Jerusalem on pain of death, and when, three years later, Shimei went searching for two runaway slaves, Solomon had him executed.

Sheba may have been a relative of Saul. Like Saul, he came from the tribe of Benjamin, and his father's name, Bichri, resembles that of Saul's ancestor Becorath. After the end of Absalom's rebellion but before David had returned to Jerusalem, he raised a revolt of the northern tribes. These tribes had remained loyal to David and were offended when David invited his fellow tribesmen of Judah (who had supported Absalom) to accompany him back to Jerusalem (2 Samuel 19:12, 42).

David's forces chased Sheba right into upper Galilee, to the city of Abel, which they beseiged. There a wise woman begged their commander, Joab, not to destroy the city and he answered that he would be satisfied with Sheba's severed head. The citizens promptly supplied it.

Though this rebellion was quashed, it was symptomatic of the continuing division between the northern and southern tribes, and foreshadowed the break-up of the kingdom after the death of David's son and successor Solomon.

The Books of Kings and Chronicles

The Books of Kings and 2 Chronicles begin with the prosperous reign of Solomon (961—922 BC) and describe the events that followed his death. The kingdom was divided into two, Judah in the south and Israel in the north. Judah's capital was Jerusalem, Israel's became Samaria. Over the next two hundred years, the kingdoms were threatened by various powerful nations and also warred against each other. Israel was eventually destroyed by the Assyrians in 722 BC. In 587 BC the kingdom of Judah was overrun by the Babylonians, who had succeeded the Assyrians as the dominant near-eastern power. Most of the inhabitants of Judah were carried into exile in Babylon.

Solomon (reigned 961—922 BC) was the son of David and Bathsheba. Though not the eldest of David's sons, he was anointed king in David's lifetime (1 Kings 1:39), and soon disposed of his rival and elder brother Adonijah, Adonijah's supporter Joab and his father's enemy Shimei. After this, his rule was a peaceful one, although he made heavy demands on his subjects.

Solomon commissioned many buildings during his reign. The finest was the Temple that David had desired. His ally Hiram, King of Tyre, supplied both timbers and craftsmen and the Temple was built in the traditional Canaanite and Syrian style, in three

SOLOMON
Solomon inherited a strong, united kingdom and ruled it peacefully but despotically for almost forty years. Israel lay at the centre of a network of trade routes and Solomon, an astute businessman, negotiated profitable tariffs on goods travelling through the country and married the daughters of surrounding kings to seal commercial contracts. Under his rule, Israel prospered but he spent lavishly on his hundreds of wives and concubines, his elaborate building programme and his large army. His subjects paid a high price in crushing taxation and forced labour and at his death, the country was close to rebellion.

sections: an outer vestibule, the main temple area and the inner 'holy of holies'. Solomon, who offered the first sacrifices himself, recognized that God could not be contained in any temple, but asked God to heed the prayers uttered there whether by Israel or by strangers (8:42).

Next to the Temple (too close, Ezekiel later complained), he built palaces for himself and his Egyptian wife, with his armoury and judgement hall nearby. He also rebuilt the cities of Hazor, Megiddo and Gezer and set up countless store cities and barracks. In the remains of the three cities archaeologists have found an identical six-chambered gateway. Chariotry became the basis of his army, which had 1400 chariots and 12,000 horsemen; David, who had no use for horses, had simply hamstrung the few that he captured (2 Samuel 8:4). Solomon also expanded his administration, with an eleven-man cabinet (1 Kings 4:2—6) and thousands of officials.

Solomon retained most of the empire left to him by David. It covered most of today's Israel, Jordan, Syria and eastern Lebanon, though he lost some land in Edom (south of the Dead Sea) and Syria. He profitably controlled the routes linking Cilicia (on the north-eastern corner of the Mediterranean), which raised the finest horses, and Egypt, which exported chariots. The Queen of Sheba in Arabia visited him, probably because the caravans exporting her spices, gold and jewels northwards passed through his territory. She was dazzled by the magnificence of his court. He fortified Ezion-Geber (just west of Eilat, on the Red Sea) and with Phoenician technical aid, ran a merchant fleet which imported wood, gold and silver, ivory (his throne was of ivory and gold), monkeys and peacocks (10:22). His exports were grain and olive oil.

Solomon loved women and sustained his commercial empire through diplomatic marriages. Even the Pharaoh of Egypt offered his daughter, with the city of Gezer as dowry. Altogether, Solomon had 700 princesses and 300 concubines. Because he encouraged their worship of heathen gods, God told

THE QUEEN OF SHEBA
Sheba or Saba was a wealthy country by the Red Sea, in what is now North Yemen. Saba's wealth was founded on trade and the Queen made the 1300-mile journey to meet Solomon. She had intended to impress him with her riches but instead was herself dazzled by the splendour of his court. In Arab legend she bore his son, whose descendants became the kings of Ethiopia.

him that his descendants would lose power over all but one of the tribes. The people, too, found that supporting his magnificence was a heavy burden. He divided Israel into twelve districts (apparently exempting Judah), each responsible for his needs for one month of the year (1 Kings 4). He also imposed a 'heavy yoke' of forced labour (12:4) on Israel, as well as enslaving the conquered Canaanites living within his territory (9:21).

Solomon was renowned for his wisdom (10:1), a quality he chose when God offered him whatever he asked (3:9). In a famous story, two harlots who had lived together once came before him. Each had one son and one mother had accidentally smothered her child while asleep. Each woman claimed to be the mother of the surviving boy. Solomon ordered that the boy should be cut in half; and when one woman offered to drop her claim and save the boy's life, Solomon declared her the true mother (3:27). He uttered 3000 proverbs, about trees, animals, birds and fish (4:32). These can hardly be the biblical Proverbs of Solomon, which are primarily concerned with human behaviour, and unlike Solomon scorn wealth (Proverbs 15:16) and commend monogamy (18:22). The Book of Ecclesiastes, which calls all human effort vanity, but concludes that man's purpose is service of God, also claims to be by him—though this is unlikely.

He also wrote 1005 songs: the Song of Songs, composed of songs of love, is ascribed to him, though it, like Proverbs and Ecclesiastes, was probably written by someone else. Some understand it as a drama in which Solomon courts and marries a beautiful maiden or—because of his terror before her (6:4—5) and her references to her beloved as a shepherd (1:7, 6:2)—tries unsuccessfully to woo her from a rustic lover. Others treat it as a collection of independent songs. Though Solomon may not have written all these works, his court provided an environment in which such literature could flourish. It was a period of peace and prosperity, a contrast with the wars and intrigues of his father David's time. Solomon was succeeded by his son, Rehoboam, last king of united Israel.

The Queen of Sheba (Saba) in south-west Arabia, came with gifts of spices, gold and jewels to test Solomon's wisdom and stayed to be dazzled by the splendour of his court. The statement 'Solomon gave her all her desire' (1 Kings 10:13) probably means that during her visit they agreed tolls on her country's overland export routes to Syria and the north, which Solomon controlled.

Pharaoh The Pharaoh who lived at the time of David and Solomon became Solomon's father-in-law. As a dowry for his daughter, he gave Solomon the city of Gezer, which was still inhabited by Canaanites and lay close to the Philistine coastal strip (1 Kings 9:16). Some scholars suggest that the Pharaoh had started out to conquer the whole of Canaan but turned back when he realized how strong Solomon's army was. In spite of the fact that his daughter was married to Solomon, Pharaoh gave refuge to one of Israel's enemies, Hadad, crown prince of Edom, which had been conquered by David. After David's death, Hadad returned to lead Edom in revolt against Israel (11:14—25).

Kings and queens of Judah

Rehoboam (reigned 922—915BC) was Solomon's only named son, born of an Ammonite mother. When Solomon died, Rehoboam was 41 and was acclaimed King of Judah. The northern tribes, however, did not accept that the throne should automatically pass from father to eldest son and when Rehoboam presented himself to them in Shechem as king, they did not agree unconditionally; they demanded relief from the heavy taxes and forced labour imposed by Solomon. Rehoboam's older courtiers counselled him to agree; once accepted as king, they perhaps thought, he could always change his mind. Advisers of his own age group, however, preferred a show of strength and on their advice he declared he would be even harsher than his father, replacing his father's whips by scorpions. At this the northern tribes declared rebellion, appointing their own

king, Jeroboam, over what now became the Kingdom of Israel.

Rehoboam was so badly out of touch with the mood of the people that he sent his minister for forced labour to put down the rebellion; the minister was stoned to death, and Rehoboam fled home. A prophet dissuaded him from full-scale war against the north but there were continual battles (1 Kings 14:30)—perhaps attempts by Judah to clear the northern approaches to Jerusalem, which lay only 8 miles south of the border with Israel. He ringed his territory with fortresses (2 Chronicles 11:5), except in the north—where he recognized no border since he denied that his territory ended. In spite of the fortifications, Judah was invaded by the Pharaoh Shishak, who plundered the Temple and the royal treasuries. Among the treasures he took were Solomon's golden shields—which Rehoboam replaced in bronze.

During Rehoboam's reign the Judeans began to build illegal shrines and practise Canaanite worship, with sacred groves and pillars and even temple prostitutes. Rehoboam died aged 48 and was succeeded by his son Abijam.

Abijam (or Abijah), King of Judah (reigned 915—913 BC), though not Rehoboam's eldest son, was born to his favourite wife and inherited the throne. He expanded Judah's territory into the northern kingdom, capturing Bethel (2 Chronicles 13:19). Under his reign the Judeans continued to practise Canaanite worship, as they had under Rehoboam.

Asa, King of Judah (913—873 BC), is called Abijam's son, but may in fact have been his brother. He abolished the worship of idols, which had become widespread under his predecessors and even removed his own mother from office for making an image of the Canaanite fertility goddess Asherah. He continued, however, to tolerate shrines other than the Jerusalem Temple. According to 2 Chronicles 14:8, he repulsed a massive invasion by Zerah the Ethiopian and built many fortresses to protect his kingdom. At one point, Baasha, then King of Israel, threatened Jerusalem by fortifying the city of

Ramah, just 5 miles to the north. Asa bribed Ben-Hadad I, King of Damascus, to attack Israel, offering him the treasuries of the Temple and palace as a reward. Baasha was forced to withdraw, and the Judeans used the fortifications of Ramah to strengthen their own neighbouring cities of Geba and Mizpah (1 Kings 15:22).

Asa seems to have believed in self-help. A prophet who rebuked him for not relying on God alone was placed in the stocks; similarly, when Asa was dying of dropsy he did not pray to God for a cure but consulted doctors instead (2 Chronicles 16:12). He was succeeded by his son Jehoshaphat.

Jehoshaphat, King of Judah (born 908; reigned 873—849 BC), was the son of Asa. He abandoned Asa's hostile policy towards the north, almost becoming effectively its vassal. He joined two Israelite campaigns. In one, against the Syrians at Ramoth-Gilead (see *Micaiah*), he agreed to wear Ahab's clothes, while Ahab, the King of Israel, dressed as a common soldier. Jehoshaphat escaped being killed in Ahab's place when the Syrian charioteers came close enough to penetrate the disguise (1 Kings 22:30—33). He later joined Ahab's son, Jehoram, when he marched against Mesha of Moab; Elisha, who revealed a plan for victory, declared that he would have remained silent if Jehoshaphat had not been with them (2 Kings 3:14).

In his own kingdom of Judah, Jehoshaphat tried to revive the gold trade of Solomon's navy, but his ships (perhaps Solomon's ships, now rotted) were wrecked at their home port of Ezion-Geber.

The Book of Chronicles paints a brighter picture. Jehoshaphat built fortresses and storehouses, strengthened his army and received tribute from Philistines and Arabs. He reorganized his administration, appointing district governors and judges in every city. He commissioned the Levites to travel about Judah, teaching the law of God. When the Moabites and Ammonites attacked Israel, Jehoshaphat led his people into the wilderness, and the Levites sang, whereupon Israel's enemies slaughtered one another. The

REHOBOAM
Rehoboam, Solomon's son, was not a strong enough monarch to preserve his father's kingdom. He remained king of the southern tribes of Judah and Benjamin but in the north, the people demanded relief from the heavy taxes they had paid during Solomon's reign. When Rehoboam tried to subdue them by force, they broke away to form the independent kingdom of Israel.

Book of Chronicles adds that his ships were wrecked because the wicked Ahaziah of Israel had been his partner; according to 1 Kings 22:49, however, he refused Ahaziah's aid.

Jehoram, King of Judah (born 881; reigned 849—842 BC), was the son of Jehoshaphat. He married Ahab's daughter Athalia. He began to worship Canaanite gods, and, according to 2 Chronicles 21:4, executed all his brothers. He lost control of Edom, which had paid tribute to Judah since David's day. While trying to crush the rebellion there, he was surrounded by the rebel army and only escaped by breaking through their ranks under cover of darkness (2 Kings 8:21). The Book of Chronicles adds a bleak end. Judah was invaded by Philistines and Arabs, who plundered his palace and killed all but the youngest of his sons. He died of a disease of the bowels; they eventually came out of his body.

Ahaziah, King of Judah, reigned during 842 BC. He was the son of Jehoram of Judah and Athaliah, daughter of Ahab. He came to Jezreel to visit his wounded uncle Jehoram of Israel, and was present when Jehoram was assassinated by Jehu. Ahaziah tried to escape but was fatally wounded (2 Kings 9:27). According to 2 Chronicles 22:9, however, Jehu's agents found him hiding in the city of Samaria, brought him to Jehu and executed him.

Athaliah (reigned 842—837 BC), daughter of Ahab, was the sister of Jehoram of Israel, wife of Jehoram of Judah and the mother of King Ahaziah. She went mad when her brother and son were killed in Jehu's revolution in Israel. In her frenzy, she destroyed the whole royal family of Judah, except for Ahaziah's infant son, Joash. He was hidden in the bedroom of his aunt, Jehosheba.

Jehosheba's husband was Jehoiada, the Chief Priest, and he hid the boy in the Temple. Athaliah vandalized the Lord's Temple (2 Chronicles 24:7) and established another for Baal. Six years later, Jehoida conspired with the royal bodyguard to march Joash into the

ATHALIA
Athalia was Judah's only woman ruler and her history gives a vivid picture of the violence of the time in which she lived. Her parents, Ahab and Jezebel, both died violently and when her brother, Jehoram, and son, Ahaziah, were killed in Israel, she murdered the rest of the royal family in a frenzy of grief and seized the throne herself. Only her infant grandson escaped.

Temple one sabbath, the day of the changing of the guard, where they would crown and anoint him king. On hearing the commotion, Athaliah rushed into the Temple, shouting: 'Treason!' At Jehoida's command, she was marched out and killed by the sword in her palace (2 Kings 11:16). Her temple to Baal was desecrated and destroyed

Joash, King of Judah (reigned 837—800 BC), was the son of Ahaziah and grandson of Athaliah. Rescued when the rest of the royal family were killed by Athaliah, he was brought up in the Temple by his uncle Jehoiada, the

Chief Priest. At the age of 6 he was anointed king (see *Athaliah*) and his uncle continued as Regent with overwhelming popular support. When Joash grew up, however, he criticized Jehoida for neglecting to use all Temple taxes and donations for the maintenance of the building. Joash instead invented the collection box; its contents were kept separate from other sources of income and used exclusively for Temple repairs. Later, however, the Temple funds and even its vessels were stripped to pay off Hazael of Syria when his army threatened to attack Jerusalem (see *Hazael*). Joash was assassinated by his servants in 800 BC. According to 2 Chronicles 24:25 he was on his sickbed, having been wounded by the Syrians.

Amaziah, King of Judah (born 825; reigned 800—783 BC), was the son of Joash and executed his father's murderers. He defeated the Edomites, capturing Sela; according to 2 Chronicles 25:12, he threw the Edomite soldiers from the top of the rock (Hebrew *sela*) there. Made over-confident by this victory (or, according to Chronicles, as a punishment for worshipping captured Edomite idols), he challenged Jehoash of Israel to battle, and was not only defeated but briefly captured. Jerusalem was plundered and hostages taken back to Samaria. Later, hearing of a plot to assassinate him, he fled to Lachish, only to be killed there by Jehoash's men.

Uzziah, also called Azariah, King of Judah (reigned 783—742 BC). Uzziah was the son of the murdered Amaziah. He was made King of Judah by popular acclaim at the age of 16 and enjoyed a long and peaceful reign. A keen farmer with large herds, he dug many cisterns and built towers to deter desert marauders. He also built defensive towers around Jerusalem and recovered the Red Sea port of Eilat; according to 2 Chronicles 26, he also occupied Philistine cities and received tribute from the Ammonites. Chronicles adds that he re-equipped his standing army and had machines designed to discharge missiles from his many towers. With the growing prosperity of landed farmers and merchants, however, the gap between rich and poor widened, as Isaiah complained. Towards the end of his reign Uzziah contracted leprosy—a punishment, according to 2 Chronicles 26:19, for trying to take away the priests' right to be the sole people entitled to offer incense in the temple. Because of his disease he had to be isolated, while his son Jotham served with him as co-regent to govern the country (2 Kings 15:5).

Jotham, King of Judah (born 777, reigned 742—735 BC), was the son of Uzziah. He reigned with his father as co-regent and eventually succeeded to the throne. He was a great builder, both in Jerusalem and elsewhere in Judah. He repaired the northern gate of the Temple (2 Chronicles 27:3) although he never entered the Temple itself. This was in punishment for his father's action against the priests' right to offer incense.

Like Uzziah, Jotham subdued the Ammonites but it was in his reign that the first raids by the newly allied powers of Syria and Israel took place.

Ahaz, King of Judah (reigned 735—715 BC), was the son of Jotham. Soon after he became king, Syria and Israel mounted a full-scale invasion of Judah in an attempt to force Judah to join with them against the Assyrians. The Edomites and Philistines saw their opportunity to attack from the south and Eilat was lost to Judah forever. At the same time, the Syrians and Israelites besieged Jerusalem. Isaiah promised the terrified Ahaz that they would fail and advised him calmly to wait for God to save him. Instead, Ahaz emptied the Temple and palace treasuries to bribe Assyria to attack the allies and rescue him.

Isaiah, who had thought that Assyria would attack the allies even without a bribe, was probably right. And, as he had feared, the Assyrians now demanded that Judah should worship their gods as part of the price of the rescue.

When the Assyrian emperor Tiglath-Pileser III conquered the Syrian capital, Damascus, Ahaz visited him to submit to him personally. He sent back instructions instructions to his Chief Priest Uriah to build a great altar in Assyrian style in the Temple, while the old bronze altar was reserved for Ahaz's personal divination—another Assyrian practice. The Assyrian king made Ahaz break up some of the Temple bronze (presumably as tribute) and even made him change the architecture of the Temple (2 Kings 16:18). According to 2 Chronicles 28:24, he closed the Temple altogether and built altars all over the rest of Jerusalem. Ahaz had paid a high price for his rescue from the Syrians and Israelites, for later Assyrian kings were to make even harsher demands.

Hezekiah, King of Judah (born 740 reigned 715—686 BC), was Ahaz's son and became a powerful king. He purified worship in Judah, destroying the idols that had been introduced on Assyrian instructions and even shattered the bronze serpent made by Moses (Numbers 21:9) but since worshipped. He reopened and cleansed the Temple (2 Chronicles 29:3), inviting any Israelites remaining in the north to join him in celebrating the Passover Festival, in the second month (May). (Moses had specified the first month, but Hezekiah made this concession to the northern Israelite calendar, which was one month behind—1 Kings 12:32.) These religious reforms also expressed defiance of Assyria, while the increased importance of the Temple in Jerusalem enhanced the king's power and strengthened his claims even in the north. He also achieved foreign conquests, against the Philistines and Edomites (2 Kings 18:8; 1 Chronicles 4:42). Now his confidence grew, and he prepared for open revolt against Assyria. He built storehouses, reorganized the army, strengthened all city fortifications, and built a tunnel to carry water from the Gihon spring, outside the walls of Jerusalem, into the Siloam pool within. The prophet Isaiah disapproved; he advocated trust in God alone.

Yet Hezekiah had miscalculated. The Assyrian emperor Sennacherib overran Judah, and Hezekiah was forced to beg forgiveness and pay a penalty of 300 talents (about 9 tonnes) of silver and 30 talents of gold, some of which was stripped off the Temple doors. In spite of accepting this heavy fine, the Assyrians treacherously returned to besiege Jerusalem. Hezekiah sent a delegation to Isaiah, begging for God's help and Isaiah promised the delegates a speedy end to the siege. He later passed on to Hezekiah God's promise to defend Jerusalem. The next night the Assyrian soldiers miraculously died; Sennacherib, apparently hearing of a revolution at home, hurried back to his capital, Nineveh, only to be assassinated by two of his sons.

Hezekiah continued to intrigue against Assyria by showing his treasures and armoury to the King of Babylon who, like Hezekiah, also paid tribute to Assyria. Isaiah warned that the Babylonians would one day return as plunderers —as they did, more than a century later.

In the same year as the Assyrian siege (701 BC), Hezekiah fell sick, and when Isaiah told him to make his will, Hezekiah begged God to consider all the good things he had done. God promised, through Isaiah, to lengthen Hezekiah's life by fifteen years. Hezekiah's sickness is called—presumably with some understatement—a boil and Isaiah cured it with a fig plaster. The grateful Hezekiah composed a psalm, acknowledging that his suffering had been for his own good (Isaiah 38:9—20). He also commissioned an edition of Solomon's proverbs (Proverbs 25:1).

Manasseh, King of Judah (born 698; reigned 686—642 BC), the son of Hezekiah, was named after one of the northern tribes—perhaps a gesture by his father to the survivors of the northern kingdom. He strengthened Jerusalem's fortifications, but also rebuilt the local shrines and altars which had been destroyed under Hezekiah, and generally cancelled Hezekiah's reforms. He worshipped the Canaanite gods and goddesses and even sacrificed his son to them as a burned offering. He also served the astral gods popular in Assyria. Altars to these foreign gods were set up in the Temple itself. To be fair to Manasseh, he may have been forced to do this by his Assyrian masters. They understood that a national religion gave the people a strong sense of their own identity. By replacing the national religion, they hoped to prevent the growth of nationalism.

In his struggle against those loyal to the Lord, Manasseh 'filled Jerusalem from end to end with blood' (2 Kings 21:16). He is condemned in the Book of Kings as the worst king either Judah or Israel had ever had and his sins were said to have caused the Exile in 587 BC. The Book of Chronicles, however, tells that he was carried in chains to Babylon, where he repented and prayed. (A 'Prayer of Manasseh' appears in the Apocrypha). According

Hezekiah's reign was marked by religious reform and the kingdom remained at peace. It was during this time that many of the proverbs which now form the Book of Proverbs were written down for the first time. However, Judah was still part of the great Assyrian empire and Hezekiah was determined to regain its freedom. He prepared the city of Jerusalem carefully for a long siege. To make sure that the supply of fresh water did not end, he extended the city walls to surround a pool, and built an underground tunnel running from a spring outside the walls to supply it. The tunnel was rediscovered in 1880; water still flows through its stone channel today.

JOSIAH (right)
The sixteenth king of Judah was a strongly religious ruler, eager to bring the people back to traditional ways of worship. He carried his reforms into Samaria, where, since the destruction of the kingdom of Israel, pagan rites were practised unopposed.

to Chronicles, he then returned to Jerusalem where he cleared the Temple of foreign gods and idols and ordered his people to worship only the Lord (2 Chronicles 33:16).

Amon, King of Judah (born 666; reigned 642—640 BC), was Manasseh's son and successor. He continued Manasseh's worship of foreign gods and idols (according to Chronicles he restored them after Manasseh had repented). He was soon assassinated in his palace (2 Kings 21:23).

Josiah, King of Judah (born 648; reigned 640—609 BC), was the son of Amon and was only 8 years old when his father was assassinated and he was placed on the throne. In 622 BC, he instructed the High Priest Hilkiah, through his scribe Shaphan, to empty the collection box in order to finance Temple repairs. Shaphan brought back and read to him a book (possibly Deuteronomy) which Hilkiah had found in the Temple. The book contained divine laws and threatened curses on anyone who disobeyed them. Josiah, knowing that these laws had not been observed, tore his garments. He then arranged a covenant ceremony in which the book was adopted by the people, and set about a religious reform. (2 Chronicles 34, however, places the reform *before* the book's discovery.) He removed and burned all the images and signs of idol worship in the Temple, which he made the sole centre of worship in Judah. Rival shrines and holy places—whether sacred to idols or to the Lord—were desecrated and their priests killed. Wizards and sacred prostitutes were banished. At the Temple in Jerusalem he revived the long-neglected Passover sacrifice. The Assyrian government was losing control over its possessions and did nothing to hinder him from carrying his reforms into Samaria.

In 612 BC the Assyrian Empire collapsed and the Egyptian Pharaoh Necho tried to take control of the area. Josiah tried to prevent this but was killed at Megiddo by the Pharaoh's archers. According to 2 Chronicles 35:21, Necho had commanded him in God's name to desist, and Josiah died for ignoring God's command.

Jehoahaz, King of Judah (born 632; reigned 609 BC) also called Shallum, was a younger son of Josiah. Although not the eldest son, he was enthroned by popular acclaim on his father's death. He reigned just three months before Pharaoh Necho deposed him in favour of his elder brother Jehoiakim. When he went to Riblah to make his vows of submission to Necho, he was imprisoned and brought to Egypt, where he died.

Jehoiakim, King of Judah (born 634; reigned 609—598 BC), was Jehoahaz's elder brother. He was made king over Judah by Pharaoh Necho, who had replaced the Assyrian Emperor as Judah's overlord. Jehoiakim raised 100 talents (about three tonnes) of silver and one talent of gold as tribute to Pharaoh, through a poll tax. During those dark days for Judah, he used forced labour to build a sumptuous new palace painted in vermilion, with panels of cedar (Jeremiah 22:13-19). He reversed the reforms his father Josiah had made and threatened the prophet Uriah when he prophesied Judah's doom. Uriah fled to Egypt, but was extradited by Jehoiakim's agents and executed (26:20—23). Jehoiakim also persecuted Jeremiah and burned his prophecies.

ZEDEKIAH
The last king of Judah was little more than a figurehead, controlled by the Babylonians. In an attempt to win back independence, Zedekiah led a hopeless revolt. When it failed, Jeremiah's prophecies of doom were finally fulfilled: Jerusalem was sacked, the Temple and city buildings destroyed and the people exiled. Zedekiah himself was blinded and led away in fetters to Babylon.

Pharaoh Necho was soon defeated by the Babylonians, and Jehoiakim acknowledged their Emperor, Nebuchadnezzar, as his overlord. Three years later, however, he rebelled, no doubt expecting Egyptian support. The Babylonians controlled many of Judah's neighbouring states and encouraged them to raid Judah's territory, while Nebuchadnezzar himself marched on Jerusalem. Jehoiakim died (he was probably murdered) just before Nebuchadnezzar's arrival. (Daniel 1:2 and 2 Chronicles 36:6 state instead that he was captured and taken to Babylon.)

Jehoiachin, King of Judah (born 615; reigned 597 BC), was Jehoiakim's son. He became king at the age of 18 when his father died just before Nebuchadnezzar began the siege of Jerusalem. He surrendered after just three months. Nebuchadnezzar's army ransacked the Temple and palace and the king was exiled to Babylon, along with his mother, his wives and thousands of leading citizens—officers, soldiers and craftsmen. Tablets listing deliveries of oil for his use during Nebuchadnezzar's reign have been discovered in Babylon. Jehoiachin outlived Nebuchadnezzar, whose successor Evil-Merodach released him from prison and fed him at his own table.

Zedekiah, King of Judah (born 618; reigned 597—587 BC), was a younger son of Josiah. He was made king of Judah at the age of 21 by Nebuchadnezzar in place of his nephew Jehoiachin. Yet he revolted against Babylon, probably under pressure from ministers too confident of Egyptian support (Ezekiel 17:15). The Babylonian army began a siege of Jerusalem that was to last eighteen months.

Zedekiah was an irresolute character, inconsistent in his policies. His dealings with Jeremiah during the Babylonian siege highlight this. He secretly asked Jeremiah how the siege would end; but then, because he knew his ministers disapproved of Jeremiah, forbade him on pain of death to mention the interview. Jeremiah advised him to surrender but Zedekiah refused—fearing those Judeans who had gone over to the

Babylonian side. When Jeremiah had been imprisoned for desertion, he had him moved from a dungeon to the court of the guardhouse; but when the officers protested, he declared himself powerless to do anything about it (Jeremiah 38:5) and allowed them to throw Jeremiah into a pit. Later, when a servant warned him that Jeremiah would die there, he ordered the prophet to be returned to the guardhouse.

The walls of Jerusalem were breached in the summer of 587 BC after eighteen months siege. Zedekiah fled from the

city at night but was captured and brought before Nebuchadnezzar at Riblah. The last thing he saw was the killing of his sons; he was then blinded and taken in captivity to Babylon.

Kings and queens of Israel

Jeroboam I (reigned 922—901 BC) became the first King of Israel. He was from the tribe of Ephraim and a man of outstanding industry. Solomon put him in charge of forced labour among the northern tribes. However, Solomon

JEROBOAM
After Solomon's death, a prophet foretold that Jeroboam would divide the kingdom and he fled to Egypt to avoid assassination. Before long, the prophet's words came true: the northern tribes rebelled against Solomon's successor and acclaimed Jeroboam king.

discovered that the prophet Ahijah had promised Jeroboam kingship over ten of the twelve tribes, and Jeroboam fled to Solomon's enemy, Pharaoh Shishak for protection.

In spite of the fact that he had organized forced labour, he was overwhelmingly popular among the northern tribes and after Solomon's death they recalled him to lead their negotiations with Solomon's son, Rehoboam. When Rehoboam threatened to treat them even more harshly than his father had done, they refused to accept his rule and acclaimed Jeroboam king of a separate kingdom of Israel.

Jeroboam had official residences in three different cities—Shechem, Penuel and Tirzah—apparently moving regularly from one to the other so that his presence would be felt throughout his new realm. To prevent people from making pilgrimages to Jerusalem, where the people might hear Rehoboam's propaganda, he set up golden calves in the south and north of his kingdom, in Bethel and Dan. (These were probably not intended to be worshipped as gods, but as pedestals on which the Lord might alight.) 1 Kings 13 tells how, as Jeroboam was about to sacrifice in Bethel, a prophet announced that the altar would one day be desecrated; the altar was then miraculously split and Jeroboam's hand withered (though it was soon healed). Jeroboam also put the traditional autumn festival one month back. Because Jeroboam made these changes in worship, the prophet Ahijah announced that his descendants would not survive as kings. He lost his son Abijah in infancy. Another son, Nadab, succeeded him, but was assassinated during a war against the Philistines.

Nadab, King of Israel (reigned 901–900 BC), was the son of Jeroboam and succeeded him, briefly, as king. He was assassinated by his countryman Baasha while fighting against the Philistines. He may have gone to war in order to win the support of his people, who did not accept that kingship passed from father to the eldest son. His death fulfilled the prophecy that Jeroboam's descendants would not be kings.

Baasha, King of Israel (reigned 900–877 BC), seized the throne from Nadab and wiped out Jeroboam's family. He was succeeded by his son, Elah (reigned 877–876 BC) who was soon assassinated in turn during a drinking bout. Elah was killed by a man named Zimri, who commanded half the chariotry. Zimri's ancestry is not mentioned; perhaps he was a Canaanite. He killed all Baasha's relatives and even his friends. He was not supported by the army, however, and they acclaimed their general, Omri, as king. Omri besieged the city of Tirzah, where Zimri was living and Zimri committed suicide by setting his palace ablaze. He had reigned only seven days (1 Kings 16:18).

Omri, King of Israel (reigned 876–869 BC) was acclaimed king by the army, in place of the upstart Zimri. After disposing of Zimri, he bought the hill of Samaria and there founded a new capital. The Bible dismisses him in six verses, complaining that he continued Jeroboam's sins, but he must have been a vigorous ruler; the Assyrians called Israel 'the house of Omri' until they conquered it in 722 BC, long after Omri's own dynasty ceased (842 BC).

Ahab, King of Israel (reigned 869–850 BC), built many cities and even a palace decorated with ivory (1 Kings 22:39). He married Jezebel, a Phoenician princess. Ahab could not decide whether to worship the Lord or the Canaanite gods of Phoenicia and built a temple for the god Baal in Samaria (16:32–33). During Ahab's reign the prophet Elijah appeared, seemingly out of nowhere, and correctly predicted three years of drought. Ahab recognized his prophetic power by calling him 'troubler of Israel', and helped him to gather all Israel to Mount Carmel for a trial between the Lord and the god Baal; yet he did nothing to stop Jezebel from threatening Elijah's life.

Another episode (21) shows that Ahab sinned by turning a blind eye to his wife's crimes. He had wanted to buy a vineyard next to his palace, but the owner, Naboth, refused to exchange or sell it, because it was inherited land. Aware of the laws binding an Israelite king, Ahab could only sulk. Yet when Jezebel told him shortly afterwards that Naboth was dead (murdered, in fact, on her command), Ahab asked no questions, but went to take possession of the vineyard. Elijah announced that Ahab's dynasty would be destroyed, to avenge Naboth's death. Ahab replied by calling Elijah his enemy but in fact fasted and mourned so contritely that the punishment was delayed by God for one generation.

Ahab was once condemned by a prophet for excessive kindness. Early in his reign, the Syrian king Ben-Hadad II besieged Samaria and demanded Ahab's treasures, wives and children. Ahab agreed, but was encouraged by his advisers and by a prophet to order a sortie that routed the besiegers. The next year Ben-Hadad attacked Israel at Aphek, and was roundly defeated. When he begged for his life, Ahab called him 'my brother' and accepted his offer of compensation. Ahab's co-operation with Syria is supported by archaeological evidence. An inscription from the time of the Assyrian king Shalmaneser III reports that Ahab contributed 2000 chariots and 10,000 foot soldiers to an anti-Assyrian coalition which Shalmaneser defeated. A prophet declared that because Ahab had spared Ben-Hadad, the Syrians would one day defeat and kill him (1 Kings 20).

During Ahab's reign the kingdoms of Judah and Israel made a joint campaign against the Syrians, who had captured the city of Ramoth-Gilead. Before the battle, Ahab consulted the prophet Micaiah, but ignored his warning to turn back—though he took the precaution of disguising himself as a common soldier while Jehoshaphat, the King of Judah, dressed in Ahab's clothes. The deception did not save him. Wounded by an arrow, he courageously had himself propped up in his chariot until he died that evening.

Jezebel was a princess from the Phoenician city of Sidon and married King Ahab. In Israel, she encouraged the worship of Baal, the god she had worshipped in her native land. She fed hundreds of his prophets at her table (1

Kings 18:19) and ordered the prophets of the Lord to be murdered. When Elijah proved on Mount Carmel that the Lord was mightier than her god, Baal, she was unimpressed.

She could not understand why Ahab, as king, felt he had to obey the law which prevented him from taking a neighbour's vineyard. Raised by a despot, she was used to kings who took what they wanted without question. In order to help Ahab, she ordered the city elders to proclaim a fast (as if some serious offence had been committed), arrest Naboth (the owner of the vineyard) and produce false witnesses to testify that he had cursed God and his king. The elders obeyed without question and Naboth was stoned to death.

After Ahab's death, Jezebel got her just deserts: when Jehu had killed her son and claimed the throne, she appeared at her window in the palace, dressed and with eyes painted as befitted a queen. Defiantly she addressed Jehu as Zimri, the man who had seized the throne from an earlier king and ruled for just seven days (see *Baasha*). Hearing this insult, Jehu shouted to her servants, who threw her to her death.

Ahaziah, King of Israel (reigned 850–849 BC), was the son of Ahab and Jezebel. Like his father, he permitted the Israelites to worship pagan gods. Continuing Israel's friendly relationship with Judah, he offered to join Judah's King Jehoshaphat in reviving sea trade, but the project was not a success (see *Jehoshaphat*). He was injured falling off his balcony in Samaria, and sent messengers to Baal-zebub ('Lord of the flies'), the god of the Philistine city of Ekron. When the messengers returned they reported that Elijah had told them Ahaziah would die for consulting a foreign god. He summoned Elijah, who repeated that the king would never rise from his bed. He died without leaving a son to succeed him.

Jehoram, King of Israel (reigned 849–842 BC), was a younger son of Ahab. With Jehoshaphat of Judah and the vassal king of Edom, he fought

AHAB
Ahab, Israel's seventh king, was dominated by his wife Jezebel. As a Phoenician, she encouraged the worship of the Phoenician god, Baal and Ahab did nothing to prevent her. In fact he built a temple for Baal next to his palace, with luxurious quarters for its priests. Under his rule Israel was prosperous but because of Ahab's religious laxity, the Bible calls him one of Israel's worst kings.

against the Moabites. Their king, Mesha, had withheld the annual tribute first imposed on them by David. When the allies ran out of water in the wilderness of Edom, they consulted the prophet Elisha, who angrily told Jehoram to consult the prophets of the pagan gods worshipped by Ahab and his wife Jezebel. Jehoram acknowledged that their plight was the Lord's doing. This appeased Elisha, and he advised them to dig trenches. At dawn, the

trenches were filled with a miraculous downpour. The Moabites mistook the water (which reflected the red sky) for blood and decided that the allies had turned on one another. As they rushed to plunder the camp, the Israelites attacked, routed them and devastated the land of Moab. In desperation, Mesha sacrificed his first-born son. This caused 'great anger against Israel' (2 Kings 3:27) and, according to Mesha's own inscription, found in Diban in

Jordan, the Moabites were inspired to fight with such wild courage that they freed themselves from Israelite domination for ever.

Jehoram's bitterest enemies were the Syrians, who had twice been spared by Israel's kings: once by Ahab and then by Jehoram himself (see *Elisha*). The Syrians now beseiged Samaria, and starvation drove the inhabitants to cannibalism. Jehoram swore to behead Elisha, who might have been expected to perform some miracle but instead sat at home. When Jehoram appeared at Elisha's door, Elisha promised that there would be plenty of food next day—and that night the Syrians mysteriously panicked and abandoned camp.

Jehoram was wounded while trying to recover Ramoth-Gilead from the Syrians and withdrew to recover in his capital Jezreel. While he was there, his commander Jehu was anointed king by Elisha. Jehu returned to Jezreel and Jehoram rode out to meet him in Naboth's vineyard. There Jehu killed him for tolerating Baal worship—though Jehoram had at least restricted it (3:2).

Jehu, King of Israel (reigned 842—815 BC), was commander of Jehoram's army in the battle against the Syrians at Ramoth-Gilead. After Jehoram was wounded and retired to Jezreel, Jehu was suddenly summoned from a meeting with fellow officers by a follower of a prophet Elisha. He was then secretly anointed king of Israel, with a mission to wipe out Baal worship. One officer asked what the madman (as he called Elisha's disciple) had wanted and Jehu—anxious not to be branded a traitor—replied that it was nonsense; but when pressed, Jehu admitted the truth and they acclaimed him king on a makeshift throne. He swore the officers to silence and drove with a squadron of chariots to Jehoram's palace in Jezreel, pulling aboard the scouts sent out by the anxious king.

As they approached Jezreel, the lookout recognized Jehu's wild driving and Jehoram himself rode out to ask if all was well. Jehu replied that all could not be well while Baal worship continued, and he shot an arrow through Jehoram's heart. He also

JEHU
Jehu was an army commander who seized power in a bloody coup to become the tenth king of Israel. One of the most brutal of Israel's 19 kings, he executed all of Ahab's surviving relatives and, in an attempt to cleanse Israel of foreign gods, butchered thousands of the followers of Baal. Israel turned back to God but, weakened by so much bloodshed, was forced to submit to the earthly power of Shalmaneser III, ruler of the Assyrian empire.

ordered the murder of Jehoram's nephew Ahaziah, King of Judah, who happened to be there at the time. At the palace, he had Jezebel thrown from the window, and casually ate a meal before ordering her burial.

Seventy grandsons of Ahab still lived in Samaria and Jehu challenged the city elders to choose a king and defend themselves. When they fearfully accepted his authority, he wrote asking for 'the heads of your master's sons' (2 Kings 10:6). The 'heads' might have meant the chiefs, delivered alive, but the elders played safe and sent baskets of severed heads—contrary, Jehu pretended, to his intention. After displaying the baskets, he murdered forty-two visitors from Judah's royal family, which had intermarried with Ahab's.

Jehu next announced a great sacrifice at Baal's temple in Samaria. All the prophets and worshippers of Baal attended, and all had to wear sacred garments —so that Jehu could identify them and make sure that they left their weapons outside. When he had offered the sacrifice, he signalled to his men to slaughter all the worshippers. The temple of Baal was demolished and turned into a latrine.

All this bloodshed must have weakened Israel's military strength. An inscription from the time of Shalmaneser III, emperor of the rising superpower of Assyria, shows that in Jehu's first year as king he asked protection from Assyria, becoming a voluntary vassal of Shalmaneser. In spite of this powerful protector, he lost his land east of the Jordan to Syria.

Jehoahaz, King of Israel (reigned 815—801 BC), was the son of Jehu. During his reign the Syrians continued to harass the Kingdom of Israel and were said to oppress him 'like the dust in threshing'; his army was left with just ten chariots, in contrast to Solomon's 1400 (2 Kings 13:7).

Jehoash, King of Israel (reigned 801—786 BC), was the son of Jehoahaz and recovered territory that had been lost to the Syrians. When Amaziah of Judah challenged him to battle,

Jehoash answered with a parable: the thistle (Judah) sought a marriage alliance with the cedar (Israel) but was trampled by a beast. Amaziah nevertheless insisted on fighting; Jehoash routed his army at Beth-Shemesh (15 miles west of Jerusalem), capturing Amaziah himself. He destroyed the northern defences of Jerusalem, plundered the Temple and palace, and took hostages back to Samaria.

When Elisha was dying, Jehoash visited him, weeping and using the words Elisha himself had used to Elijah, calling him 'my father, the chariots and horsemen (i.e. the glory) of Israel'. Elisha laid his hand upon Jehoash's and told him to shoot an arrow out of the window, as a sign of victory over Syria, and to strike the ground. Jehoash struck only three times, and the disappointed Elisha declared that he would win only three victories. Elisha's words proved true, but in the three victories Jehoash recovered the land on the eastern side of the Jordan which had been captured by Hazael in Jehu's time.

Jeroboam II, King of Israel (reigned 786—746 BC), succeeded his father Jehoash. He continued the fight against the Syrians, overwhelming them and extending Israel's borders almost as far as in David's day—east of the Jordan, as far south as the Dead Sea and past Damascus. The Bible explains that God had taken pity on Israel's sufferings at Syria's hands (2 Kings 14:26). Assyria was also attacking Syria successfully and for a time, therefore, Israel and Judah were not threatened from the north-east—until the Assyrians themselves arrived. Israel also controlled the trade routes and this added to the kingdom's new wealth. The riches, however, were concentrated in few hands and the prophets Amos and Hosea both attacked this inequality and the over-confidence brought by Jeroboam's long and prosperous reign.

The year of Jeroboam's death saw three more kings. His son Zechariah (746—745) reigned six months before being publicly assassinated by Shallum, who was in turn murdered by Menahem.

Menahem, King of Israel (reigned 745—738 BC), was the fourth king to rule Israel in the year Jeroboam II died. He sacked an Israelite city that had refused to recognize his accession, attacking even pregnant women. He voluntarily offered tribute to Assyria, inventing the poll tax to raise it: 60,000 men of wealth each paid 50 shekels (about 20 ounces) of silver. He was succeeded (briefly) by his son, Pekahiah (reigned 738—737), who was murdered in his palace by his captain Pekah.

Pekah, King of Israel, reigned 737—732 BC, not for the twenty years stated in 2 Kings 15:27. He served as captain to King Pekahiah and came to the throne after assassinating him. Pekahiah's father had submitted voluntarily to Assyrian domination but Pekah joined with Rezin, King of Damascus, to fight them. In 735 BC the allies overran Judah and besieged Jerusalem, determined to force Judah to join them, by installing a puppet king if necessary (Isaiah 7:6). Egypt had probably encouraged the coalition, and if Judah had not co-operated, the supply lines from Egypt might have been blocked. The Assyrian emperor Tiglath-Pileser III responded by capturing Israel's lands in Galilee and east of the Jordan and exiling the inhabitants to Assyria. In 732BC he conquered and annexed Damascus, killing Rezin. Only the assassination of Pekah saved Israel from immediate destruction.

Hoshea, King of Israel (reigned 732—722 BC), submitted to the Assyrian emperor Shalmaneser V. Later, however, he intrigued with Pharaoh So (whose identity continues to perplex Egyptologists) and withheld tribute. This time the Assyrians overran the whole land, imprisoned Hoshea, captured Samaria after a three-year siege, and exiled the Israelites (mainly to the area that is now northern Iraq). To replace the Israelites, the Assyrians brought in a new mixed population (mainly from southern Iraq), later called the Samaritans. The Bible, perhaps out of sympathy, calls Hoshea the best of the northern kings. He was the last.

Prophets and priests

Ahijah was a prophet from Shiloh during Solomon's reign. He once tore the coat of Solomon's minister, Jeroboam, into twelve pieces. He then told Jeroboam to take ten pieces as a token that kingship over ten of the tribes would be torn from Solomon and become his (1 Kings 11:31). Yet when Jeroboam's queen later consulted him about her sick son, he foretold only gloom: the boy would die, the rest of Jeroboam's household would be killed and lie unburied, and the northern tribes would one day be exiled, all because of Jeroboam's sins. Jeroboam had expected Ahijah to be hostile and had told the queen to go in disguise. But Ahijah, though now blind, knew her immediately (14:6).

Hilkiah was Chief Priest at the Temple in Jerusalem under Josiah. He found a scroll of the Law while gathering Temple donations; it had apparently been buried under the coins in the collection box. Hilkiah passed it (apparently unread) to his scribe Shaphan. Soon afterwards, a distraught Josiah asked him to consult a prophet because the scroll gave details of laws which, he knew, had been neglected. Later, he supervised the removal of cult objects of foreign gods from the Temple.

Huldah was a prophetess in Jerusalem in Josiah's time. She was consulted by Hilkiah after he discovered a scroll in the Temple collection box. The scroll included curses on those who failed to keep its laws and Huldah declared that these would be fulfilled. They would, however, be delayed until after Josiah's death, as a reward for his repentance.

Huldah was the wife of the 'keeper of the wardrobe' (of the Temple priests or king), and this may be why she was consulted rather than Jeremiah.

Obadiah was Ahab's god-fearing steward. Ahab's wife, Jezebel, worshipped the heathen god Baal and when Elijah killed the prophets of Baal, she attacked the Lord's prophets in a murderous fury. Obadiah hid 100 prophets of the Lord in two caves and fed them until the danger was over. Once, while searching for water and grass for the royal horses and mules in the three-year drought, he met Elijah. Elijah asked to be taken to Ahab. Obadiah warned that Ahab had been hunting for him and protested that he himself would be killed if Elijah now suddenly disappeared—as he had a habit of doing. When Elijah promised to stay, however, Obadiah did as he asked.

Micaiah was a prophet consulted by Ahab to discover whether Israel and Judah could successfully dislodge the Syrians from Ramoth-Gilead. Jehoshaphat, King of Judah, had insisted on consulting him, even though 400 other prophets had already predicted victory (1 Kings 22:8). Micaiah first answered in the same words as the 400, but when Ahab rightly accused him of mimicry, Micaiah declared that he saw Israel scattered like lost sheep on the mountains. In a second vision, God in his heavenly court asked who would lure Ahab to fall at Ramoth-Gilead, and a spirit volunteered to spread false prophecies of victory.

Ahab decided that Micaiah was simply speaking out of hatred and ordered him to be imprisoned until his return from battle; but Micaiah's prophecy was correct: Ahab did not return alive.

Another prophet, Zedekiah, had made himself iron horns, promising that the Syrians would be gored to death. When he jealously struck Micaiah on the cheek and claimed he was not inspired by God, Micaiah warned that Zedekiah would hide in shame when the true outcome became known.

Jehonadab, son of Rechab, founded the sect of Rechabites, who lived in tents and did not drink wine or till the soil. They thus perpetuated the life of Israel's desert wanderings, despising the

ELIJAH
Elijah first appeared when Ahab was king in Israel. A stern, implacable enemy of Baal worship, he cursed the king for allowing the people to turn away from God and dedicated his life to bringing Israel back to the true religion. He spent long periods in the wilderness, alone in the company of God. By tradition, he did not die, but instead was carried to Heaven on a chariot of fire.

luxuries of settled life—and particularly of the court of Ahab and his sons. This fanatic helped Jehu to exterminate Ahab's family in Jezreel (2 Kings 10:17). His descendants still observed his rules of life in Jeremiah's day (Jeremiah 35).

Elijah ('the Lord is God') came from Gilead, east of the River Jordan, in the kingdom of Israel. He was a great prophet. He appeared suddenly at Ahab's court, where he announced a three-year drought, God's punishment for Ahab, who allowed the worship of

pagan gods in Israel. Three years later he reappeared and told Ahab to assemble the people of Israel at Mount Carmel. When everyone was together, he asked them how long they would hesitate between the Lord and Baal, the Canaanite god. When they made no reply, he challenged the prophets of Baal to place a bullock on an altar and see whether Baal could set it alight. As Baal's prophets prayed, danced and cut their flesh, Elijah mockingly told them to shout louder, in case Baal was asleep or away; it was no use. Towards evening, Elijah repaired the Lord's altar, which had been broken and neglected, laid a bullock on it and prayed. At his request, the people had drenched the altar with water, but in spite of this, fire from heaven consumed sacrifice and altar together, and the whole assembly shouted: 'The Lord is God'. Elijah told them to seize the prophets of Baal, whom he slaughtered. Then he announced to Ahab that the drought would end (1 Kings 18). He later rebuked Ahab when the king was about to take possession of Naboth's vineyard (see *Ahab*), predicting that dogs would lap his blood and eat Jezebel's flesh, and that his family would be wiped out. His prophecy came true.

On another occasion Ahab's successor Ahaziah was injured and sent messengers to consult a Philistine god. Elijah intercepted them and announced that Ahaziah would die. Ahaziah was furious and despatched fifty men to bring Elijah to him. They found him on top of a hill but were consumed by fire. Elijah disposed of a second company in the same way but the captain of the third company asked him humbly to go with him to the King and Elijah agreed. On arriving, Elijah repeated his stern prediction.

Elijah was a hairy man (2 Kings 1:8) and possessed superhuman strength, at least when under the 'hand of the Lord'. He once ran in front of Ahab's chariot all the way from Mount Carmel to Jezreel—a distance of more than 20 miles—out of respect for Ahab's office.

Not all Elijah's time was spent at royal courts. During the drought he asked a widow in Zarephath (between Tyre and Sidon) for food. When she answered that she had only a handful of flour and a small flask of oil, he told her to make him a small cake nevertheless (to show faith). He promised that the remaining flour and oil would be miraculously renewed until the drought ended; and so they were.

When the widow's son later died, she blamed Elijah, apparently thinking that his saintly presence had made God notice her sins. Elijah reproved God for striking a hospitable widow, and prayed that the child should be brought back to life. After stretching himself upon the child three times, Elijah returned him alive to his mother.

In many cities he attracted followers, called 'sons of the prophets'. At other times he was alone in God's company. At the beginning of the three-year drought, for example, God told him to camp beside a stream named Cherith a few miles north of Jerusalem. He stayed there, drinking the stream water and fed by ravens, until the stream dried up. On another occasion, when Ahab's wife Jezebel threatened his life after his victory over Baal's prophets, he fled to the wilderness of Beersheba and prayed that he would die. An angel led him to Mount Horeb (i.e. Sinai), where God had revealed himself to Israel. There Elijah complained of his persecution. A mighty wind, an earthquake and a fire passed before him, but God was in none of these; and then Elijah heard the sound of a light whisper, and covered his face in his cloak. God asked why Elijah had come, and, when Elijah repeated his complaint, gave him three new tasks: to anoint Elisha as his own successor, Hazael as King of Syria and Jehu as King of Israel. Hazael would fight Ahab's idolatrous kingdom and Jehu would destroy Ahab's dynasty. Elijah immediately found Elisha and threw his mantle over him; Hazael was in fact anointed by Elisha, and Jehu by Elisha's representative.

In old age, Elijah knew that God was about to take him and travelled to various cities to say goodbye to the 'sons of the prophets', coming last to Jericho. Elisha stayed with him. His last miracle was to divide the Jordan, which he struck with his rolled-up cloak. Soon after the two had crossed eastwards, a chariot and horses, all of fire, carried the immortal Elijah away in a storm wind to heaven. At the end of the Old Testament his return is expected, to herald the Messianic age (Malachi 4:5). Jesus identified him with John the Baptist and once appeared to his disciples standing between Moses and Elijah (Matthew 17:3; Mark 9:4).

Elisha was successor to the prophet Elijah. Elijah came to him as he was ploughing and threw his cloak over him as a sign that he was to take over Elijah's role. Since he was ploughing with eleven assistants, his family was evidently wealthy. Nevertheless he immediately accompanied Elijah, pausing only to kiss his parents farewell and to sacrifice the oxen on their wooden plough. He became Elijah's devoted disciple and remained with him until Elijah was taken to heaven. When Elijah invited a last request, Elisha asked to inherit a double portion—as was the right of a first-born son—of Elijah's prophetic spirit.

Elisha's miracles outnumbered Elijah's. As soon as he took on Elijah's cloak, he repeated Elijah's miracle of dividing the Jordan. When a poor widow who owned only one flask of oil cried that creditors were about to seize her sons, Elisha told her to borrow as many containers as she could and, miraculously, she filled them all with oil from the flask. He rewarded a hospitable woman with the promise of a son, and, when the boy died, revived him (2 Kings 4:34); later he predicted a famine and counselled the family to move temporarily abroad. He cured the Syrian general Naaman of leprosy, testing his faith by casually sending a messenger to tell him bathe in the Jordan; Naaman had expected to be cured by Elisha's prayers and gestures but when the treatment worked, he offered Elisha gifts in gratitude. Elisha refused them but his servant Gehazi was determined to get something in return for the cure. He asked Namaan for money and clothes 'for the sons of the prophets'. Elisha, however, had seen a vision of a man turning back from his chariot and so knew what Gehazi had done. He cursed Gehazi with leprosy.

Elisha performed many other miracles. He cured the poisonous waters of Jericho by pouring salt on them from a new flask; made a poisonous soup harmless by adding flour; fed a hundred disciples with twenty barley loaves (4:44) and raised an axe-head from the River Jordan. Even the touch of his bones revived a man who was buried in his grave.

There was a certain coldness about him however. Forty-two children once made fun of his baldness. Elisha cursed them and two she-bears tore them to

ELISHA
Elisha was actively involved in state affairs and used his prophetic powers to help the armies of Israel and Judah. His miracles show that he was compassionate, but he could also be severe and once cursed children for mocking his baldness.

Syrians besieged Samaria. Jehoram was about to behead Elisha for not miraculously saving the city when Elisha predicted the end of the siege just in time.

Elisha performed two tasks inherited from Elijah—he anointed Hazael king of Syria, and sent a disciple to anoint Jehu king of Israel.

Jehu's revolution was marked by violence (he killed not only Jehoram and his nephew the king of Judah, but also the 70 remaining grandsons of Ahab). The bloodshed was thought justified in order to prevent Ahab's descendants from claiming the throne of Israel. A third task for Elisha (1 Kings 19:17) had been to kill any Baal worshipper who escaped Jehu's sword; but none did. He next appears over forty years later, when he promised Jehu's grandson Jehoash three victories over Syria; and then he died.

Gehazi was the servant of the prophet Elisha. Elisha often accepted the hospitality of a wealthy woman whose home he passed from time to time. Elisha wanted to reward her in some way and Gehazi suggested the birth of a son. Yet when the woman fell upon Elisha's feet with the news that the boy had died, Gehazi tried to push her away. Elisha told him to go ahead and place his staff on the boy, but this did no good; only Elisha in person could revive him (2 Kings 4:31). On a later occasion, Elisha cured Naaman, commander of the Syrian army, of leprosy. The prophet refused to accept any reward, but Gehazi ran after Naaman and asked for money and clothes in Elisha's name for two 'sons of the prophets' who had unexpectedly arrived. Naaman gave gratefully, but Elisha angrily punished Gehazi with leprosy for obtaining the goods on false pretences (5:27). People suffering from leprosy had to live apart from others, yet Gehazi was later admitted to Jehoram's palace (8:4). As he was recounting Elisha's miracles, the very woman whose son had been revived entered. Strangers had taken her land while she was away for seven years and she had come to plead for its return. Jehoram immediately gave her what she asked.

pieces (2:24). Even when planning how to reward the woman who had been hospitable to him, he first told Gehazi to call her and then spoke at length with Gehazi about her, in the third person, as if she was not there (4:12—15).

Elisha was involved in state affairs even beyond Israel's borders. When the armies of Israel and Judah, marching against Moab, were short of water, his prophetic powers had to be awakened by a minstrel's playing; he then told the armies to dig trenches (to show faith) and promised that the next day would

bring abundant water—and victory. The next day, his promise was fulfilled. He knew prophetically where Ben-Hadad II lay in ambush, and always warned Jehoram. On one occasion the Syrian Ben-Hadad had sent an army to capture Jehoram. They were all temporarily blinded and Elisha led them to Jehoram in Samaria. Elisha would not allow Jehoram to slaughter them; prisoners, especially those captured supernaturally, could not be killed in cold blood. Instead, he told Jehoram to feed them and send them home. Later those same

The Egyptians

Pharaoh Shishak (reigned about 935–914 BC) founded the 22nd Egyptian dynasty. He harboured Jeroboam in the hope of dividing and ruling Solomon's realm. When the kingdom divided into Judah and Israel after Solomon's death, he invaded Judah and plundered Jerusalem (1 Kings 14:25). According to Shishak's own (perhaps exaggerated) list of conquered cities, inscribed on the northern wall of the temple at Karnak, he also overran the northern kingdom.

Pharaoh Necho (Neko II) marched eastwards in 609 BC to try to take the city of Harran from the Babylonians. The Assyrian empire was collapsing and the Babylonians had taken its capital Nineveh. They were moving southwards, bringing them into conflict with the Egyptians, who were moving northwards into Israel and Syria. Pharaoh Necho intended to help the Assyrians recapture Harran (in northern Syria) and so to create a small buffer state that would both block the Babylonian expansion and also become an ally of Egypt. Josiah, then King of Judah, tried to prevent Pharaoh from taking over the area and intercepted him at Megiddo, where Josiah himself was killed. The assault on Harran failed—partly, perhaps, because Necho had been delayed by Josiah's army. Necho returned to Judah in a vengeful mood. He deposed Josiah's son Jehoahaz, set his brother Eliakim on the throne (renaming him Jehoiakim) and imposed heavy tribute on the Judeans. Egypt's domination of Canaan and Syria soon ended, however, when they were overwhelmingly defeated by the Babylonians under Nebuchadnezzar at Carchemish in 605 BC (Jeremiah 46:2).

The Syrians

Hazael (reigned c.842–806 BC) was minister to the Syrian King Ben-Hadad II, but God had commanded the prophet Elijah to anoint him king. Elisha arrived in Damascus to complete Elijah's task and found that Ben-Hadad was sick. Not knowing the purpose of Elisha's visit, Hazael asked if he would recover. Elisha at first replied that he would, but then saw in a vision that Ben-Hadad would die. When Hazael saw him staring and then breaking into tears, Elisha explained his vision; Hazael would become king and mercilessly attack the Israelites. Hazael protested that he was too insignificant—rather than too good—to aspire to 'this great thing' (2 Kings 8:13). However, on returning to Ben-Hadad, he reported only that Elisha had predicted his recovery, and the next day smothered him with a wet bath-cloth. As king, Hazael occupied all Israel's territory east of the Jordan, and then marched west to capture Gath; only a bribe of Temple vessels and gold from the palace of Joash of Judah stopped him from attacking Jerusalem. His son Ben-Hadad III (2 Kings 13:24) was defeated three times by the Israelite king Jehoash, who recovered the cities captured by Hazael.

Naaman was commander of the Syrian army when Jehoram was King of Israel. He suffered from leprosy and heard from a captured Israelite maid that a prophet in Israel could heal him. The Syrian king sent him to Jehoram, with rich gifts and a royal letter requesting his cure. Jehoram thought that the Syrians were preparing a pretext for war, but the prophet, Elisha, asked to receive Naaman himself. When Naaman reached Elisha's home, Elisha sent a messenger telling him bathe seven times in the Jordan. Naaman angrily left, shouting that there were greater rivers in Syria, but his servants persuaded him to do as the prophet advised. He was fully healed, and in gratitude he declared before Elisha that the God of Israel was the only god. He asked to take two mule loads of Israelite earth to Syria so that he could worship the Lord there on Israelite soil. He asked hesitantly whether Elisha could forgive him if he continued to worship the Syrian god Rimmon in his king's presence; Elisha replied diplomatically: 'Go in peace' (2 Kings 5:19). Elisha refused gifts, and the unsuspecting Naaman was later glad to give twice as much as he was asked to Elisha's villainous servant Gehazi.

The Assyrians

Rabshakeh is not a name but an Assyrian title—literally 'cup-bearer', in fact a high official. When the Assyrians besieged Jerusalem (see *Hezekiah*), it was the Rabshakeh who demanded surrender, shouting over the walls in Hebrew, which this diplomat knew well. He was equally familiar with religious affairs and declared that the Lord had commanded him to invade Judah as Hezekiah's punishment for closing the local religious sanctuaries. He scornfully bet 2000 horses that Hezekiah could not supply 2000 riders. The Judean leaders asked him to speak in Aramaic, the language of international diplomacy, but he replied that he wanted to reach the common people, who were now reduced to eating dung and drinking urine. He pointed to Assyria's many conquests—including Samaria, which the Lord had failed to save—and asked them to accept exile to a land as fertile as their own. Met with silence, he reported their reaction to Sennacherib. With the Rabshakeh were the Rab-saris ('chief eunuch') and the Tartan ('field marshall'). Among the Judean officials who negotiated with them were Eliakim, minister 'over the palace' and Shebna, the scribe.

Sennacherib was King of Assyria from 704 to 681 BC. During his reign, the kingdom of Judah was part of the Assyrian empire but, under its King Hezekiah, rebelled against Assyrian rule. Sennacherib invaded and besieged Jerusalem. He demanded its surrender first through his minister the Rabshakeh and later by letter. During the siege he was attacked by the army of Pharaoh Tirhaka but soon defeated it. Just when victory seemed to be in his hands, his entire army died outside the walls of Jerusalem (see *Hezekiah*). Downhearted, he returned to his capital Nineveh, where his sons murdered him at his temple (2 Kings 19:37). His own account of the campaign against Judah has survived. In it he claimed to have captured 46 cities and over 200,000 prisoners, and to have besieged Hezekiah 'like a bird in a cage'.

The Book of Daniel

The Kingdom of Judah was overrun by the forces of Nebuchadnezzar, Emperor of Babylon in 587 BC. Jerusalem was besieged, then destroyed and most of the people in the kingdom were exiled to Babylon.

The Book of Daniel is set during the period of exile, when the Jews, living in a foreign land, tried to remain loyal to their faith.

The exile in Babylon

Nebuchadnezzar, Emperor of Babylon (from 605 to 562 BC), overran the Kingdom of Judah in 587. He is more correctly called Nebuchadrezzar by Jeremiah and Ezekiel. The original form of the name is *Nabu* (a Babylonian god) + *kudurri* (my boundary stone) + *usur* (guard thou!). He built up an empire covering the present-day states of Iraq, Syria, Jordan, Lebanon and Israel, taking over many countries previously ruled by Assyria. When Assyria conquered a state, the population was usually exiled and replaced by people from another area. This had already happened to the northern tribes in 722. Nebuchadnezzar followed the Assyrians' example in sending the majority of the people as captives to Babylon but did not replace them.

The Book of Daniel (2) tells how through Daniel's interpretation of a dream, Nebuchadnezzar came to

SENNACHERIB
At the height of its power, the Assyrian empire stretched from Babylonia to the Mediterranean. When Sennacherib came to the throne in 704 BC, its power was beginning to decline and many of its satellite kingdoms, including Judah, were trying to gain independence. Sennacherib attacked Judah, and his records claim that he captured 46 cities and took 200,000 prisoners. He never succeeded in taking Jerusalem, however, for on the verge of victory, his army was devastated by a plague. Sennacherib returned home, to be murdered by his sons.

NEBUCHADNEZZAR
It was Nebuchadnezzar who, as emperor of Babylon, finally destroyed the kingdom of Judah, blinded its king and drove the people of Jerusalem into exile. The Book of Daniel tells how God punished his arrogance with years of madness when he lived in the fields like an animal. Later, it says, he converted to Judaism but records from Babylon do not confirm this.

acknowledge the Lord as supreme God. A contradictory story in Daniel 3, however, tells that he condemned to death anyone who refused to worship a great golden image he had made. The Book of Daniel also relates how Nebuchadnezzar was suddenly banished while boasting of his achievements in Babylon. He spent seven years in the wet fields, his hair and nails uncut, eating grass like oxen, before returning to kingship (Daniel 4). The story is written in the first person, as if from Nebuchadnezzar's own hand. Babylonian sources give no hint of Nebuchadnezzar's conversion to Israel's faith—nor of his banishment.

Nebuzaradan was the Babylonian general who sacked Jerusalem, burning down the Temple and all the other buildings and pulling down the city walls. He also brought the chief priests and some seventy other prominent citizens to Riblah, where Nebuchadnezzar executed them. On Nebuchadnezzar's orders, however, he treated the prophet Jeremiah kindly. All but the poorest of the population were then carried off to Babylon.

Daniel and three other men (Shadrach, Meshach and Abed-Nego) were chosen, for their good looks and wisdom, to be taken to the Babylonian court after King Nebuchadnezzar's invasion of Judah. There Daniel continued to practise his religion fully and openly. He refused to eat the king's food and wine, which did not satisfy the Jewish dietary laws; he and his three companions ate only vegetables—and looked the healthiest people at court. In time Daniel became governor of the province of Babylon.

Daniel was inspired to interpret messages received but not understood by the Babylonian kings. Nebuchadnezzar once had a dream but could not remember its content. He threatened to put everyone at court to death if it could not be recalled and interpreted. Daniel and his companions prayed for inspiration and Daniel was given the answer—in a dream of his own. Nebuchadnezzar had seen a great statue with a gold head, silver breast, bronze thighs and feet of iron mixed with clay. Daniel interpreted these as four empires, of which Babylon was the first and mightiest. Nebuchadnezzar later dreamed that a great tree was cut down, only the stump remaining; Daniel was at first too terrified to speak, but then explained that Nebuchadnezzar would temporarily be banished and live as an animal. During the reign of Nebuchadnezzar's heir, Belshazzar, he also interpreted four words written by a disembodied hand on Belshazzar's palace wall. The words pointed to the immediate fall of Babylon.

Later, according to Daniel 5, Darius the Mede conquered Babylon. Daniel became Darius's right-hand man. Darius, however, was persuaded to pass a law forbidding his subjects to pray to anyone except himself for thirty days. Undeterred, Daniel continued to pray to God three times a day, with the

DANIEL
Daniel was a courtier in Babylon, a Jewish exile who insisted on practising his religion openly. He became a provincial governor under Nebuchadnezzar and later, adviser to Darius. A prophet and an interpreter of dreams, his visions foretold the downfall of the Babylonian empire and the rise and fall of its successors.

windows open towards Jerusalem. As punishment he was thrown into a den of lions—whose mouths God miraculously closed (see *Darius*).

More detailed pictures of God's scheme of history came in Daniel's own visions (Daniel 7—12), which came when he prayed for the restoration of his exiled people. In spite of his insight into the visions of other people, Daniel could not understand his own; he

simply turned pale or lay sick and once hardly ate for three weeks (10:3) until an angel explained them. Like Nebuchadnezzar, he saw symbols of four cruel kingdoms—a lion, a bear, a leopard and a ten-horned monster with iron teeth—followed by a man, symbolizing a benign kingdom that would endure for ever. Traditionally these empires were taken as Babylonia, Persia, Greece and Rome. Christian

tradition sees this as a prophecy of either the first or second coming of Jesus. Jewish tradition, too, sees it as a prophecy of the future Messiah.

Daniel's prediction (Daniel 11) of the events leading to 'the end' is in fact an accurate account of relations between the Seleucids ('the north') and the Ptolemies ('the south'), down to 167BC, with details of wars and marriage alliances. In that year, the Seleucid Antiochus IV sacrificed a pig ('the abominable thing that causes desolation'—11:31) on the altar in the Temple and banned the Jewish religion. At this point, Daniel's vision parts with history. The persecution provoked a revolt, led by Judah the Maccabee, which soon won Judah's political independence; Daniel, however, expected the archangel Michael to intervene and the resurrection of the dead to take place (12:1—2).

Shadrach, Meshach and **Abed-Nego** were companions of Daniel. They were taken with him to the Babylonian court (see *Daniel*) and these names were given to them by the Babylonians. Daniel became governor of the province of Babylon, and he entrusted his three companions with its administration (Daniel 2:49). They were arrested, however, for not worshipping Nebuchadnezzar's great golden statue, and were sentenced to be thrown into a furnace. They were prepared for martyrdom, and told Nebuchadnezzar that even if their God could not save them, they would not bow down to an idol. The furnace was so hot that the men who threw Shadrach, Meshach and Abed-Nego inside were themselves burned and Nebuchadnezzar was astonished to see the three walking unscathed through the flames, together with a fourth man resembling an angel (3:25). In the Apocrypha, Azariah (Abed-Nego's original name) confesses his people's sins while in the furnace and all three sing a hymn of praise. Nebuchadnezzar released them and then promoted them to higher office in Babylon.

Belshazzar, according to Daniel 5, was Nebuchadnezzar's son and Babylon's

DARIUS
Despite being ruler of Babylon, Darius had to obey the law. His courtiers became jealous of the way he promoted Daniel to be his close councillor and tricked him into passing a law they knew Daniel, as a devout Jew, must break. Darius was forced to punish Daniel by throwing him to the lions. To Darius's relief, Daniel survived unhurt and Darius fed the courtiers and their families to the lions instead.

last king—though the Babylonian sources say he came from a different family and was only regent. At a great feast, he and his guests were drinking wine from the golden vessels of the Jerusalem temple, and praising their idols, when four words that no-one could understand suddenly appeared on the palace wall. Belshazzar promised to appoint the person who could interpret them as third in command of his kingdom but no-one could help. Eventually the queen mother told him that Daniel was an inspired interpreter. He was summoned and fearlessly declared that the writing announced that Belshazzar would be punished for his arrogance: he had been weighed and found wanting, and his kingdom would be divided between the Medes and Persians. Belshazzar kept his promise to give the interpreter power; but that very night he was killed and Babylon was captured.

Darius the Mede (522—486 BC), according to Daniel 5, conquered Babylon at the age of 62. Daniel was appointed to his cabinet of three, and soon became second only to Darius. Jealous courtiers, however, persuaded Darius to pass a law forbidding anyone to pray except to Darius for thirty days; offenders were to be thrown into the lions' den. Darius was distraught when Daniel was found guilty, but as his courtiers insisted, the laws of the Medes and Persians could not be changed. Having locked Daniel in with the lions, Darius anxiously refused food, sleep and concubines, and at dawn ran to the den—to be greeted by Daniel. Darius released him, fed his accusers to the lions—with their wives and children—and commanded his subjects all over the world to fear the God of Daniel (Daniel 6:26).

This Darius puzzles historians for all other evidence (including biblical evidence) shows that the Babylonian Empire fell to Cyrus the Persian (who appears as a separate character in 6:28). Many consider this Darius an invention by someone who had read prophecies of Babylon falling to the Medes alone (Isaiah 13:17, Jeremiah 51:11), and therefore viewed the Medes as the succeeding world power.

The Book of Esther

The Book of Esther is set in the reign of Ahasuerus, Emperor of Persia. By this time, the Jews had been permitted to return home to Judah but only a minority had done so. Many remained in other parts of the empire where, like other peoples conquered by the Persians, they were allowed to practise their own religion freely. The story of Esther, however, shows that persecution was always possible: the Jewish festival of Purim commemorates the successful outcome of the events it describes.

Ahasuerus was the Persian emperor known to the Greeks as Xerxes (486—465BC). His empire stretched from India to Ethiopia. The Bible portrays him as foolish and sensual. In his third year, he feasted for six months with all his officers and servants, then held a seven-day feast for the men of Shushan, his capital city. His queen, Vashti, feasted separately with the women and when she refused to appear at the men's feast, he banished her. Four years later he desired another queen, and beautiful young women were brought to spend the night with him (Esther 2). The woman that he chose was Esther.

Some time later, his prime minister, Haman, offered an enormous bribe to destroy 'a certain people scattered over your kingdom' (3:8); Ahasuerus did not ask which people he meant; he simply agreed, even waiving the bribe. Just over

VASHTI
Vashti's husband, Ahasuerus, was so proud of her beauty that he ordered her to join him at the drunken banquet attended only by men. She refused and Ahasuerus immediately banished her, afraid that her disobedience would encourage women to despise their husbands.

a month later, however, his beloved wife revealed that she was herself Jewish, from the people Haman intended to have killed. Ahasuerus stormed out of the palace. On his return he found Haman begging for mercy on Esther's couch, accused him of trying to assault her and had him hanged. He then appointed Esther's uncle Mordecai as prime minister in Haman's place.

Under Persian law, a decree could not be revoked so the order to destroy the Jews had to remain. However, Ahasuerus invited Esther and Mordecai to draft a second decree in his name, authorizing the Jews to defend themselves on the day fixed for their destruction.

Vashti was the wife of Ahasuerus, Emperor of Persia. In his third year as emperor, he held a seven-day feast. The men celebrated together and, according to the custom of the time, Vashti and

Esther, a young Jewish girl living in Shushan, the capital city of ancient Persia, was the second wife of the emperor Ahasuerus. An intelligent and courageous woman, she saved the lives of her uncle—and of the whole Jewish community.

enraged that he planned to kill all the Jews. He easily obtained from Ahasuerus a decree to wipe out 'a certain people scattered over your kingdom whose laws differ from other peoples, and who do not keep the king's laws' (Esther 3:8). The king did not even ask who they were. Haman chose the date for the extermination eleven months ahead, by drawing lots. A month later, however, he could bear Mordecai's insolence no longer. On his wife's advice, he built a gallows and in the middle of the night went to ask Ahasuerus if he might hang Mordecai at once. The king, however, had been unable to sleep, and had been listening to the royal records. He had just learned how Mordecai once foiled an attempt on his life and when Haman appeared, Ahasuerus commanded him honour Mordecai: he was to lead Mordecai around the city, dressed in the king's robes and riding the king's horse, proclaiming, 'Thus shall be done to the man whom the king wishes to honour!'

When she heard this, Haman's wife commented that Haman would not be able to stand against Mordecai: the next night, Haman was denounced by Esther and hanged on his own gallows. His ten sons were also killed and their corpses hanged at Esther's request. Some 75,000 of his supporters were later killed when the Jews fought back against the men sent to destroy them.

her women had a separate feast. On the last day of the celebration, Ahasuerus summoned Vashti to 'show her beauty' at the men's feast. When she refused, one of Ahasuerus's ministers warned the emperor that she had set a bad example. Her disobedience would encourage women throughout the empire to despise their husbands. Ahasuerus promptly banished her and issued a decree that 'every man be master in his house'.

Haman was prime minister under the Persian emperor Ahasuerus. He was a descendant of Agag who had been King of the Amalekites in Saul's time. The Amalekites were traditional enemies of Israel: they had attacked the Israelites in the desert without cause (Exodus 17:8), and God had commanded Israel to blot out their memory (Deuteronomy 25:19). Ahasuerus commanded that everyone bow down to Haman, and when the Jew Mordecai refused, Haman was so

Esther was an orphan, brought up by her uncle Mordecai. She was beautiful and charmed all who saw her. At the time when she became old enough to marry, King Ahasuerus was looking for a new queen. His servants arranged for a contest: beautiful virgins were to be brought from all over the land; the one that pleased him the most was to become queen.

Esther was taken (apparently against her will) to the palace, where, like the

MORDECAI
Mordecai was a Jewish official at the court of Ahasuerus. The prime minister became jealous of Mordecai's influence and a law was passed which meant all the Jews in the city would be killed. Too subtle to take any direct part in the course of events, Mordecai persuaded Esther to act, pointing out that if the law was carried out, even she would not be safe.

join her in a three-day fast, and then entered the royal court. Ahasuerus received her favourably and promised to give her anything she asked for, 'up to half my kingdom'. She invited him and Haman alone to a feast, and when the king repeated his promise, she invited them to another. At the second feast she revealed that she was a Jew and denounced Haman to the king.

Ahasuerus stormed out in a rage and Haman flung himself on Esther's couch to plead for mercy. Returning suddenly, Ahasuerus accused him of assault. Esther did not deny it and allowed the king to condemn Haman to death.

Since the order to kill the Jews had already been given, a second one had to be given to cancel it out. Together with Mordecai, Esther drafted a decree authorizing the Jews to kill their enemies, including women and children. She added her royal authority to Mordecai's letter by instituting the Purim festival.

Mordecai was Esther's uncle and foster-father. He was a courtier, who 'sat in the king's gate', and he won King Ahasuerus's gratitude when he overheard two officers plotting against him, and informed Queen Esther. He won the hatred of the king's prime minister, Haman, because, for no obvious reason, he refused to bow to him. Haman was furious, and managed to have a decree passed ordering the extermination of the Jews. Mordecai persuaded Esther to plead with the king on behalf of the Jews, telling her not to imagine that she would be safe in the king's palace; if she remained silent, she would perish, and salvation would come 'from another place' (4:13—14). Esther secured Haman's downfall, but Persian law made it impossible for Ahasuerus to cancel the decree. However, he allowed Esther and Mordecai to draft a second decree authorizing the Jews to defend themselves. They did so—successfully. After their victory, he wrote to all the Jews in the empire, telling them to keep that day as a festival each year. It became the festival of Purim, 'lots'.

Mordecai became Prime Minister immediately after Haman's fall, and was 'popular with most of his countrymen'.

other girls, she spent six months being treated with oil and myrrh and six months with spices and perfumes (Esther 2:12). Her turn to spend the night with Ahasuerus came by chance in the month of Tebet (December/January), a time when, as the rabbis said, body warms to body. She was chosen to be queen, but did not reveal her Jewish origin. Strangely, the prime minister, Haman, never suspected this, even though he knew

that Mordecai, who frequently visited her, was a Jew. Haman hated Mordecai, so persuaded the emperor to pass a decree ordering the killing of all Jews. Mordecai told Esther about this and asked her to plead with Ahasuerus. Esther was reluctant to risk her own life, for Ahasuerus had not summoned her for a month, and the penalty for disturbing him without permission was death. When Mordecai insisted, however, she asked all Jews in the city to

The Books of Ezra and Nehemiah

The exile of the people of Judah in Babylon lasted almost 50 years, from 587 BC, when Nebuchadnezzar of Babylon conquered them, to 538 when Cyrus of Persia, having conquered Babylon, allowed the Jews to return home. The city of Jerusalem, with all its buildings, had been totally destroyed and not all the exiles wished to return to these harsh conditions. Some 43,000 of the tribes of Judah, Benjamin and the priestly tribe of Levi returned to rebuild their devastated land. The Books of Ezra and Nehemiah describe the gradual reconstruction of their city and of their way of life.

Cyrus the Great was Emperor of Persia from 550—530 BC. Isaiah hailed him as the future conqueror of Babylon (Isaiah 44:28, 45:1). In 539 BC he defeated the Babylonian army, and his troops entered Babylon without a fight. There Cyrus restored the worship of Marduk, the chief Babylonian god, neglected under the previous Babylonian emperor. Cyrus's policy was to allow subject peoples religious freedom, and he returned exiles together with their captured gods to their cities. As the Jews had no idols, he charged the Jewish prince Sheshbazzar to restore the sacred vessels of the Temple to Jerusalem and then authorized Jews to return with him to Jerusalem and rebuild the Temple. Cyrus promised to pay for the materials, and took the precaution of specifying the dimensions (Ezra 6:3). Sheshbazzar was appointed Governor of Judah and laid the foundation of the Temple (5:16), but no more progress was made until 520 BC when Haggai and Zechariah called for a new effort. (In other references, it was Zerubbabel, not Sheshbazzar, who was put in charge of the return.)

Zerubbabel was a descendant of David (apparently Jehoiachin's grandson). According to several passages, it was he, not Sheshbazzar, who led the exiles returning from Babylon to Jerusalem (see *Cyrus*). He was appointed Governor of Judah, and laid the foundation of the Temple (Haggai 1:1; Ezra 2:2; Zechariah 4:9). Together with Joshua the High Priest, he rebuilt the Temple altar and resumed sacrifices. Later, at the request of the prophets Haggai and Zechariah, he and Joshua began the rebuilding of the Temple itself. The Samaritans offered to help, but their help was refused. These were not members of the tribes from the old northern kingdom (they had been scattered by the Assyrians) but foreigners who had been granted the land. They were suspected of worshipping idols. The resentful Samaritans hindered the restoration of Jerusalem for generations.

Haggai (2:21—23) expected the Persian empire to fall, and Zerubbabel to become king, the Lord's 'signet'. Zerubbabel is not mentioned after the completion of the Temple in 515BC; some wonder whether the anxious Persians eliminated him.

Tattenai was the Persian governor of 'Beyond Euphrates' (which included Judah). In 520 BC he questioned whether the Jews had the right to rebuild the Temple (see *Cyrus*); perhaps he knew Zerubbabel had hopes of kingship. When he was told that the rebuilding had been authorized by Cyrus, Tattenai allowed the work to proceed, but wrote to check with the current ruler, Darius I. Darius's servants discovered Cyrus's decree and Darius replied forbidding anyone, on pain of death, to hinder the rebuilding. He also commanded Tattenai to provide whatever funds, animals or materials the Temple required; the conscientious Tattenai did as he was asked (Ezra 6:13).

Artaxerxes I was Emperor of Persia from 465 to 424 BC. Early in his reign he heard from the Samaritans that the Jews, who had begun to rebuild the walls of Jerusalem, planned a rebellion. He discovered Jerusalem's long history of ambitious kings from palace records, and ordered the rebuilding to be halted immediately. In his seventh year, however, with no recorded prompting, he despatched Ezra to organize religious life in Judah. With him he sent a decree (Ezra 7:12—26) promising funds for sacrifices and other temple needs, and exempting temple personnel from taxation. The decree also authorized Ezra to teach the law of his God, to administer it—together with the law of the king—and to appoint judges who could even exact the death penalty.

In his twentieth year, Artaxerxes allowed his cup-bearer Nehemiah to go to Judah; he was to remain there for twelve years and rebuild the province of Judah. Artaxerxes even granted him timber from the royal park for use in the rebuilding. This reflects the general tolerance of the Persian kings, but in addition Artaxerxes hoped that the prayers offered in the Temple would benefit his family and his whole realm; he may also have wanted loyal allies near the border with Egypt.

The Bible mentions Ezra and Nehemiah as contemporaries (Nehemiah 8:9, 12:26), implying that both served under the same Artaxerxes. This would have been Artaxerxes I: Sanballat, Nehemiah's enemy, had already retired when Artaxerxes II (404—358 BC) ascended the throne. On this evidence, Ezra's mission (in Artaxerxes' seventh year) began before Nehemiah's (in the twentieth). Other clues in the text, however, seem to show that Ezra and Nehemiah were not contemporaries but that Ezra began his mission in 428 BC, under Artaxerxes II. For example, 'Johannan, son of Eliashib' (Ezra 10:6) seems to have been the son of the High Priest under Nehemiah.

CYRUS THE GREAT
In 25 years, Cyrus's conquests built the powerful Persian empire which at its height reached from the Mediterranean to India. Cyrus was an outstanding general and an enlightened ruler who allowed religious freedom and permitted the exiled Jews to return to Jerusalem and rebuild the Temple.

Nehemiah was cup-bearer to the Persian emperor Artaxerxes I. He heard of the wretched conditions in which the returned exiles were living in Jerusalem and longed to go there. The people of Jerusalem had lacked leadership since the completion of the Temple some seventy years earlier (see *Cyrus*). Nehemiah mourned and fasted until Artaxerxes asked what the matter was. Nehemiah asked to be posted to 'the city of my fathers' graves' in Judah. Diplomatically he did not mention Jerusalem, which Artaxerxes had once called a centre of insurrection (Ezra 4:19). He was granted a twelve-year stay (445–433 BC), and was later allowed a second visit. On arrival he secretly inspected Jerusalem by night, and saw his first task as the rebuilding of the ruined city wall. This he completed in just fifty-two days, despite the strenuous opposition of Sanballat, Governor of Samaria, and other neighbours. Nehemiah supervised the many teams working simultaneously in different parts of the city, and even slept in his working clothes. Building continued from dawn to nightfall—though towards the end, Nehemiah had to divert half his workforce to guard duty for fear of invasion.

The plan to rebuild the wall of Jerusalem was opposed on all sides—to the north, by Sanballat, governor of Samaria; to the east by Tobiah, the Ammonite; to the south, by King Geshem the Arabian; and in the west by the Ashdodites. When mockery and threats failed, they invited Nehemiah to meet them on the plain of Ono (in the north-west corner of the province of Judah) but Nehemiah declined, suspecting an assassination plot. Eventually Sanballat threatened to tell the Persian Emperor that Nehemiah was planning a revolt and had produced prophets to proclaim him king. When Nehemiah remained unmoved, they bribed a prophet to help them. This prophet told Nehemiah to lock himself in the Temple because a squad of men had been sent to kill him. Nehemiah, however, knew that as a commoner he could not enter the Temple (Numbers 18:7), so realized that the prophecy was a ploy to discredit him. Still more prophets and one prophetess were hired to terrorize him, but the walls were completed with astonishing speed. Nehemiah's opponents had to acknowledge that it was God's doing.

Even after the walls were completed, however, few volunteered to settle in Jerusalem itself, and so Nehemiah allocated one tenth of Judah's people to Jerusalem by lot (Nehemiah 11:1).

Nehemiah was also concerned with the survival of the Jewish religion and fear of the influence of pagan religious practices prevented him from accepting the Samaritans' offers of help (see *Zerubbabel*). On his second visit he

stamped out religious abuses that had grown up during his absence. He beat those who had taken foreign wives (he had first noticed the children's foreign dialects), tore out their hair, and made them swear to allow no such marriages in future (13:25). To prevent merchants, whether Jewish or foreign, from trading in Jerusalem on the Sabbath, he locked the city gates and threatened traders who encamped just outside (13:21). He was also horrified by the neglect of ethical laws. Starvation had forced many to mortgage their lands and even sell their children into slavery to their richer fellow Jews. Nehemiah (who had himself lent money and corn) made the creditors swear before the assembled priests to return every pledge and cancel the debts. To set an example, he

NEHEMIAH
Nehemiah, a cup-bearer to King Artaxerxes, was sent to Jerusalem as its governor. He was not just an inspired leader, he was also a careful and meticulous organizer. Under his guidance, the walls and gates of the city were rebuilt in a record 52 days.

never drew the salary which, as governor, he was entitled to raise by taxation.

In all this activity Nehemiah recognized God's guidance and the Book of Nehemiah is full of prayers asking God to remember his good deeds. He recorded his achievements himself, in the first person—and had just cause for pride.

Ezra was a priest and scribe skilled in the Torah (better translated as 'teaching' than 'law') of Moses. In 458 BC he was sent to Jerusalem by Artaxerxes I, with full authority to teach the Torah among the Jews and put its rules into action. He brought some 4000 more exiles and royal funds (with power to raise grants from local governors) for the Temple. On the New Year festival Ezra spent all morning—from dawn to midday—reading from the Torah to the people assembled in Jerusalem . The Levites provided interpretation—a task later assumed by the rabbis. The people wept, because they had not observed the Torah's commands. (The reason, according to most biblical critics, is simply that Ezra had originated many of them himself.) He spent many more days proclaiming the Torah during that month. All the Jews then assembled swore to uphold it—and in particular to contribute money and offerings in kind to the Temple, never to marry heathen women or to desecrate the sabbath (Nehemiah 10:31—40).

Ezra observed the Torah scrupulously. On his first journey, he ensured that vessels dedicated to the Temple were carried only by priests and Levites. He told the people to observe the New Year festival with feasting and good works, and later that month gather branches to celebrate a Feast of Booths (Nehemiah 8:15). He demanded the banishment of heathen wives together with their children; over a hundred offending husbands are named.

Ezra's faith sometimes stopped him from taking practical action. Not daring to ask the king for an armed escort to Jerusalem, he told his treasure-laden followers to fast and pray—and they arrived safely. When told of Jews who

had taken foreign wives, Ezra tore his clothes, pulled out his hair and then uttered a long confession on behalf of all Israel; Nehemiah in the same situation pulled out the husbands' hair. Critics doubt whether Ezra can really have been so passive.

In Ezra's day, as ever since, only a minority of Jews lived in the Holy Land. His emphasis on the Torah preserved Jewish identity through a religion that

EZRA
Ezra was a scholar and a priest, an expert in the teaching of Moses, a man of deep conviction and strict discipline. His main aim was to re-educate the people, to bring back the moral and religious laws that had been neglected and corrupted during years of exile and hardship.

could be practised not just in Judah but anywhere in the world.

Eliashib was the High Priest who began the rebuilding of the walls of Jerusalem. He was ready to conciliate the Jews' opponents, making a chamber for Tobiah in the Temple; his grandson married Sanballat's daughter. The uncompromising Nehemiah, however, ejected Tobiah and expelled the couple.

The Book of Job

The Book of Job bears no date, but Job's style of life, as owner of vast flocks and herds suggests that his story is set in the age of the Patriarchs, before the time of Moses.

Job came not from Israel but from the land of Uz. Genesis 10:23 places Uz in Syria, but Lamentations 4:21 equates Uz with Edom. He was a righteous man, but Satan (in one of just two appearances in the Old Testament) had a bet with God that Job would curse God if he became poor. God authorized Satan to kill Job's livestock and his ten children, and to cover him with boils, but Job accepted God's will without complaint—for the moment. Three friends visited him, each from a different land east of Israel. For seven days everyone was silent, and then Job spoke, wishing himself dead and asking why God created man only to suffer.

Eliphaz, presumably the oldest of the friends, replied that no-one suffered unless he deserved it. 'Remember, who ever perished, being innocent?' he asked Job, ostensibly to encourage him, but in fact insinuating that Job was not wholly righteous. God, declared Eliphaz, was all-powerful and just; no man was sinless, and if Job would only take note of God's rebuke and repent, his prosperity would return. The two other friends made the same points. Bildad was less tactful, remarking that

JOB
Job was subjected to a terrifying series of tests in order to prove how much suffering he could bear without questioning God's justice. He bore the loss of his children, his possessions and his health with patience, but at last broke down in despair, overwhelmed by grief and doubt.

Job's children must have deserved to die (Job 8:4); and Zophar called Job a 'man full of talk' (11:2), who ought not to question God's unfathomed wisdom. To each of the friends' speeches Job replied that he had done no wrong, and that God was unfair to him: 'What is man, that you...turn your heart to him, only to punish him every morning?' (7:17—18, a bitter parody of Psalm 8:4).

In a second round of speeches, the friends continued to insist on God's justice, and offered pointed descriptions—in which they hoped that Job would recognize himself—of the punishment of the wicked. Eliphaz then opened a third round by reciting a list of sins (such as robbing the poor) which Job must have committed, since his sufferings must have been deserved. Job continued to protest that he was innocent, rejecting his 'miserable comforters' (16:2). As for God, Job on the one hand denied his justice ('he destroys both the blameless and the wicked'—9:22) and complained that God could not be summoned to court; on the other hand, Job trusted in his 'witness on high' (16:19) and declared: 'I know that my vindicator lives' (19:25).

The real reason for Job's sufferings, the fact that a power other than God had interfered, never occurred either to Job or to the friends; and the later Jewish and Christian belief that in a life after death justice would be done, is mentioned only to be dismissed (14:12—15). Eventually the friends gave up the attempt to reform Job, who remained 'righteous in his own eyes' (32:1).

A new character, named Elihu, had been listening, but, being younger than the others, had kept silent; he now harangued Job for six chapters (32—37). Like the friends, he described the supreme power of God (which Job had not denied); and he saw suffering as a way of education and deliverance (36:15). Before Job could reply, God himself appeared, declaring that his works were beyond human understanding and asking whether Job could run the world better than he. At this Job repented abjectly (42:3) of his doubts about 'things too wonderful for me' (although he had argued strenuously when the same arguments were put by his friends). God then rebuked the friends for 'not speaking of me aright like my servant Job' (although they had defended his justice throughout). Job became twice as rich as before, was again blessed with ten children, and died at the age of 140.

Eliphaz, Bildad, Zophar and **Elihu** came from different parts of Edom to visit Job and comfort him in his sufferings. All four believed in God's justice and were convinced that Job must be guilty of some serious sin and so deserved his punishment. Elihu, the youngest, advised him angrily to accept and learn from his sufferings. Job, certain of his own innocence, rejected their advice.

The Books of the Prophets

The Books of the Prophets are usually divided into two groups—the major prophets, Isaiah, Jeremiah and Ezekiel, and the twelve minor prophets. Major and minor does not mean that one group was more important than the other but that more actual speeches and prophecies have survived from the major than from the minor ones. Here, the characters are arranged in date order.

Amos ('load bearer') came from Tekoa in Judah but felt a divine compulsion to prophesy in the northern kingdom. His ministry probably coincided with the long reigns of Jeroboam II (786—746 BC) in the north and Uzziah (783—742 BC) in the south. Both kingdoms were prosperous, but the gap between rich and poor was wide and Amos was horrified by the way the poor were forced to live. He began by condemning Israel's neighbours—Damascus, Gaza and Tyre, ending with Judah. Having thus won their sympathy, he attacked the Israelites themselves, for 'selling the righteous for silver' (Amos 2:6). He condemned the ivory houses and luxurious feasts of those who 'trample the poor', (5:11) and he called their wives 'cows of (the fertile region of) Bashan' (4:1). God hated their sacrifices while justice continued to be ignored (5:24). Israel was not the only nation God cared for (God had guided the migrations of other peoples as well as

the Israelites' exodus from Egypt (9:7)) but because of his special relationship with Israel, he would punish them for their sins (3:2). The spoken oracles were reinforced by visions of God preparing to mete out punishment; in the first two Amos saw himself successfully interceding for Israel, but afterwards he despaired (Amos 7). The punishment, which Amos foretold at the height of Israel's prosperity, was to be destruction and exile at the hands of the Assyrians (though Amos never named them); in 722 BC they indeed overthrew the northern kingdom.

The priest Amaziah once expelled Amos from Bethel, the national shrine of the northern kingdom, because of his doom-laden prophecies, which had reached a wide audience: 'Be off to Judah, and earn bread prophesying there!' (7:10—12). Amos replied that he was not a prophet but a herdsman and a 'dresser' of sycamore trees (probably one who nips the fruit at the right time to make it edible). He apparently meant that prophecy was not his sole livelihood. He added that Amaziah himself would die in exile, his children would be killed and his wife would become a whore.

Almost at the end of the book, Amos shifts in mid-verse from foretelling Israel's doom to promising that they will be restored to their land in prosperity. Many scholars believe that this happy ending was added by a later editor; but perhaps Amos was looking here to a more distant future.

Hosea ('salvation') prophesied in the northern kingdom and was active there just before it fell in 722 BC. We know that his ministry began no later than 745 BC, for he predicted the end of Jehu's dynasty (Hosea 1:4), which occurred that year (with the assassination of Jehu's great-great-grandson, Zechariah).

The Israelites had begun to worship the Canaanite god Baal alongside—or even instead of—the Lord. Hosea was commanded to marry a wanton woman in order to make his personal life a symbol of God's love for an unfaithful people. His bride, Gomer, bore him two sons and a daughter to whom he gave ominous names: Jezreel (the scene of

love and fidelity' (2:19—20).

Hosea ruefully described Israel's rebellions. He condemned the north for breaking with David's dynasty and the Temple in Jerusalem, for their shifting alliances, for the assassinations which removed king after king and for using the fertility rites of Baal as an excuse for promiscuity. Northern Israel's punishment would be destruction and exile. Although Hosea's audience considered him mad (9:7), these prophecies were soon fulfilled when the Assyrians conquered the northern kingdom in 722 BC. Nevertheless, Hosea foresaw a time of reconciliation in the more distant future when the repentant Israelites would return and become as numerous as the sand on the seashore (1:10).

Isaiah ('the Lord's salvation') was born in the southern kingdom of Judah and became a prophet in 742 BC, on a visit to the Temple in Jerusalem. The smoke swirling from the altar appeared as the robes of God, who was attended by winged beings called seraphim. From the altar, one seraph took a coal and flew to Isaiah, touching his mouth with it so as to purify him. Then he heard God ask: 'Whom shall I send?' and replied, with none of the reluctance of Moses and Jeremiah: 'Here am I; send me.' He was to deliver the bleak message: 'Listen but do not understand!' until the day his prophecies were fulfilled. Perhaps this account was written some years later and coloured by disappointment for his prophecies were widely rejected.

Isaiah was able to speak directly to King Ahaz and King Hezekiah, both of Judah, and to the High Priest Uriah. In the first political crisis of his ministry, however, in 735 BC, King Ahaz refused to act on Isaiah's prophecy. The northern Israelites and Syrians had marched on Jerusalem, taking vast numbers of prisoners (2 Chronicles 28:5—8). Their aim was to force Judah to join a coalition against the growing menace of Assyria. Isaiah told Ahaz not to fear 'these two smouldering firebrands' and not to ask for Assyrian protection. The names of Isaiah's two sons, born in this period, emphasize his

AMOS
Amos, a country herdsman, prophesied in Israel during the rule of Jeroboam II. This was a period of peace and prosperity and Amos was shocked by the contrast between the way the rich and the poor lived. His grim prophecies of destruction and exile did not bring the social revolution he longed for but were fulfilled when the Assyrians overran the kingdom in 722 BC.

Jehu's revolution), Lo-ruhama ('unpitied') and Lo-ammi ('not my people'). Later, in the slave market, God ordered Hosea to buy a prostitute who was to live in his house but lead a celibate life (Hosea 3). God meant this as a sign that Israel would one day return to him; it seems, then, that the prostitute was Gomer who had deserted Hosea as Israel had deserted God, but

eventually returned to him.

Baal's followers believed that their god made the earth pregnant through rain. Hosea took up this concept of divine marriage, but transformed its meaning; instead of the land, it was the people of Israel who became God's bride, and their relationship, begun during the wilderness wanderings, meant 'righteousness, justice, devotion, message. Shear-Yashub means 'a remnant shall return': if Judah became Assyria's vassal, the Assyrians would not be satisfied until they had conquered Judah and reduced its people to a mere remnant—which would turn in repentance to God. The other name, Maher-Shalal-Hash-Baz, means 'spoil hastens, booty speeds': the invading Syrians and northern Israelites would themselves soon be conquered. He also announced that a young woman (the Hebrew word need not mean 'virgin') would soon conceive and bear a son, to be called Immanuel ('God is with us'), and that by the time the child grew up Syria and northern Israel would be desolate. In spite of Isaiah's warnings, Ahaz submitted voluntarily to Assyria.

In 701BC Assyria overran Judah, just as Isaiah had predicted, and besieged Jerusalem. Isaiah, however, promised Hezekiah, now King of Judah, that the Assyrians would never enter the city; and that night a plague wiped out the besiegers. In 2 Kings 18:13—16 Hezekiah is said to have lifted an Assyrian siege of Jerusalem that same year by paying a massive tribute. Conservative scholars suppose that the Assyrians accepted the tribute but treacherously renewed the attack; sceptics instead consider the plague story a mere legend.

Isaiah describes the compulsion to prophesy as 'the grip of the hand' of God upon him (Isaiah 8:11). In his oracles, God often speaks in the first person, as if invading him. At one stage (c. 711 BC) Isaiah obeyed a divine command to walk naked and barefoot for three years (20:3). His wife was called a prophetess, although this may merely mean 'prophet's wife'. He viewed his sons and himself as 'signs and portents in Israel'. He also founded a circle of disciples, who 'sealed up the teachings' that king and court had ignored, for a future age.

Among his people, Isaiah demanded social justice, condemning those in power who 'grind the faces of the poor' (3:15) and 'join house to house' (5:8). God took no pleasure, Isaiah announced, in the rich sacrifices and lengthy prayers of those whose 'hands were full of blood'. Repentance would

ISAIAH
Isaiah was born in Jerusalem. He was adviser to both King Ahaz and King Hezekiah and probably came from a wealthy family, brought up to be involved in state affairs. His grim visions of the future and his emotional pleas for justice were widely rejected but many of his prophecies came true within his own lifetime.

bring prosperity, but if they continued to rebel they would be destroyed by the Assyrian army, which considered itself mighty but was merely the tool of God's anger. Ultimately, all nations would come streaming to Zion and beat their swords into ploughshares; a king of David's line would rule Israel, and the wolf would live with the kid. Many of his prophecies referred to foreign nations, foretelling their destruction, warning Judah against their intrigues, or predicting their conversion to the worship of the Lord.

He was also remembered as a miracle worker. As a sign to Hezekiah that he would recover from an apparently fatal illness, Isaiah caused a shadow cast by the sun on the stairway to move back ten steps (38:8). To persuade Ahaz not to fear the Syrians and Israelites, he is said to have offered to perform any wonder Ahaz asked—though Ahaz preferred not to put God to the test.

Between chapters 40 and 66, Isaiah's name is not mentioned, and the exile in Babylon (587—538 BC) seems to be the background. The prophet 'proclaims freedom for the captives', tells his audience to leave Babylon, and even names Cyrus as the king who will shortly conquer Babylonia. These chapters are usually ascribed to a later prophet, sometimes known as the second Isaiah. Perhaps they were once copied on to a scroll that contained Isaiah's prophecies and had space for more writing. They mention the Lord's 'servant', tortured and executed for the sins of others, but finally vindicated. Christians interpret the 'servant' as Jesus (Acts 8:32—35). In Jewish tradition, however, he represents the exiled Jewish community. Some scholars suggest that the prophet had been condemned to death by the Babylonians for subversion and that he was referring to himself.

The Bible does not mention the death of Isaiah, nor of any other of the prophets, perhaps to show that their books are of undying relevance. Legend tells that Isaiah died at the hands of Manasseh, Hezekiah's wicked successor.

Micah ('who is like the Lord?') was a prophet who came from Moresheth-gath, some 20 miles south-west of Jerusalem. He was a younger contemporary of Amos, Hosea and Isaiah, and, like them, attacked those who exploit the poor and 'rob their skin from off them' (Micah 3:1). He condemned corruption, in ruler, judge, priest and prophet, and advised: 'Trust not in a friend; a man's enemies are the men of his own house.' (7:5—6). Man needed only 'to do justly, love mercy and walk humbly with God'. (6:8).

Micah foresaw the fall of the northern kingdom, and was the first to predict the ruin of Jerusalem and the Temple. Yet he prayed for God's compassion (7:19), and predicted that Israel would return from exile in Babylon (although the Jews were not carried there until more than a century later). Their king, he said, would be from Bethlehem. Matthew 2:6 applied this prophecy to Jesus, although the reference may simply be to a descendant of David, who came from Bethlehem (1 Samuel 17:12). He looked forward to the day when nations would stream to Zion, beat their swords into ploughshares, and give up war (4:1—4). When, over a century later, the priests wanted to kill Jeremiah for predicting the fall of Jerusalem, the elders protested that Micah had foretold it long before and had not been put to death.

Jonah ('dove'), son of Amittai, came from Gath-hepher (just north of Nazareth) and prophesied in the northern kingdom under Jeroboam II (786—746 BC), predicting his conquests (2 Kings 14:25). Jonah's prophecies, had they survived, would provide a cheering contrast to those of his contemporary, Amos. Instead of giving prophecies at all, however, the Book of Jonah tells how God commanded him to travel east to Nineveh, the Assyrian capital, and denounce its wickedness. Jonah was reluctant to go. If he predicted the downfall of Nineveh, and if they then repented and were saved, his predictions would be proved wrong. To avoid this, he boarded a ship bound for Tarshish, in the opposite direction (perhaps in Sardinia or North Africa). Once aboard he fell asleep.

But there was no escape from God: a storm threatened to wreck the ship, and the sailors, deducing that someone on board was to blame, drew lots and identified Jonah. He confessed that he was fleeing from God and suggested that they throw him into the sea. At first they refused and tried to row back to shore, but the storm soon forced them to do as he said. Jonah was then swallowed by a great fish, in whose belly he spent three days and nights—prefiguring, according to Matthew 12:40, the three days between Jesus's death and resurrection. There he offered a prayer of thanksgiving (Jonah 2) for having escaped drowning; strangely, the prayer does not mention his distress in the belly of the fish. The fish disgorged him and Jonah at last reached Nineveh and announced (even though God had commanded a rebuke rather than a prediction) that in forty days the city would be overthrown. The Ninevites fasted, mourned, improved their ways, and were spared. This was just what Jonah had feared: he had been proved wrong. He left the city, made himself a shelter from the sun, and prayed for death. So God created a gourd to give Jonah shade; but the next day God created a worm which killed it, and a scorching east wind. 'Are you angry now?' God asked him. 'Mortally angry,' Jonah replied. To this God rejoined: 'You were sorry to lose the gourd...Should I not be sorry to lose the 120,000 bewildered Ninevites, men, women and children?' Jonah would be wrong to regret his part in the salvation of Nineveh, even though the Assyrians were soon to destroy his homeland.

Zephaniah ('the Lord treasured') prophesied in Judah in the reign of Josiah (640—609 BC). His ancestry is traced back to his great-great-grandfather, who was named Hezekiah. The exceptionally long family tree suggests that this was King Hezekiah of Judah, born c. 740 BC. Zephaniah denounced corruption, injustice, desecration and the adoption of foreign methods of worship, foreseeing a 'day of wrath...of darkness and gloom, of the trumpet and alarm' (1:15—16) at the hands of an unnamed invader. He also

JEREMIAH
JEREMIAH
Jeremiah, a lonely, anguished man was a reluctant prophet and struggled constantly against the compulsion to prophesy. His message was the bleakest possible: Jerusalem was sinful and its destruction inevitable. When his words were about to come true, however, he saw a more hopeful vision of the future, when the Jews would return from exile and a new covenant with God would be established.

announced punishment for foreign nations, and especially for proud Nineveh. Yet he also foretold that one day all nations would call upon God's name (3:9), and that the righteous survivors of Israel would return from captivity and sing for joy.

Nahum ('comfort') was a prophet from Elkosh, which was probably in Judah, but may have been either in Galilee (Capernaum means 'village of Nahum') or the city of el-Kush, near ancient Nineveh. His book denounces Nineveh, the Assyrian capital, 'the city of blood, filled with deceit and spoil' (3:1) and predicts its imminent fall, which happened in 612BC. Some passages read so realistically—the attackers' red shields, their jostling cavalry, the forcing of the sluice gates on the Tigris—that they may have been composed after the battle. Unlike the other prophets, he never criticized Israel; instead he celebrated God's power in bringing down the Assyrians, the oppressors of the whole Near East.

Jeremiah became a prophet in 627 BC as a young man, and must have been born around 645 BC. His birthplace was Anathoth, a village 4 miles north-east of Jerusalem. At God's command, he never married, because any children born in Judah would die by the sword, sickness or famine in the Babylonian conquest (Jeremiah 16:4) which was about to take place.

Unlike Isaiah, Jeremiah was reluctant to prophesy, claiming that he was too young to speak (Jeremiah 1:6). God, however, promised him strength, and warned him not to lose heart: 'Do not let your spirit break before them (i.e. your countrymen), lest I break you before them' (1:17). His was a horrifying message: the sinfulness of Judah and its inevitable destruction. The sins he condemned were violence and injustice; he seems less concerned with ritual, although he was of priestly descent, and he even declared that God had never commanded Israel to make sacrifices (7:22).

Jeremiah first clashed with authority when, at God's command, he publicly broke an earthenware flask, to symbolize the destruction of Jerusalem. The Temple priest Pashhur put him into the stocks for a day, but Jeremiah defiantly repeated his prophecy, adding that Pashhur would die in exile in Babylonia. In 609 BC he announced that if the Jews (a more appropriate term than 'Israelites' now that the northern kingdom had fallen) did not repent, the Temple would be destroyed. When the priests and Temple prophets wanted him put to death for blasphemy, he replied that he had merely delivered God's message (26:12), and the people spared him. Three years later God commanded him to have his prophecies written down and read to the people. His scribe Baruch went to the Temple (from which Jeremiah was now banned) and read the scroll. It so shocked the royal officers that they confiscated it and read it to King Jehoiakim. The king tore it up, column by column, and threw it into the fire, ordering the arrest of Jeremiah and Baruch. God, however, hid them from the king's men.

In 593 BC Jeremiah put a wooden yoke around his neck to symbolize the approaching Babylonian captivity. A false prophet named Hananiah broke it and, at God's command, Jeremiah replaced it with a yoke of iron. He announced that Hananiah would die

that year—as, indeed, he did.

The siege of Jerusalem by the Babylonians began in 588 BC. During the siege Jeremiah was repeatedly consulted by King Zedekiah, sometimes being smuggled into the palace through a secret entrance (38:14). He always declared that the Babylonians would triumph, and that deserting to them was the only way anyone could hope to survive. When the siege was briefly lifted, and Jeremiah left the city, he was promptly arrested by the royal officers, charged with desertion and thrown into a dungeon. Zedekiah, who believed in Jeremiah's prophecies but also feared his own officers, moved him to the court of the guardhouse, and gave him a daily bread ration. Eventually, however, the officers insisted that Jeremiah should be thrown into a muddy pit. He would have suffocated or starved if Ebed-Melech, an Ethiopian eunuch, had not reported his plight to Zedekiah. The king ordered thirty men to pull him out but Jeremiah continued to be held prisoner in the guard house and was only released when Jerusalem fell. It was the Babylonian general Nebuzaradan who set him free. Nebuzaradan knew that Jeremiah had foretold his victory and gratefully offered him the chance of a comfortable life in Babylon. Jeremiah chose to stay in Judah and was put under the charge of Gedaliah, the governor appointed by the Babylonians. When Gedaliah was assassinated, the Jewish leaders who remained in Judah were afraid of Babylonian reprisals and fled to Egypt, taking Jeremiah with them—against his will and in spite of his prophecy that Nebuchadnezzar would also conquer Egypt. In fact this prophecy was not fulfilled. In his last oracle, Jeremiah denounced these refugees, especially the women among them for abandoning the Lord for the 'Queen of Heaven' (44:18). Jeremiah declared that they would die by the sword and famine. No doubt he himself died in Egypt.

Jeremiah took no pleasure in his calling. He pleaded for his people, but God would not save them. He was mocked and shunned, his life was threatened and he wished himself unborn. Yet he was unable to stop

prophesying, for God's message 'was in my heart like a burning fire, locked into my bones; I try to hold it in but cannot' (20:9). His angry arguments with God were unprecedented. 'You have duped me, oh Lord', he cried. 'You have overpowered me'.

Not all of Jeremiah's prophecies were gloomy. The Book of Lamentations, which has added to his reputation as a herald of woe, is probably not his. It ignores his ministry; all it says of the Prophets is that they were sinful and failed to foresee the fall of Judah.

During the siege of Jerusalem, Jeremiah was offered a field by his cousin Hanamel, and bought it from him at full market value as a sign of his confidence that the Jews would one day return from exile. He expected that return to come seventy years later, and in fact it came sooner, in 538 BC. Then, he declared, the mourning of the Jews would turn to joy, and God would establish with them a new covenant, writing his teaching upon their heart. Jesus interpreted the 'new covenant' as the Eucharist (Luke 22:20; 1 Corinthians 11:25); indeed 'new testament' is merely an alternative English translation of the Greek for 'new covenant' (kaine diatheke). In Jewish tradition the verses mean that God will renew his covenant with Israel, a covenant based on the laws revealed at Sinai; and that Israel will never again violate it.

Baruch ('blessed') was Jeremiah's scribe. In 606 BC he read publicly a scroll of Jeremiah's prophecies in the Temple. He was soon summoned to read it again to the royal officers (who had not been present). The officers warned Baruch that they would have to inform the king, and advised him to flee. Baruch sometimes lost courage: 'Woe is me . . . I find no rest.' Jeremiah promised that he would survive the fall of Jerusalem, but should not seek 'great things' for himself. The Apocrypha includes a Book of Baruch, which places him in Babylon, where he is said to have called upon the Jewish exiles to repent, and promised their return; the author apparently forgot that Baruch was removed, with Jeremiah, to Egypt.

Habakkuk's name may mean either 'embrace' (Hebrew *chabaq*) or 'fruit tree' (Akkadian *hambaquq*). His ancestry and period are not stated but his prophecy that a Chaldean (i.e. Babylonian) invasion would take place suggests that he lived in the period around 612 BC, when Nineveh, the Assyrian capital, fell to the Babylonians. Habakkuk complained of strife and injustice, apparently under the wicked King Jehoiakim (609—598 BC). God replied that the Babylonians would sweep the tyrant away, but Habakkuk objected that the Babylonians would be just as cruel. He retired to his watchtower (2:1) (probably meaning his solitude) to await God's answer: 'The righteous shall live by his faith.' Habakkuk condemned the greed and idolatry of the invaders, probably referring to the Babylonian campaigns against Judah. The book ends with a vision of God coming from the desert and shaking the earth in order to deliver his people and destroy his enemies—a vision which made Habakkuk's belly quake and his lips quiver.

According to the apocryphal book Bel and the Dragon, Habakkuk survived the Babylonian conquest of Jerusalem, and was carried miraculously from Judah to Babylon and back, to bring food to Daniel in the lion's den.

Daniel See page 96.

Ezekiel ('God strengthens') lived in Babylonia, and was probably among the earliest groups of Jewish aristocracy whom Nebuchadnezzar exiled there after the Babylonians had captured Jerusalem for the first time in 597 BC (2 Kings 24:14). He prophesied for twenty years, from 593 to 573 BC; his prophecies include dates which are exact to the day. The enigmatic '30th year' to which his first prophecy is dated, may mean that he was then 30 years old. The fall of Jerusalem in 587 BC and the exile of the remaining Jews divided his ministry into two eras: before it, his message was denunciation and doom; after it, he prophesied restoration.

He was married; God called his wife 'the desire of your eyes' and she died at

EZEKIEL
Ezekiel lived through the fall of Jerusalem in 587 BC and went into exile in Babylon. His detailed, poetic visions were not taken seriously although he often illustrated them dramatically. On one occasion he shaved his head and beard and divided the hair into three parts to symbolize the people's fate. On others he ate a scroll covered in messages of doom, and baked his bread in cattle dung.

the time the final siege of Jerusalem began, in January 588 BC. God forbade Ezekiel to mourn for her, as a token that the Jews would lose their beloved Temple but not mourn over it—presumably because the Babylonians would immediately exile them. His familiarity with luxury goods (Ezekiel 27) suggests that he may have come

from a wealthy family; and he owned a house, where the exiled leaders visited him.

Some have suggested that he was a craftsman because he had an excellent knowledge of mechanical intricacy. His first vision described God (looking like a man) seated on a throne carried by four winged creatures, each having four faces and moving on a 'wheel within a wheel' (1:16). To symbolize Jerusalem's fall he drew on a tile a map of the city, surrounded by siege works; and as a symbol of the people's fate, he shaved his head and beard, divided the hair into three equal parts by weight, and then burned one third, cut up another third with a sword, and scattered the rest in the wind. With the same mechanical exactitude he described the restored Temple, giving exact measurements of the gates, altar and courts and details of the rituals to be performed there (40—48). He was of priestly descent, and probably remembered the Temple from his youth.

In his first vision, God made him eat a scroll which was inscribed with messages of woe yet tasted sweet as honey, to symbolize his preaching (2:8—3:3). Ezekiel's behaviour—at God's command—remained bizarre right up to the fall of the Temple. He lay for 390 days on his left side, and 40 days on his right, to atone for the sin of the northern and southern kingdoms respectively. He was commanded to bake his bread in human excrement, and, when he protested, was permitted to substitute cattle dung—as a token of Israel's exile from the land of holiness. Struck dumb, he could speak only in order to prophesy publicly. As soon as he heard of the fall of Jerusalem, his dumbness and other abnormalities disappeared. His only symbolic action afterwards was, however, a significant one: he joined two sticks to show that the two Israelite kingdoms would be reunited (37:15—28).

Although he lived in Babylonia, he travelled in vision twice to Jerusalem, once to see the Lord's chariot leave the doomed Temple, once to see it return; 'The Lord took me', he wrote, 'by a lock of my head'. On the first occasion he saw foreign worship taking place in the Temple itself. Only those who wept over such abominations would be saved, and a man dressed in linen passed through the city, drawing a cross on the forehead of each. At the Temple gate he saw a certain Pelatiah, together with twenty-four other high officials, who had 'filled the streets with slain' (11:6);

Ezekiel rebuked them and Pelatiah immediately fell down dead. Again, Ezekiel predicted the exact date when the siege of Jerusalem began. If he lived permanently in Babylonia, as the book states, he must have possessed remarkable psychic powers. Some suggest, therefore, that he might have spent several years in Jerusalem. God declared that Ezekiel would be personally responsible for the death of any sinner whom he did not warn to repent, and he could hardly have given effective warnings by speeches and symbolic actions in a distant land.

Whereas Moses held that God visited the sins of the fathers on the children, Ezekiel taught that people were rewarded or punished for their own deeds alone. He also emphasized God's holiness and the gulf between God and man. When Israel sinned, God showed his holiness in punishment; but when Israel suffered, he would save them, so that the nations would recognize his holiness. Ezekiel's vivid vision of dry bones being returned to life symbolized the deliverance of Israel from disaster. He expected this to be preceded by a horrific war, when Gog, prince of the land of Magog, would be struck down miraculously by God (38—39).

Ezekiel's audience found his prophecies entertaining, 'like love songs beautifully sung', but did not take them to heart. It was perhaps in an effort to find the best medium to convey his message that Ezekiel wrote sometimes in poetry, sometimes in prose, sometimes in elaborate allegories half-way between the two. God comforted him with the assurance that his prophecies would be fulfilled.

Obadiah ('servant of the Lord') wrote the shortest book in the Old Testament—just twenty-one verses. He announced punishment for Israel's neighbours, the Edomites, because they gloated over the fall of Jerusalem (587 BC) and trapped and betrayed the fugitives. The Babylonian conquerors, too, would be punished, while the Jews would return from exile and possess the lands of Edom and Philistia as well as their own. In spite of the fact that he mentions the fall of Jerusalem, he has

traditionally been identified with Obadiah, the steward of King Ahab, who lived in the ninth century BC (1 Kings 18:3). This identification was made only because the two share the same name.

Haggai ('born on a festival') prophesied between August and December in the second year of Darius I (520 BC). Eighteen years earlier, when Cyrus the Persian had swept away the Babylonian Empire, the Jews had been allowed to return to Judah. The Samaritans, however, who lived in what had been the northern kingdom, had prevented the rebuilding of the Temple (Ezra 4:1—5). Haggai, together with Zechariah, called for a new effort: 'is it time for you to dwell in panelled houses while this Temple lies desolate?' (Haggai 1:4). He blamed the droughts and bad harvests on their failure. The second Temple, he declared, would be even more glorious than the first, for all nations would worship there (2:9). Haggai expected God to intervene soon in history, shaking heaven and earth and overturning the heathen kingdoms. He apparently expected Zerubbabel, the Jewish governor appointed by the Persians, to be the Messiah (2:21—23). The fact that the Emperor Darius (522—486 BC) had problems controlling his empire at the beginning of his reign probably encouraged his hopes

Under Haggai's encouragement, the rebuilding of the Temple was immediately resumed and completed four years later (Ezra 5:2, 6:15).

Zechariah ('the Lord remembered') began to prophesy in 520 BC, just two months after Haggai, whom he joined in urging the Jews to rebuild the Temple. He was of priestly descent, and had been born in Babylonia. In contrast to Haggai's straightforward preaching, Zechariah described eight complicated visions (Zechariah 1—6) all apparently witnessed in a single night in February 519 BC. These were all interpreted for him by 'the angel who spoke within me', who was present throughout, as an intermediary between God and the prophet. In the first vision, for example, horses that had roamed the world reported to the angel that all was still; the angel begged God to stir events and bring relief to Jerusalem; God answered with 'comforting words', and the angel assured Zechariah that the Temple would be rebuilt. Zechariah also called for justice and kindness (7:9).

Chapters 9—14 of Zechariah contain visions of the dawning of the Messianic age. The nations attack and pillage Jerusalem, but the Lord himself stands to confront them on the Mount of Olives (14:2—3). The Messiah, 'humble and riding an ass', enters Jerusalem (9:9). The Jews suddenly becomes contrite over 'him that they pierced' (12:10). Chapter 11 is probably the most mysterious in the Bible. God commands the prophet to act as shepherd to a hitherto neglected and ill-treated flock, doubtless Israel. The prophet removes three shepherds in one month. Yet he, too, decides to neglect the flock. As payment for his month's work he receives 30 pieces of silver, which he flings into the Temple treasury. God then orders him to play the part of a negligent shepherd, for he is preparing to inflict just such a shepherd on Israel. The identity of the 'pierced one' and the shepherds remains obscure, though the New Testament interpreted the former as Jesus (John 19:37) and the 30 pieces of silver as the price of his betrayal by Judas Iscariot (Matthew 27:9).

Joel ('the Lord is God') was a prophet who lived in Judah, probably in the fourth century BC. The Jews had been allowed to return to Judah by the Persian emperor but they found extremely harsh conditions there. In Joel's time there was a terrible plague of locusts, made worse by a bad harvest, drought and outbreaks of fire. To Joel, these disasters indicated that 'the Day of the Lord' was near (Joel 1:15), so he summoned the people to the Temple for a day of repentance and prayer. In answer, God promised to remove the locusts, renew the harvest, and also protect them from invaders. The spirit of prophecy would be poured out on all flesh (2:28) before the Day of the Lord, when the Jews would be saved and the nations that had oppressed them would be punished.

Joel was traditionally listed early among the prophets, identified either with Samuel's first son, Joel (1 Samuel 8:2) or with the unnamed prophet who had announced a famine in Elisha's day (2 Kings 8:1). However, the references to Jews 'scattered among the nations' and 'sold to the Greeks' (Joel 3) and the fact that no king is referred to, make a date of the fourth century BC likely.

Malachi. Nothing is known of Malachi's ancestry and birthplace. He was traditionally identified with Ezra but it is more probable that the book was originally written anonymously and that an editor anxious to have twelve prophets supplied the name from Malachi 3:1: '(behold I send) my messenger' (Hebrew *malachi*). Whoever he was, he denounced layman and priest alike for sacrificing blemished animals in the Temple, and blamed outbreaks of drought and pests on failure to pay tithes. He also condemned mixed marriages, and yet was broadminded enough to declare that all other nations recognized the greatness of God and unlike Israel offered him 'pure gifts'. He was aware of social issues: he denounced injustice and exploitation, declared divorce hateful to God (2:16) (even though Moses in Deuteronomy 24:1 had permitted it), and ended his book with the hope that God would one day 'reconcile fathers to sons and sons to fathers'. The people's retorts are also heard: they doubted God's justice and said of sacrifice: 'what weariness!'. His disillusionment with the Temple and the mixed marriages fit best into the years just before the mission of Ezra and Nehemiah in the mid-fifth century BC.

In Christian tradition, the Old Testament books are arranged chronologically: first, records of the past (Genesis down to Esther); second, speculation about the present (Job, Psalms and so on); and finally, prophecies of the future, when God would visit his people in judgement and salvation. Malachi thus ends the Old Testament, and his final prophecy of a day 'burning as an oven' for the wicked, but bringing healing to the righteous, demands a sequel in the New Testament.

The Books of the Apocrypha

The Apocrypha comprises 15 books from the second and first centuries BC which were not included in Hebrew scripture. Most do appear in the Latin Vulgate Bible, used by the Roman Catholic Church: for example, the 'Book of Susanna' and 'Bel and the Dragon' (Daniel 13—14). The Apocrypha is omitted or printed separately in Protestant Bibles.

Judith was living in Bethulia, Judah when it was besieged by the Assyrians under Holofernes. She convinced Holofernes that she would betray her own people, then killed him as he lay in a drunken stupor. The leaderless Assyrians abandoned the siege.

Tobit, a devout believer, was taken to Nineveh when Israel was conquered. Blind and near death, he sent his son Tobias to recover some money from a relative. An angel guided Tobias, and on his return Tobit was healed

Susanna lived in Babylon during the Exile and was falsely accused of adultery by two elders whom she had rejected. She was condemned to death, but Daniel ordered a retrial at which she was acquitted and the elders condemned.

Judas Maccabeus led a revolt against the Seleucids in 167BC. He fought a long guerilla war, and became a national hero.

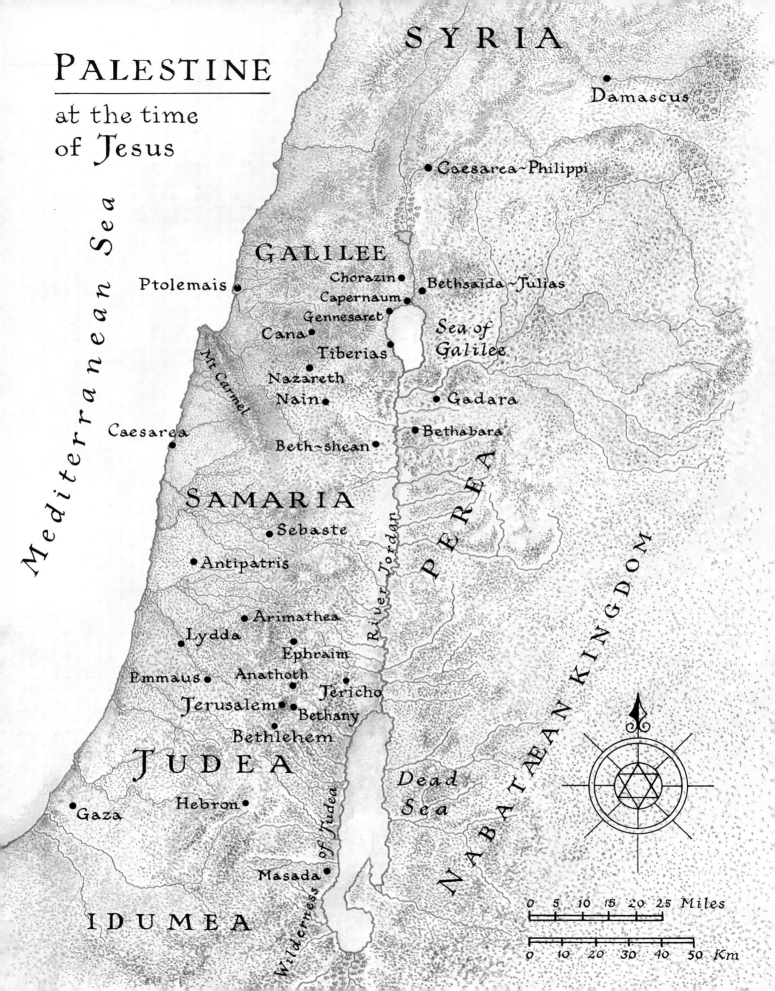

The New Testament

Introduction to the New Testament

The New Testament consists of twenty-seven books, written by various Christians during the first century of the church's existence. They tell the story of Jesus and of the work of some of his followers after his death and resurrection. Letters written by early Christians show how they argued in favour of their positions, admonished and inspired their followers, and laid the foundation for the continuing spread and influence of Christianity.

The entire New Testament was written in Greek. Jesus and his immediate followers spoke Aramaic as their first language. They probably knew Hebrew and could read and understand the Jewish scriptures (later the Christian Old Testament) in Hebrew. They may also have known some Greek, which was the common language of trade and diplomacy in the eastern part of the Roman Empire. It is probable that the original teaching of Jesus was written and circulated for some time in Aramaic, but for the most part the traditions about Jesus were fully translated into the common language of most of the Roman empire.

The books of the New Testament fall into several major divisons:

1. The four Gospels: Matthew, Mark, Luke and John. These narrate events from the life of Jesus and give his teaching.

2. The Acts of the Apostles. This work, written by the same person who wrote the Gospel according to Luke, gives a partial history of the early church in Jerusalem and of Paul's missionary activity.

3. The letters of Paul. This is a collection of thirteen letters attributed to Paul. They provide first-hand evidence of the activity and thought of a key figure in the history of Christianity. Many are extremely argumentative, as he wrestled with the other leaders of the church over such crucial issues as the role of the Mosaic law and the status of the Gentiles. The collection as it now exists contains some letters written in Paul's name by his followers, in some cases after his death. There are some scholarly disagreements over which letters were written by Paul himself, but almost universal agreement about the major ones. Romans, 1 and 2 Corinthians, Galatians, Philippians, 1 Thessalonians and Philemon were almost certainly dictated by Paul. Ephesians, Colossians and 2 Thessalonians are grouped as early letters possibly not by Paul and 1 and 2 Timothy and Titus are considered to have been written later.

4. The Epistle to the Hebrews was included under Paul's name but there is no mention in it that Paul wrote it; the author is unknown.

5. The Epistles known as the 'catholic' (universal) epistles are James, 1 and 2 Peter, 1, 2 and 3 John and Jude. These were written by various Christian leaders, at various times and in different circumstances. Jude and 2 Peter are usually considered to be very late, possibly as late as 150. The Epistles of James and John come from near the end of the first century. 1 Peter is harder to date, with estimates ranging from 60 to 90.

6. The Book of Revelation, or The Apocalypse. This is a visionary work, written by someone named John, but the precise identity of the author is unknown.

The authors of these books were not conscious of writing 'scripture'. In the first years of Christianity, the scripture was the Jewish Bible, either in the original Hebrew or translated into the local language, in most Christian churches, Greek. There was at the beginning no 'Old Testament' or 'New Testament', just the Law, the Prophets and the Writings of the Jewish scripture. The Greek version of the Jewish scripture was somewhat longer than the Hebrew, including the books now often called 'apocryphal', such as 1 and 2 Maccabees, Judith, Ben Sira (or Ecclesiasticus) and others.

The New Testament authors quoted the Greek version, using principally the five books of Moses, Prophets (especially Isaiah) and the Psalms. The Christian church retained the Jewish Bible as 'the Old Testament'.

The early Christians, then, quoted the Jewish Bible as scripture and wrote as had the Hebrew prophets: to meet the needs of the time. These needs were diverse. The early Christians formed small, scattered groups in numerous cities from Jerusalem to Rome, and soon beyond. Travel from church to church, and correspondence from the leaders to their sometimes distant flocks, was surprisingly frequent. Letters were written on parchment with a pen and ink or, if in Hebrew, with a brush. Many people could not read or write and even those who could, dictated letters to a scribe. Paul, who was literate in Hebrew, Greek and Latin, would have dictated to save time. The roads and sea lanes of the Roman empire were safe: safer than at any other time until the nineteenth century. The reader of Acts or of the Letters of Paul meets a world in movement. One also sees a world in which advice was asked and given, arguments were necessary and admonition was frequent. We can still read the questions and answers exchanged between early converts and their leaders.

The scattered churches also needed information about Jesus. They looked to him as their saviour and guide, but many, even within the first fifteen years of Christianity, knew little about him. The disciples told stories about him and passed on aspects of his teaching. These came to be collected and circulated and the collections eventually became the four Gospels.

The Gospels and the letters of Paul are the heart of the New Testament. The

Gospels as we have them were written in the last third of the first century (about 65-90). Paul's letters were written between the early forties and mid fifties. The letters which we have were collected and published about the year 90. Thus before the end of the century, Matthew, Mark, Luke, John and the main letters of Paul were well known and widely used. Other works were, however, also in use, and Christian literature greatly increased in the early second century. They were copied, circulated and read, both in church meetings and for private devotions. The writings which were known by the year 125 include most of the present New Testament, plus other works not now included.

After the year 150 the idea of expanding the scriptures beyond the Jewish sacred texts, to include some of the new Christian works, began to take hold. Which books were included as scripture varied from church to church and from time to time. There were, even then, scholarly arguments.

Two local councils of bishops at the end of the fourth century named just the twenty-seven books which we now have as 'scripture', but these decisions were not binding on the whole church, and variations in usage continued at least through the 6th century. The contents of the New Testament were finally settled just by use: the twenty-seven books which we now have are those which proved themselves worthy over the years.

No original manuscript of a New Testament book has survived. As they were used, they were copied and passed on, and then the copies were copied. Scribes made small changes, either by accident or to 'improve' the text. The earliest fragments of manuscripts come from the second century and from the third and fourth centuries there are hundreds. The text of the New Testament was standardized in the fourth century under the influence of the Emperor Constantine, but nevertheless in some parts of the Empire, divergent readings were maintained. Some uncertainties remain, but the New Testament is the best-attested ancient document in the world, and the remaining questions about the original wording are relatively minor.

The historical background

When Jesus was born, the world had greatly changed since the days of the Hebrew kings and prophets.

In 538 BC and the years that followed, Cyrus the Persian conquered the Babylonian empire and allowed the Jews to return home. The Persians were in turn defeated by Alexander the Great of Macedonia. Alexander was in Palestine from about 332 to 331 BC and after his death in 323 his empire was divided among some of his leading generals. Palestine lay between the territory of the Seleucids in Syria and of the Ptolemies in Egypt, and belonged first to one empire then to the other. The Ptolemies controlled it from about 300 to 200, the Seleucids from about 200 to about 165. They lost the country to the Hasmoneans (or Maccabees), who led a Jewish revolt and founded a ruling dynasty. Successive stages of independence were achieved, and full autonomy was gained in 142. Rome recognized the Jewish state in 139 and the Hasmoneans remained in power until the Romans appointed Herod the Great.

In 63 the Roman general, Pompey, conquered Jerusalem but reinstated a Hasmonean king, Hyrcanus II. Antipater, a leading military figure in Idumea (a subject state to Israel) was also given some power. Both rulers were, however, subject to Rome. After much internal strife Antipater's son Herod emerged as a strong man who could control the country and protect the Roman Empire from the Parthians to the east. He was declared king by the Roman Senate in 40. He died in 4 BC, which is approximately when Jesus was born (see page 176). After Herod's death, various of his descendants controlled different parts of his kingdom at different times, but Rome directly governed Judea (including Jerusalem) from AD 6 to 41 and again from 44 to 66. In 66 revolt against Rome broke out. Led first by Vespasian, then by his son Titus, the Roman legions defeated the rebels, destroying the Temple in 70. The last rebel fortress, Masada, fell to the Romans in 73.

Christianity began as a Jewish sect. After Jesus's death (c.30), churches were established in Jerusalem, elsewhere in Judea and in Samaria and Galilee. The church soon spread to Antioch in Syria, and then across Asia Minor, to Greece, and even to Rome. The fate of the churches in Palestine during and after the revolt against Rome is not known, but the lack of information after this time makes it likely that the war effectively destroyed Christian groups and organizations. There is a later legend that some Christians in Jerusalem fled to Pella, just east of the Jordan. The future of the church, however, lay elsewhere. By the end of the first century the principal churches were Antioch and Rome, though Ephesus and other cities in Asia Minor and Greece also had large Christian communities. It is not known how Christianity was taken to Egypt, but by the end of the second century Alexandria had assumed a major role, and the principal churches became Rome, Alexandria and Antioch. Christianity had become predominantly Gentile, though Jewish Christianity did not altogether disappear. Its continued existence is attested as late as the fourth century.

The Gospels

There are four Gospels in the New Testament, the Gospels of Matthew, Mark, Luke and John. They were all written anonymously, and the titles by which they are known were given to them only in the second century. The Gospels of Matthew and John were thought to have been written by the disciples whose names they bear. Mark's Gospel was attributed to John Mark, who was for a time the companion of Peter, and Luke's was attributed to a physician who was one of Paul's converts.

The Gospels of Matthew, Mark and Luke are called 'the synoptic Gospels'. They all follow the same general outline, and many of the stories and sayings in them are the same. Scholars often find it convenient to study these Gospels in a work with parallel columns, one for each of them, called 'a synopsis'—from which the term 'synoptic' comes. John's Gospel is very different. The outline of events is different, only a few of the stories are the same, and the sayings attributed to Jesus do not appear in the other three.

The preparation

Zechariah, the father of John the Baptist, was a priest. While he was serving in the Temple one day, an angel appeared and announced that his longstanding hope for a child would be fulfilled. Zechariah's wife, Elizabeth, was beyond the normal years for having children and Zechariah doubted the angel's word. He was struck dumb and remained so until the birth of the child. When the boy was born, the relatives wished to name him after his father, but Elizabeth insisted on 'John'. Zechariah wrote 'His name is John' on a tablet and immediately was able to speak. The writer of the Gospel then attributes to Zechariah one of the beautiful and moving hymns which are a feature of the first chapters of Luke. Zechariah's is called the Benedictus, after the first word of the hymn in Latin translation: 'Blessed be the Lord God of Israel'. The focus of the hymn is on the coming saviour, and the child John is mentioned at the end, as the one who 'will go before the Lord to prepare his way' (Luke 1:5—25, 39—80).

Zechariah and the other characters in the first chapters of Luke (Elizabeth, Simeon, Anna, Mary and Joseph) are perfect depictions of common Jewish piety and devotion in the first century.

Elizabeth, the mother of John the Baptist, was the wife of Zechariah and a kinswoman of Mary. They lived in the hill country of Judea, although the city is not named. Elizabeth and Zechariah had given up hope of having children when an angel announced to Zechariah that Elizabeth would conceive, and soon she did so. While Elizabeth was pregnant, she was visited by her kinswoman, Mary. When they met, the child leaped in Elizabeth's womb and Elizabeth took this as a sign that Mary would be the mother of the Lord. When her own child, a boy, was born, Elizabeth insisted that his name be John, although that was not a usual name in their family, and the relatives preferred the father's name, Zechariah. Zechariah supported his wife, and the boy was named John. (Luke 1:24—25, 39—45, 57—66).

John the Baptist, the son of Elizabeth and Zechariah, was a contemporary of Jesus (according to Luke 1:36 he was a cousin, six months older than Jesus) who became a well-known prophet. As a prophet he apparently modelled himself on Elijah, wearing a camel's hair garment, a leather belt or girdle, and eating locusts and wild honey (Matthew 3:4; see 2 Kings 1:8; Zechariah 13:4). If he did have Elijah as a model, he would also have been 'a hairy man', allowing his hair and beard to grow freely. In his preaching he echoed Isaiah 40:3—'A voice crying in the wilderness: prepare the way of the Lord' (Matthew 3:3). John applied this to himself, preaching in the Wilderness of Judea, and near the Jordan river, where he baptized those who repented. The Wilderness itself is a steep, rocky and barren area, almost without vegetation. Although the river Jordan runs through part of it, this section is very difficult to get to and lay outside the domain of Herod Antipas in Galilee where we know that John worked for at least part of the time. It is usually thought that he preached and baptized either at Aenon, south-east of Beth-shean (in the Jordan valley near the Wilderness but not actually in it) or at Bethabara, near the Dead Sea.

Baptism as Christians understand it today, as a sign of forgiveness and inner conversion, was not usual in John's time although a religious community living near the Dead Sea (the Essenes) practised periodic ritual washings and other small sects may have used a form of baptism.

John's message was that the kingdom of God was at hand, that the people of Israel should repent and mend their ways, and that those who did not repent would be destroyed. The one who would follow him, he said, had in his hand a winnowing fork, 'and he will clear his threshing floor and gather his wheat into the granary, but the chaff he will burn with unquenchable fire' (Matthew 3:12).

John's prophecy of a coming kingdom (and king) was probably taken literally by many who looked forward to liberation from the rule of Rome. Prophets preaching similar messages appeared as the Jews grew more discontented with Roman rule and many were destroyed by the Romans. John himself attracted several disciples, though according to the Gospel of John two of them, including Andrew, left him to follow Jesus.

ELIZABETH
Elizabeth was the wife of a priest and the mother of John the Baptist. She had given up all hope of having a child when an angel announced that she would conceive. Unlike her husband, she accepted the angel's message without question.

While John was preaching in the territory of Herod Antipas, he was arrested and thrown into prison. According to the gospels this was because John had denounced the marriage of Antipas to his niece Herodias. At a banquet Antipas became inflamed by the dancing of Salome, Herodias's daughter, and promised to give her whatever she wished. Prompted by her mother, Salome asked for, and received, the Baptist's head on a platter (Mark 6:14—29). The Gospels say that Antipas was reluctant to kill John but was forced to do so by his wife Herodias. According to Josephus, John was executed by Antipas because he feared that the Baptist's preaching would lead to an uprising. Josephus's explanation of the execution is more likely, but it is quite probable that John had criticized the marriage of Antipas and Herodias, and more than one motive for his execution may have been at work. Although Josephus tried to conceal John's distinctive message, he does reveal how important many people considered John the Baptist. He relates that, when Herod Antipas was defeated in battle (see *Herod Antipas*), some Jews regarded it as divine punishment for his execution of John.

In their accounts of John's baptism of Jesus, Matthew and John both tell that John recognized Jesus as the subject of his prophecy. Later, however, it seems he was not so certain. When John was in prison, he sent disciples to ask Jesus, 'Are you he who is to come, or shall we look for another?' (Matthew 11:1—3; Luke 7:18—19). Jesus replied indirectly (as he often did), and he sent back to John a paraphrase of a passage in Isaiah, 'the blind receive their sight and the lame walk, lepers are cleansed and the deaf hear, and the dead are raised up, and the poor have good news preached to them' (compare Isaiah 35:5—6). We do not know whether or not John found this convincing.

Jesus valued the work of John the Baptist highly: 'Among those born of women there has risen no one greater than John the Baptist', but he added, 'yet he who is least in the kingdom of heaven is greater than he' (Matthew 11:11). Another incident shows John's

Jesus was one of those who came to John to be baptized. Mark and Luke give no indication that John paid special attention to Jesus. According to Matthew, however, John said to Jesus, 'I need to be baptized by you, and do you come to me?' (3:14). The Gospel of John repeatedly says that the Baptist pointed to Jesus as the one who really mattered: the one who would follow him and to whom his work referred (John 1:29, 33—34, 36).

John the Baptist is also mentioned by Josephus, the historian (Antiquities 18:116—119). He shows John as someone who preached virtue and baptized those who turned their backs on sin, making no mention of John's message of a coming kingdom and a coming king. This is not surprising since Josephus systematically deleted from his history anything that would make it appear that many Jews wanted another kingdom, not Rome's.

importance, both to Jesus and to the general public. When Jesus attacked the moneychangers in the Temple, officials asked who gave him authority to act in this way. Jesus replied with this question: 'Was the baptism of John from heaven or from men?' This stifled the opposition, since John was generally regarded as a spokesman for God (Mark 11:27—33). Jesus appears to have been claiming not John's authority but the authority of the one who inspired John: God himself.

John the Baptist's influence lived on long after his execution. Jesus appealed to it near the end of his own life, and from Acts, it is known that John's message had spread even beyond Palestine. In Ephesus an Alexandrian Jew named Apollos is mentioned as having received John's baptism, but not baptism into Jesus (Acts 18:24-25). John's activity as a preacher did not last long, but nevertheless made a deep impression on his generation, and, through Jesus, on many subsequent generations.

Gabriel From very early times, the Israelites believed that God spoke through envoys, called 'angels'. These were often identified as men (see for example Genesis 18), but especially under Persian influence, the concept of angels became more closely identified with heavenly beings. Eventually it was thought that there were chief angels ('archangels'), and they became named and their duties specified.

Gabriel was thought to be the messenger and revealer of God's will. He appears in this role (though still called 'a man') in Daniel 8:16—17; 9:21—22. He appears again in the first chapters of Luke, first to tell Zechariah that he would have a son, and then to

JOHN THE BAPTIST
A fanatic and charismatic figure, John the Baptist was widely believed to be the greatest prophet of the age. He preached repentance and the imminent arrival of a Messiah to establish the kingdom of God. To the authorities this was a politically explosive message since some believed it threatened the power of Rome.

MARY
Betrothed as a young girl, Mary at first found it hard to believe the angel's message that she was to be the mother of the Messiah. Betrothal at a young age was common in New Testament times and Mary could have been married to the carpenter Joseph when she was only 12 or 13.

announce to Mary that she would conceive even though she had no husband (Luke 1:13—19; 1:26—38). In both cases he was able to assure the listener that he told the truth: he knew the will of God because he stood in God's presence (Luke 1:19).

Simeon was a 'righteous and devout' resident of Jerusalem at the time of Jesus's birth. When Mary and Joseph brought the infant Jesus to the Temple to present the sacrifice required after childbirth, Simeon was inspired to go there, having been told by the Spirit that he would see the Christ. When he saw Jesus he lifted him up and said a poem, now called the Nunc Dimittis: 'Lord, now lettest thou thy servant depart in peace, according to thy word; for mine eyes have seen thy salvation which thou has prepared in the presence of all peoples...' (Luke 2:25—35).

Jesus and his family

Mary, the mother of Jesus, is the most revered woman in history, yet she remains historically largely unknown, having long since been obscured behind Christian devotion and the legends that were woven around her name.

Mary spent most of her life in Galilee. Matthew and Luke disagree about whether or not she was already living there at the time of her betrothal to Joseph, but they agree that Jesus and his family lived there from the time of his infancy to his death.

Mary and Joseph had not completed the marriage procedures when Jesus was born. Both Matthew and Luke say that they were betrothed, and that when Mary conceived she was still a virgin. Joseph and Mary were living together, but this was the practice of the time, according to which the marriage agreement (betrothal) was the decisive matter, and the final ceremony less important. Before the marriage itself took place, an angel told Mary that she would bear a son, to be named Jesus.

Luke shows Mary as a devout and humble woman, ready to do God's will.

When the angel announced to her that she would bear the heir to the throne of David, she wondered how it could happen, since she was a virgin, but then made no protest, showing her willingness to he 'the handmaid of the Lord' (Luke 1:26—38). The poem which she is said to have spoken when she visited her relative Elizabeth recalls the song of Hannah in 1 Samuel 2:1—10 and its main theme is that God raises the humble and brings down the mighty (Luke 1:46—55). The one characteristic which marks every account of her is her humble and quiet devotion to God.

The two accounts of Jesus's birth are not in full agreement. According to Matthew, Mary and Joseph lived in Bethlehem at the time of Jesus's birth and fled from there to Egypt in order to escape Herod the Great. When they wished to return to Bethlehem, Joseph was warned in a dream to avoid Archelaus, Herod's successor in Judea, and so they went to Nazareth (Matthew 1:18—2:23). According to Luke they lived in Nazareth and went to Bethlehem for a census, returning to Nazareth after Jesus's birth (Luke 1:26—2.40). These two stories are designed to satisfy both history (Jesus was from Nazareth) and prophecy (the Messiah should be born in Bethlehem). Luke's view, that they were natives of Galilee, is the more probable.

Luke is the source of one of the world's best known and best loved stories. Mary and Joseph travelled to Bethlehem because of the census, but they could not find a room. They lodged instead in a stable, and it was there that Jesus was born (Luke 2:1—7). Angels announced the birth to shepherds, who came to worship the child (2:15—20). According to Matthew, the infant Jesus was visited by wise men from the East (Matthew 2:1—12).

After the accounts of Jesus's birth, Mary figures only a few times in the New Testament. Three of these passages show that Jesus prized other relations above those of family. One is a story from Jesus's childhood. The family visited Jerusalem at Passover and Jesus, aged twelve, was separated from them. When they found him in the temple he was talking with authority to the

JOSEPH
Mary's husband, Joseph, was a carpenter, a craftsman whose skills made him a respected and prosperous member of the community. He is traditionally held to have been many years older than Mary and may have died before Jesus's mission began, for nothing is said about him after the account of Jesus's birth and childhood.

teachers there. Mary scolded him and he replied, 'Did you not know that I must be about my father's business?' Mary, we are told, 'kept all these things in her heart' (Luke 2:46—52).

When Jesus had begun his ministry Mary and the other members of the family seem to have worried about what he thought 'his father' had called him to do. They once tried to seize him, saying that 'he is beside himself' (Mark 3:21). According to Mark 3:31—35, at one point Jesus's mother and brothers, perhaps concerned about him, stood outside where he was and sent a message to him. He replied, 'Who are my mother and my brothers?' and, looking around at his followers, added 'here are my mother and my brothers! Whoever does the will of God is my brother, and sister and mother'.

Other sayings attributed to Jesus reflect this critical attitude towards family, for example: 'I have come to set a man against his father. . . He who loves father or mother more than me is not worthy of me. . .' (Matthew 10:35—37).

The Gospel of John has more favourable stories. Jesus, his disciples and Mary attended a wedding feast at Cana. The wine gave out, and it was Mary who pointed out the fact to Jesus and who then said to the servants, 'Do whatever he tells you'. This confidence in her son's ability was not misplaced, and he turned jars of water into wine (John 2:1—11). Most poignant is the final story. Mary was one of those who followed Jesus from Galilee to Jerusalem, and she stood by him when he was crucified. When he saw her, with the 'beloved disciple', he said, 'Woman, behold your son!', and, to the disciple, 'Behold your mother!' (John 19:25—27)

Mary is mentioned only once more. After the crucifixion and resurrection she joined his brothers and disciples in prayer in the 'upper room' (Acts 1:14).

There is no information about the rest of Mary's life. According to the New Testament, Jesus had brothers and sisters. Mark 6:3 names four of the brothers: James, Joses, Judas and Simon. Subsequently the Christian church developed the idea of Mary's lifelong virginity and explained that Joseph had been previously married and that Jesus's brothers and sisters were Joseph's children but not Mary's (Epiphanius, fourth century AD).

One of Jesus's brothers, James, received a special resurrection appearance and he became one of the leaders of the Jerusalem church. One or more of the other brothers became travelling missionaries. Thus it seems that, whatever the tension earlier between Jesus and his family, it was overcome. One trusts that Mary too came to realize the greatness of the son whom she had borne.

Joseph was a carpenter (Matthew 13:55) who lived in Nazareth, in Galilee (Luke 2:4). He was betrothed to Mary and she became pregnant before they were married. Being a kind man, he did not wish to expose her to public disgrace, so he planned to marry her and then divorce her quietly. An angel or messenger appeared to him, however, and told him that the conception had been 'of the Holy Spirit', and that he should marry her as planned.

After the birth of the child, Jesus, an angel again appeared to Joseph, advising him that the child was in danger from King Herod. Joseph took the small family to Egypt. Matthew's story is that he continued to act on messages from God, returning first to Bethlehem after being told that Herod was dead, and then to Nazareth because he was warned also to fear Archelaus, who inherited Judea, the part of Herod's kingdom in which Bethlehem lies (Matthew 1:18—24; 2:13—23).

Nothing else is known of Joseph. He appears to have been a kind and sensible man who was willing to follow God's will as best he could.

Judas is named as one of Jesus's brothers (along with James, Joseph or Joses, and Simon) in Matthew 13:55 and Mark 6:3. The letter of Jude has sometimes been attributed to him, probably incorrectly. Its author describes himself as 'a servant of Jesus Christ and brother of James' (Jude 1). Judas the brother of Jesus was also, of course, the brother of James, but it does not seem very likely that one of Jesus's own brothers would describe himself as 'servant of Jesus Christ and brother of James'.

Jesus's family were not followers during his lifetime, as Matthew 12:46—50 makes clear. John 7:5 states explicitly that 'even his brothers did not believe in him', and one passage seems to indicate that his family suspected he might be mad (Mark 3:21). James, however, received a special resurrection appearance (1 Corinthians 15:7), and he and Jesus's other brothers became active in the Christian movement. According to Acts 1:14 they joined the disciples and Mary in prayer after

Jesus's death and resurrection. Paul states that the other apostles, the brothers of the Lord, and Cephas (Peter) travelled as missionaries along with their wives (1 Corinthians 9:5).

James, brother of Jesus. See page 153.

Simon, Joseph (Joses). See *Judas*.

Jesus of Nazareth

Jesus, who, along with the Buddha and Mohammed, ranks as one of the most influential men in history, was born in humble circumstances in Palestine. Most of our knowledge about his life comes from the four Gospels now called Matthew, Mark, Luke and John. A few fragments of information appear in Paul's letters, and Acts (written by the author of Luke) tells us that Jesus was someone who taught and performed miracles. Roman sources (Suetonius and Pliny the Younger) mention him, but they have no knowledge which has not come from the Christian movement.

Jesus became the object of devotion soon after the resurrection and the authors of the Gospels regarded him as the 'Son of God', a person to be worshipped. They do not, therefore, describe his life and teaching as a historian from a later period might. There is historical information in the Gospels but they were not written in order to convey 'mere history'. In the words of the author of John's Gospel, the early Christians wrote so that readers would 'believe that Jesus is the Christ, the Son of God, and that believing (they would) have life in his name' (John 20:31).

To make the historian's task more difficult, early Christians believed that Jesus still lived and still spoke to his followers. The Book of Revelation (or The Apocalypse) contains seven 'letters' dictated by the risen Lord (see Revelation 1:17—3:22), and in the Gospel of John, Jesus promises the disciples that the Holy Spirit will come and 'teach you all things' in Jesus's name (John 14:26). Thus 'sayings' of Jesus, in the mind of the early Christians, need not have been said by

Jesus of Nazareth during his earthly ministry. This makes it very difficult to distinguish what are now called 'authentic' sayings from 'inauthentic' ones, for early Christians saw no difference between them. They regarded revelations from the Spirit or from the risen Lord as true messages from Jesus, just as true as sayings uttered by Jesus during his life in Galilee. The category 'truth' to them was not limited to simple matters of fact. It is only in modern times that people have limited 'truth' to facts that can be proved.

Jesus was born about 4 BC, the last year of Herod's life (Matthew 2:1; Luke 1:5). His mother, Mary, had been told by an angel that she would bear a son even though she was still a virgin. His foster father, Joseph, was a carpenter from Nazareth. According to the Gospels of Matthew and Luke, Jesus was born in Bethlehem, though he grew up in Nazareth and was known as a Galilean. His birth was accompanied by signs which showed that he was no ordinary child: wise men came from the east to worship him and angels announced his birth to shepherds. When he was brought to the Temple as a baby, a devout Jew named Simeon recognized him as the promised Messiah (see *Simeon*). According to Matthew, Herod attempted to have Jesus killed to destroy a possible threat to his throne and the family fled to Egypt for a time to avoid persecution.

From Jesus's childhood there is only one story. When he was twelve, his parents took him to Jerusalem at Passover. When the holy day was over, they left, probably with a crowd of pilgrims, and did not notice that he was not with them. Returning, they found him in the Temple, debating with the teachers. Mary rebuked him but he replied, 'Did you not know that I must be about my father's business?' (Luke 2:46—52).

When he was about 30 (Luke 3:1) he was one of those who went to be baptized by John the Baptist. This tells us something about him. John was a prophet who expected the kingdom of God to arrive soon and the fact that

Jesus went to him for baptism probably indicates that he shared the same hope. Luke's Gospel tells how a voice from heaven spoke when Jesus was baptized, while the Holy Spirit in the shape of a dove flew down to him.

After his baptism, Jesus stayed in the wilderness for a period of fasting and meditation before beginning his own ministry, travelling in Galilee, and teaching and healing. He was soon joined by disciples, whom he called 'the Twelve', probably using the number symbolically to indicate his hope that the twelve tribes of Israel would be brought together once more. His teaching focussed on the kingdom of God, and he illustrated it by apt and memorable parables. The main point of many of them is that, in God's kingdom, there would be room for the weak, the sinners, and the outcasts. He called tax collectors such as Matthew and Zacchaeus, as well as other people considered to be sinners, to follow him and was known as their friend. He made a special point of eating with sinners, thus demonstrating with a symbolic gesture that they were to be included in the kingdom.

Jesus's healings attracted crowds to him. He was, however, by no means the only healer of his day and the Gospels refer to others (Matthew 12:27; Mark 9:38—41). The miraculous cures of Jesus were not different in kind from those said to have been performed by other healers of the time. Today some people consider that many of the healing miracles recorded in the ancient world were psychosomatic cures of illnesses such as deafness, dumbness or paralysis which were caused by mental disturbances not by physical diseases. Other reported healings cannot be described like this, and they remain unexplained by modern science. Jesus was reported to have raised the dead (see *Jairus* and *Lazarus*) and also to have performed 'nature' miracles, such as stilling a storm and walking on the water (Mark 4:35—41; Matthew 14:22—33). It is certain that at the time all the miracles were regarded as supernatural events and that this helped to gain Jesus a following. It also brought him to the hostile notice of the rulers of Palestine.

The Gospels make it clear that the disciples were slow to perceive the significance of the man they followed. At one point a large crowd which followed Jesus was fed when five loaves of bread and two fish miraculously multiplied (Mark 6:35—44). Immediately after this, Jesus came to the disciples in a boat by walking on the water. Mark then comments, 'they were utterly astounded, for they did not understand about the loaves' (6:51—52).

Two episodes show how the disciples began to understand. When Jesus and his followers were near Caesarea Philippi, he asked them, 'Who do people say that I am?' They replied, 'Some say John the Baptist, others say Elijah, and others Jeremiah or one of the prophets'. Jesus asked what they thought themselves and Peter answered, 'You are the Christ, the Son of the living God.' But Jesus told them to tell no-one else (Matthew 16:13—20).

Shortly after this incident, Jesus took Peter, James and John to the top of a mountain. There they had a vision in which Moses and Elijah talked with Jesus. A heavenly voice announced, 'This is my beloved Son, with him I am well pleased; listen to him.' The disciples had fallen on their faces and when they looked up again they saw Jesus only (Matthew 17:1—8).

The meaning of these events seems clearer now than it must have at the time, and perhaps they have been enhanced by Christian telling and retelling. Even after the revelation on the mountain top, the disciples showed uncertainty and a lack of full commitment, as their behaviour during Jesus's last hours shows.

It is not known just how long Jesus preached and healed in Galilee. The Gospel of John tells of three trips to Jerusalem for Passover, which would mean that his ministry lasted just over two years. All the events in the other three Gospels, however, easily fit into one year and they describe only one trip to Jerusalem for Passover.

In any case, about the year 30, Jesus and his disciples went to Jerusalem for Passover. Outside the city the disciples obtained a donkey for him and he rode into Jerusalem on it, with some of his followers hailing him as 'Son of David'— the longed-for liberator of Israel (Matthew 21:1—9). He went to the Temple, and there he created a disturbance by overturning some of the tables used for changing pilgrims' money into coinage acceptable by the priests, and for selling the unblemished doves required for sacrifices (Matthew 21:10—17).

This, like the entry to Jerusalem, was probably a small and symbolic demonstration. The two events must have been small, or Jesus would have been immediately arrested and executed. Jerusalem during holy days was like dry tinder, ready to explode. It was packed with pilgrims, most of them resentful of Roman domination, and many resentful of the chief priests who accepted it. The Roman Prefect and most of his troops were usually stationed in Caesarea, leaving Jerusalem to be administered by the High Priest and his council. At Passover, however, the Prefect resided in Jerusalem to be on hand in case of trouble, and the city, especially the Temple, was heavily guarded. A large demonstration, in which multitudes hailed Jesus as king, or a major disruption of the Temple activities, would have led to prompt intervention by the troops.

Jesus, however, was able to leave the city. He went to the house of Simon the Leper in nearby Bethany, where a woman anointed him with ointment. He explained the extravagance by saying that it was preparation for his burial (Matthew 26:6—13). He then sent his disciples back into Jerusalem, telling them to meet a man carrying a jar of water, to follow him and ask him for a room for their Passover meal (Mark 14:12—16). At the meal he performed a last symbolic act: he broke bread and drank wine, proclaiming 'a new covenant', and he said that he would not drink wine again until he drank it with his disciples in the kingdom of God (Luke 22:14—23; 1 Corinthians 11:23—26).

After the meal, Jesus took his disciples to the Garden of Gethsemene, on the Mount of Olives, just east of Jerusalem. There he prayed, asking God to spare him the coming ordeal, but

concluding by saying 'but as you wish'. The disciples, asked to watch with him while he prayed, slept instead (Matthew 26:36—46).

During the visit to Jerusalem, a disciple, Judas, had arranged with the chief priests to betray Jesus so that he could be arrested in secret (Mark 14:10). They doubtless feared that a public arrest would create a tumult, possibly a riot, which would lead to military intervention by the Roman soldiers. The chief priests did not want to lose their power and it was very much in their interests to help keep the country peaceful. As a prophet who preached a coming 'kingdom', Jesus was thought to be dangerous even if he had no military ambition, and the priests had decided that he should die. Judas led soldiers to Jesus, identifying him by kissing him. One of the followers drew his sword and cut off the ear of one of the soldiers. According to Luke, Jesus restored the ear. Then, he was led away and all the disciples fled (Matthew 26:47—56; Luke 22:47—54).

Jesus was taken to be interrogated by the High Priest and others during the night, probably not tried formally (see especially John 18:12—27), led to the Prefect Pontius Pilate, interrogated further, flogged, and crucified with two other men who were probably rebels against Roman rule rather than common thieves (Mark 15:1—41). He died relatively quickly (death by crucifixion often took days of pain) and his body was taken to be buried by Joseph of Arimathea, with faithful women looking on (Mark 15:42—47). The women returned the next day to complete the burial procedures but found the tomb empty. A figure dressed in white told them that Jesus was raised and sent them to the disciples in Galilee with a message that Jesus would appear to them there (Mark 16:1—8).

Jesus was seen by several people after his death: first by Mary Magdalene, then by various disciples both individually and when they were together. All four Gospels describe his appearances after the resurrection, over a period lasting from a day to more than a week. In Luke's Gospel his last appearance was to the eleven disciples who were

together in Jerusalem, discussing the reports that were reaching them that Jesus had been seen alive. Suddenly Jesus himself appeared and when they seemed terrified, showed them his hands and feet and asked to eat with them, proving to them that he was not a ghost. After explaining many things to them he took them as far as Bethany, blessed them and 'was parted from them and carried up to heaven' (Luke 24:36—53).

From these bare facts, what does the historian see as Jesus's own intention, his view of himself and of the kingdom he promised?

First, he expected the kingdom of God but did not think that it would come by military insurrection. His small band of followers was not regarded by either the Romans or the chief priests as a military threat. After his death, the disciples were not rounded up and killed but later returned to Jerusalem, where the Romans, if anything, protected them (see *Gamaliel; James the brother of Jesus*). The kingdom of God that Jesus expected was, therefore, one that was interior, in the heart of individuals; or one which would be in heaven; or one which would be instituted on earth by God himself, who would directly intervene in history.

The last possibility is the most likely. Jesus's action in the Temple was almost certainly symbolic: he expected it either to be purged of corrupt practice, so that it would serve its true purpose, or to be literally destroyed and miraculously replaced by God himself. His words at the last supper point in the same direction: Jesus thought that the kingdom would soon come, and that in it he and his followers would celebrate by drinking wine. One of the sayings which is most certainly to be attributed to Jesus is the prohibition of divorce (Matthew 5:31—32; 19:9; Mark 10:11—12; Luke 16:18; 1 Corinthians 7:10—11). This also seems to suppose an earthly kingdom, a world in which marriage would exist.

The disciples understood that the kingdom would involve a ruler (Jesus), who would have lieutenants, and they discussed who would sit at his right hand and at his left. Jesus rebuked them, but he did not say that there would be no real kingdom, only that 'whoever would be great among you must be your servant' (Mark 10:35—45).

If this was in fact Jesus's expectation, it was disappointed. In this case even he misunderstood God's intention for him. Many see his last intelligible words, 'My God, my God, why have you forsaken me?' (Mark 15:34), to be truly a cry of despair and disappointment. Certainly his followers thought that it was all over. The resurrection appearances caught them by surprise. The 'kingdom' which had been looked for did not come, but rather a movement which has given spiritual life to many over the centuries.

This brief reconstruction of Jesus's life is built on the direct evidence of the earliest known sources, but it is still an incomplete one: no historian can ever feel that he has fully comprehended the mystery of Jesus's life.

It is possible, however, to learn more from looking at the different ways in which Jesus impressed different people. In the Gospel of Matthew, he is above all a moral and ethical teacher. The strict demands of the Sermon on the Mount (Matthew 5—7) have permanently impressed themselves on the western conscience as pointing a way towards a higher way of life. This collection of teaching material, the most influential part of the church's most influential gospel, is not, of course, the whole of Matthew's portrayal of Jesus. But it was clearly Matthew's intention to depict Jesus as the teacher of a new law.

Mark's Jesus is more a doer than a teacher. He is, above all, the man of God locked in battle with demonic forces, and healings and exorcisms make up a much larger proportion of Mark's Gospel than they do of Matthew's and Luke's. Mark often comments that Jesus taught (for example 1:21—22; 2:13), but reports relatively little. Whereas the Sermon on the Mount sets the tone for Matthew's Gospel, Jesus's exorcism of a man in the synagogue in Capernaum sets the tone for Mark's. The demon forced the man to cry out, 'What have you to do with us, Jesus of Nazareth? Have you come to destroy us? I know who you are, the Holy One of God' (1:24—25). Jesus commanded the demon to be silent, and then exorcised it (1:26). The command to silence is important, for much of the drama of Mark's Gospel comes from the way he contrasts the public acclaim with Jesus's quest for privacy; the recognition of demons, whom he conquers, against the incomprehension of humans, including his disciples; and the outward rush through Galilee and on to Jerusalem, against the quiet inner development of the view that it is necessary for the Son of man to suffer and die (8:31). Mark's love of drama and mystery extends even to the final scene. The Gospel ends when a young man dressed in white tells the women to 'tell the disciples and Peter that he is going before you to Galilee; there you will see him, as he told you'. The women fled, 'for trembling and astonishment had come upon them; and they said nothing to any one, for they were afraid' (16:6—8).

The original Gospel ends there, with trembling and fear and only the promise of resurrection. Later writers found this ending unsatisfactory and scribes who copied and recopied the narratives of the resurrection added the verses sometimes printed as 16:9—20.

The Gospel of Luke presents a Jesus who is, above all, a sympathetic human being and the creator of magnificent parables. Luke emphasizes again and again Jesus's appeal to sinners, tax collectors, women, and even some Pharisees. But the most memorable parts of Luke's Gospel are the great parables, especially The Good Samaritan (Luke 10:29—37) and The Prodigal Son (15:11—32). The points are simple: live good and charitable lives, never hesitate to repent and turn to God, and be equally unhesitant about accepting the repentant sinner. What is impressive is the skill with which the message is conveyed.

While there are differences among Matthew, Mark and Luke, these three Gospels are in many ways much alike. The Gospel of John is quite a different work. The Jesus of Matthew, Mark and Luke speaks in short pithy sayings and in parables, and always about God and humanity, almost never about himself. The Jesus of John speaks in long and elaborate metaphorical monologues, and his own relation to God is one of the chief topics. He is more the risen Lord of the church and less the carpenter's son from Nazareth.

The theme of the monologues in John's Gospel is that Jesus 'abides' in the Father, and the Father in him; and he abides in the disciples, and the disciples in him. This union is based on love: 'thou hast sent me and hast loved them even as thou hast loved me' (John 17:23), and the disciples are commanded to love one another, 'even as I have loved you'. 'By this all men will know that you are my disciples, if you love one another' (13:34—35). The union is also based on mystical participation in the sacraments: 'He who eats my flesh and drinks my blood has eternal life' (6:54). The author explains that this flesh is 'true flesh' (6:55), but he does not use 'true' here and throughout the Gospel in the sense of 'matter of fact'. Instead he uses the word to mean not physical and short-lived but eternal and therefore 'true'. Generations of Christians have found in John the truest—in John's own sense of the word—depiction of Jesus.

Many other legends and stories were written about Jesus by the early Christians. These collections are now called the apocryphal gospels but none stands on the same level as the first four attempts to capture the significance of Jesus of Nazareth. Each Gospel surely does catch and represent something of him. He looked for a new order, one in which the meek would be blessed, in which God would welcome sinners, in which human failings (represented by divorce) would be no more. But he was not just a dreamer. He was also a stern judge of people and their motives, and he demanded of others what he did of himself: complete and total devotion to his cause. But, again, he was not just harsh and demanding. He loved all whom he met, and he tried to demonstrate God's love by being open, accepting and forgiving. And all the while he carried within himself the conviction that God had chosen him especially, that he would use him to bring about the kingdom of God.

JESUS
Jesus lived and died in obscurity in an insignificant backwater of the Roman Empire; his ministry lasted for less than two years and none of his teachings were written down in his lifetime; his followers were drawn from the poorest sections of society and were persecuted for their belief in him. Yet despite this, Jesus has become the most influential figure in history and his teaching has changed the way we think and live today.

The disciples

All four Gospels, Acts, and Paul agree that there were twelve special disciples, and they are often referred to collectively, as 'the Twelve'. Matthew, Mark and Luke give lists of the Twelve, and Luke's is repeated in Acts (Matthew 10:1–4; Mark 3:13–19; Luke 6:12–16; Acts 1:13). The Gospel of John refers to the Twelve (John 6:67–71; 20:24), but does not give a list, though some individuals are named. It is a curious fact that the sources do not agree precisely on their names. The most probable explanation is that Jesus himself used the term symbolically, and it was remembered as a symbolic figure, even though the precise number of close disciples may have varied slightly.

As a symbol, the number represents the twelve tribes of Israel. In calling the disciples and speaking of them as 'the Twelve', Jesus intended to show that he foresaw the full restoration of the people of Israel (Matthew 19:28).

There were three disciples in the 'inner circle': Simon (later called by Jesus 'Peter') and the two sons of Zebedee, James and John. In the Gospels these are often singled out, and they became prominent leaders of the Christian movement after Jesus's death and resurrection. The Gospel of John does not name James and John, though it does mention 'the sons of Zebedee' (John 21:2). Some scholars think that the unnamed 'beloved disciple' in John's Gospel is the disciple John himself.

Other disciples mentioned in the Gospels and Acts are: Andrew, the brother of Simon; Philip; Thomas; Judas Iscariot; Bartholomew; Matthew; James the son of Alphaeus; Simon the Cananaean or the Zealot; Thaddaeus; Judas the son of James; and Nathanael.

This gives fourteen named disciples. Some of the discrepancies in the Gospels have been solved traditionally by assuming that some disciples had two names. Thus Thaddaeus (mentioned in Matthew and Mark) is often thought to be the same person as Judas the son of James (in Luke) and as Judas (not Iscariot) in John.

Instead of trying to fit all the names to twelve disciples, it is much more reasonable to assume that Jesus had a group of followers, at any one time numbering more or less twelve, and that some of the minor followers fell away, so that later the early Christians did not agree precisely on who the Twelve were.

Peter is by far the most sharply etched figure among the followers of Jesus, and all the evidence indicates that he was a man of contradictions. The gospels, especially Matthew, go out of their way to describe his hesitations and fears, and Paul also attributes to him behaviour which can only be called vacillating. Yet the Gospels and Paul agree that he was the foremost of the disciples, and Jesus gave him the nickname by which he is known: 'Rock'.

Peter's actual name was Simon, son of Jonas. Jesus, speaking in Aramaic, called him 'Kepha', 'Rock', and Paul knew him by this name. Paul also used the Greek version, 'Petros', 'Rock', from which we derive 'Peter'. He was a Galilean fisherman who, with his brother Andrew, responded to Jesus's call to follow him (Matthew 4:18). He was married, and we hear of Jesus healing his mother-in-law (Matthew 8:14–15), but nothing else is known of his personal circumstances.

Either because of a vigorous personality, or a striking appearance, or both, he stood out. Along with James and John, the sons of Zebedee, he was one of Jesus's closest companions. They were not always prepared to grant his leadership (see *James* and *John*), but it appears that he was early recognized as the chief of Jesus's disciples. For example when a hostile observer hoped to catch Jesus in an act of disloyalty it was Peter he asked whether Jesus would pay the temple tax (Matthew 17:24–27). When Jesus returned from his final prayer, and found his disciples asleep, it was Peter whom he singled out for rebuke (Matthew 26:40–41).

Most significantly, it was Peter who first voiced his belief that Jesus was the anointed of God, the Messiah. When Jesus first asked, 'Who do people say that I am?', the disciples said, 'One of the prophets.' In reply to the next question, 'Who do you say that I am', it was Peter who answered, 'You are the Messiah'. The tradition is that it was this reply which earned Simon the name 'Peter' (Matthew 16:13–20). It was a bold answer, for would-be Messiahs were dangerous to the stability of the region, and Rome allowed none to live long.

Shortly after this Jesus took Peter, James and John to the top of a mountain. 'And he was transfigured before them, and his face shone like the sun, and his garments became white as light.' The three disciples had a vision of Jesus talking with Moses and Elijah. Peter attempted to make an appropriate gesture and offered to build three shrines there, one for each of the three figures of the vision. He was interrupted by a heavenly voice, repeating the words heard at the time of Jesus's baptism: 'This is my beloved Son, with whom I am well pleased; listen to him'. The disciples fell on their faces, and when they rose they saw only Jesus, in his natural state (Matthew 17:1–8).

Despite these stories of devotion and revelation, there are several incidents which reveal that Peter's deep commitment to Jesus was often not sufficient to overcome his all-too-human fears. One of the best known was that, following Jesus, he began to walk on water; but that he grew afraid and went under. This story, in Matthew only (14:22–33), is probably a colourful account intended to depict his character. When Jesus predicted that he must die, Peter rebuked him, perhaps out of concern for his own safety as well as Jesus's. Jesus returned the rebuke: 'Get behind me, Satan!' (Matthew 16:21–23), perhaps seeing Peter as tempting him towards the easy but wrong goal.

The main example of Peter's uncertainty makes one of the most poignant stories in the gospels. After the last supper, Jesus took his disciples to the Mount of Olives, where he predicted that they would desert him. Peter vowed, 'though they all fall away, I will never fall away.' Jesus said that on that very night, 'before the cock crows', Peter would deny him three times; but Peter promised loyalty to death. When Jesus was arrested, Peter followed at a distance. He waited outside the High

Priest's house, and bystanders asked if he were a follower of Jesus. Three times he was asked, and once the evidence of his Galilean accent was cited in support; but all three times he denied it, finally with a curse on himself if he were not telling the truth (Matthew 26:30—35; 26:56—58; 26:69—75). Peter, with most of the other followers of Jesus, stayed well away from the scene of the crucifixion and then apparently went into hiding. According to John, Mary Magdalene came alone to the tomb on the morning of the resurrection, found it empty, and went to tell Peter and 'the other disciple, the one whom Jesus loved' (often believed to be John). The two men ran to the tomb, found it empty and returned home; Jesus then appeared to Mary Magdalene (John 20:1—18). The other Gospels agree that Peter was not the first to see the risen Jesus, though Paul had a tradition that he was (1 Corinthians 15:5). What does seem certain is that Peter and the other disciples feared that they, too, would be arrested, and so kept out of sight. Peter recovered his heart and courage only when the risen Lord appeared to him.

From the early years of the church there is one more story of his vacillation. He visited the church in Antioch, which included both Jewish and Gentile believers. At first he ignored the Jewish dietary laws, but he was rebuked by messengers sent by James, the brother of the Lord. He then withdrew from the Gentile Christians and would eat only with Jews. This led to a rebuke from the other side: Paul accused him of hypocrisy and of not walking according to the truth of the Gospel (Galatians 2:11—16). It is possible that Peter did not want his work of converting Jews to be compromised by charges that he broke the law. Still, though, we see the same indecisiveness which appears in the Gospel accounts.

Despite his failings, Peter was recognized after Jesus's death and resurrection as the foremost apostle. Even Paul, who once accused him of hypocrisy, granted that he was the chief apostle to the circumcised (Galatians 2:7). During the early days of the church in Jerusalem, Peter was more than once

PETER
Simon Peter is by far the most sharply etched figure among the followers of Jesus and all the evidence indicates that he was a man of contradictions. The Gospels go out of their way to describe his hesitations and fears; yet Paul, and the writers of the Gospels and the Acts of the Apostles all agree that he was the foremost of the disciples.

arrested, and was once flogged, but he bore up bravely, being strengthened now by the conviction that Jesus had survived death (Acts 4:1—12; 5:17—42).

In his role as chief apostle to the circumcised, Peter travelled extensively, accompanied by his wife (1 Corinthians 9:5), and he exerted wide influence on the developing Christian church.

Two letters in the New Testament are attributed to him, but it is unlikely that he wrote either one himself. 1 Peter is written in excellent Greek, certainly beyond the ability of a Galilean fisherman, and it seems to come from a period later than Peter's lifetime. Scholars believe that 2 Peter was the latest book to be included in the New Testament and was probably written by someone who thought that he wrote in the spirit of the apostle. This was common practice in the early Christian church. Neither letter shows any first-hand knowledge of Jesus.

The church historian Eusebius in the fourth century quoted Papias, who wrote about the year 140, as saying that Mark was the interpreter of Peter and 'wrote down accurately all that he remembered of the things said and done by the Lord, but not however in order'. This may mean that at least some of the Gospel of Mark is based on Peter's own recollection of events, although scholars consider that parts must certainly have been added at different times.

There is no firm evidence about how Peter died. At the end of the Gospel of John, there is an extended conversation between Peter and the risen Lord. Jesus asked Peter if he loved him more than did the others. Peter replied, 'Yes, Lord; you know that I love you.' Jesus commanded him, 'Feed my lambs'. The same question and answer was repeated twice more, and Jesus then said to Peter that when he became old he would stretch out his hands, 'and another will gird you and carry you where you do not wish to go'. The author comments that this statement shows how Peter would die (John 21:15—19) but scholars feel that this was written with hindsight, after Peter had in fact died.

In 1 Peter 5:13 (written not by Peter himself but in his name) the author speaks of writing from 'Babylon',

SIMON THE ZEALOT
The Zealots were a Jewish revolutionary movement whose members believed in overthrowing the Roman occupying powers by force. Simon may have been a man of violent temperament, perhaps first attracted to Jesus by his promise of a new kingdom.

probably a code word for 'Rome'. Putting these two clues together, we can guess that Peter died in Rome by crucifixion, fulfilling Jesus's prophecy that he would 'stretch out his hands'. A letter written from Rome to Corinth near the end of the first century states that Peter 'suffered not one or two but many trials, and having thus given his testimony went to the glorious place which was his due' (1 Clement 5:4). Since the letter was also sent from Rome, this may be another clue that Peter died there. By the end of the second century the tradition had arisen that Peter was crucified in Rome upside down. This became a popular story, and it appears in the Acts of Peter, a

fictional romance from around the end of the second century.

It seems likely that Peter did travel to Rome and that he died there. From Roman sources we learn that, following the fire of the year 64, Nero fixed the blame on Christians and had some executed in grisly ways: some were clothed in animal skins and attacked by dogs, others were crucified and used as torches to light one of his garden parties (Tacitus, Annals 15:44). It may be that both Peter and Paul were killed at this time.

It seems that Peter, then, overcame his vacillation and became steadfast. The character which Jesus had seen beneath the doubts and fears was really there. He was, in the end, true to the death; and he became the 'Rock', as Jesus had called him.

Nathanael is mentioned in the Gospel of John as one of the twelve disciples. According to John 1:45—51 Philip brought Nathanael to Jesus, who immediately knew who he was and told him what he had just been doing (sitting under a fig tree). Nathanael exclaimed, 'Rabbi, you are the Son of God! You are the King of Israel!' Jesus said he had not done anything very impressive, but promised, 'You shall see greater things than these'. This prophecy was fulfilled, too, and John subsequently named Nathanael as one of the seven disciples to whom Jesus appeared by the Sea of Galilee after the Resurrection (John 21:2).

Simon the Zealot was one of the twelve disciples, and one who is not mentioned apart from the name lists in Matthew, Mark, Luke and Acts. Matthew and Mark refer to him as 'the Cananaean', Luke and Acts as 'the Zealot'. 'Cananaean' is probably the Aramaic word *qanana*, which means 'zealous'.

In the sixties the Zealots were the Jews who not only wished for liberation from Roman domination, but who had resolved on war as the necessary means towards that end. Thirty years earlier, in Jesus's day, there probably was not a clearly identifiable group called 'the Zealots', but it is likely that the word was already used for those who were especially zealous for Israel's liberation and who were prepared to fight for it. Jesus himself hoped for the restoration of Israel, but he did not see armed revolt as the way to obtain it. It appears that he attracted at least one follower who had previously thought in military terms.

Thomas is named as one of the twelve special disciples of Jesus in the gospels of Matthew, Mark and Luke but nothing further is said about him there. He plays an important role, however, in John 20:15—29. In John's account of the resurrection, Jesus appears first to Mary Magdalene and then to 'the disciples' (John 20:15—23). We are then told, however, that Thomas was not with the

THOMAS
Because he asked for concrete proof of Jesus' resurrection, Thomas has traditionally been labelled as 'doubting'. Earlier, he showed a more impulsive side to his character. When Jesus decided to visit Bethany at great risk to his life, it was Thomas who volunteered to go with him and, if necessary, die with him.

disciples at the time of the appearance, and that he doubted the resurrection when he was told of it by the other disciples, saying 'Unless I see the nail marks in his hands and put my finger where the nails were, and put my hand into his side, I will not believe'. A week later the disciples, including Thomas, were together, and Jesus again appeared to them. He told Thomas to look at his hands and to put his hand in his side. The story does not say that Thomas actually touched Jesus. It says, instead, that Thomas immediately said, 'My Lord and my God'.

The author then has Jesus make the point: 'Because you have seen me, you have believed; blessed are those who have not seen and yet have believed'. Thomas, in the Gospel of John, thus represents a less praiseworthy kind of faith than that possessed by others—presumably later Christians or potential Christians whom the author wished to address: they should believe without tangible proof.

James and **John** the sons of Zebedee, were fishermen, working out of Capernaum on the Sea of Galilee. Jesus called them to follow him one day while they were preparing their nets. They immediately left their father with the hired men and followed (Mark 1.19—20).

The brothers became two of Jesus's

closest disciples. They were with Jesus when he visited the house of Andrew and Simon Peter, whose mother-in-law he healed (Mark 1:29—31). James, John and Simon Peter also went with Jesus to the top of a mountain, where they had a vision of Moses and Elijah talking with him, and thus they began to perceive who he was (Matthew 17:1—8).

The most interesting story about them is that they went to Jesus and tried to get him to promise that he would fulfil whatever they asked. He asked them to be specific, and they said, 'Let one of us sit at your right hand and the other at your left in your glory'. Jesus replied with a question, 'Can you drink the cup I drink?' They confidently answered that they could, and Jesus agreed that they would drink his cup and be baptized with his baptism—referring apparently to his suffering and death. But, he added, 'to sit at my right or left is not for me to grant. These places belong to those for whom they have been prepared' (Mark 10:35—40).

This is a very revealing story. It shows that at a fairly late stage in Jesus's ministry, the disciples still expected him to be 'king' in an earthly way, and to be able to grant positions of prominence

JOHN AND JAMES, THE SONS OF ZEBEDEE

The two brothers were two of Jesus's closest disciples. Jesus nicknamed them 'sons of thunder', probably referring to their explosive tempers. John (below) may have been 'the beloved disciple' of the Gospel of John, the only disciple who stood at the foot of the cross with the faithful women. Like his brother James(left), he was a fisherman and the two gave up what was probably a thriving business to follow the man they believed would bring a new kingdom of God on earth. James became one of the earliest martyrs.

and authority. Jesus realized that things would not work out that way and that suffering lay ahead.

It also shows that although by this time Jesus had named Simon 'Peter' ('Rock'), the other disciples did not all recognize him as the chief disciple. James and John still thought that they were candidates.

James and John are not mentioned by name in the Gospel of John, though 21:2 refers to 'the sons of Zebedee'. It used to be a tradition that people writing about themselves did not mention their own names, but identified themselves by a description of some kind. John was far too important a disciple to have been left out of the account completely and it is often thought that he was the unnamed 'disciple whom Jesus loved', who is mentioned several times in John's Gospel. According to John 19:25—27, this disciple stood by while Jesus hung on the cross, and Jesus gave his mother, Mary, into his care. Later, the 'beloved disciple' went with Peter to the tomb on the day of the resurrection. At the end of the Gospel, the writer tells how Jesus, after his resurrection, addressed his last words to 'the disciple whom he loved', and adds that the Gospel was based on his testimony. Scholars do not think it likely that the Gospel which now bears John's name is his direct eyewitness report, but it is possible that it is based on special traditions handed down from the disciple John himself.

After Jesus's death and resurrection, it appears that the brothers went separate ways. John stayed in Jerusalem, where he was Peter's chief companion and, next to Peter and James the brother of the Lord, the leading follower of Jesus. In the first incident mentioned in Acts, John and Peter were going to worship in the temple when a crippled man asked for money. Peter responded by healing him (Acts 3:1—10). The event attracted a crowd, but it was Peter, not John, who seized the opportunity to proclaim the resurrection of Jesus (Acts 3:11—26). John and Peter were arrested, and subsequently brought before the high priest and other members of his family. Again, it was Peter who testified that they healed by the name of Jesus. They were eventually released (Acts 4:1—21). John was probably arrested again, with other apostles (Acts 5:17—42). On this occasion they were freed by a miracle, though they were recaptured and flogged before being allowed to go.

Acts describes another incident in which John figured. He and Peter were sent to Samaria, where they placed their hands on converts and passed the spirit on to them. On the way back to Jerusalem they preached in Samaritan villages (Acts 8:14—25).

Paul's letter to the Galatians also shows that John was a leading member of the Jerusalem church, for Paul referred to Peter, James (the brother of Jesus) and John as "those reputed to be 'pillars'" (Galatians 2:9). This was perhaps sarcastic, since Paul was locked in a serious argument with some of the members of the Jerusalem church, but it shows nevertheless that John remained a leader. After that we learn no more of John from the New Testament.

Much less is known about what happened to James, the other son of Zebedee, after Jesus's death. He does not figure in the stories of the apostles in Jerusalem, and Paul does not mention him. It is possible that he returned to his home in Galilee. He continued to be a spokesman for Jesus, however, and perhaps an aggressive one, since he was executed by Herod Agrippa I in about the year 41 (Acts 12:2). One of the books of the New Testament is said to be by James (James 1:1), but we are not told which James and it may have been by James the brother of Jesus.

It is a curious fact that no sermons by either John or James are mentioned in the New Testament. When John travelled with Peter, it was apparently Peter who preached, and of James we hear nothing except his execution. Knowledge about the thinking of these two men, chief disciples and leaders of

JUDAS ISCARIOT
The name of Judas has become a synonym for treachery: the man who betrayed the Son of God for an insignificant sum of money. Yet his motives will always be unknown. Had he lost faith in Jesus as the Messiah or did he still believe yet wish to force him into more decisive action? He may have belonged to a group which wanted to end Roman rule by violence; perhaps he finally realized that this was not Jesus's intention.

early Christianity, is regrettably limited. The Gospels are dominated by Jesus himself, and the Book of Acts concentrates on Peter and Paul to the virtual exclusion of others. Nevertheless, James and John are remembered as two of the stalwart leaders of the Christian movement.

The Book of Revelation is by a John, but it is not known who he was. The author does not claim to be John the apostle. Revelation was written in the years AD 90—100, and if the apostle John was connected with it, he would have been a very old man aged at least in his mid-eighties. Had he lived that long, there would probably have been other references to him in some other early Christian literature, such as 1 Clement or the letters of Ignatius.

Judas Iscariot was one of the twelve disciples and the one named in all four gospels as the man who betrayed Jesus to the chief priests. His motive is not known with certainty, but it may be guessed from the circumstances. Jesus and his disciples had gone to Jerusalem about a week before Passover. Jesus had entered, riding on an ass, and his followers had hailed him as 'Son of David' (Matthew 21:1—9). They regarded him as the coming king. Nothing of great consequence had followed. Jesus had spent some time teaching and had driven some of the moneychangers from the temple court, but those who expected him to be 'king' in a political sense must have been disappointed. It is likely that Judas was one of those disappointed—so bitterly disappointed that he decided on a desperate act.

Later in that week he went to the chief priests and asked what they would pay him for an act of betrayal. Mark and Luke do not specify the sum, but Matthew says that it was thirty pieces of silver (Matthew 26:14—16). Jesus became aware that he would be betrayed, perhaps sensing Judas's uncertainty and guilt. At supper together that night he said that one of those present would betray him. Matthew and John wrote that Jesus identified the traitor, either as the person who dipped his bread into the bowl with Jesus, or as the one to whom he passed the piece of bread after it had been dipped. Matthew adds that Judas directly asked, 'Surely it is not I?' and that Jesus affirmed that it was (Matthew 26:20—25; John 13:21—30).

At night Judas led soldiers from the chief priest to arrest Jesus as he was praying in the Garden of Gethsemane, and he identified him by kissing him (Matthew 26:47—50). Jesus was arrested and taken to be tried.

There are two stories about Judas's end, one in Matthew's gospel and one in Acts. The other three gospels do not discuss it. Matthew says that Judas took the money back, but that the chief priests refused it. Judas flung it down, and went out and hanged himself. The priests then used the money to buy a burial plot for foreigners. According to Acts, Judas bought a plot of ground himself, but when he went there he fell headlong and his body burst open. The

two accounts agree that the field came to be called 'the field of blood' (Matthew 27:3—10; Acts 1:18—19).

Matthew is listed in the Gospels of Matthew, Mark and Luke as one of the twelve disciples. According to Matthew he was a tax collector who was sitting in his toll booth when Jesus passed by and called him (Matthew 9:9). Later this Gospel lists the same man as one of the disciples (10:3). Mark and Luke also include the story of the tax collector but they name him Levi and do not identify

MATTHEW
Tax collectors were regarded by other Jews with contempt since they were often corrupt and were seen as collaborators with the Roman rulers. Matthew left his despised but profitable occupation to follow Jesus. The Gospel that bears his name contains careful records of Jesus's teaching and parables.

him with the disciple Matthew.

The fact that the Gospel according to Matthew says that the tax collector and the disciple were the same person probably gave the Gospel its name. Who better to tell us that the tax collector's name was Matthew, and that he became one of the twelve, than the man himself?

The tax collectors of the Gospels were minor bureaucrats, Jews who sold their services either directly to Rome or (in Galilee during Jesus's lifetime) to a Roman puppet, Herod Antipas. They

137

were therefore criticized for aiding and abetting the occupying power. It was a special feature of Jesus's ministry that he accepted outcasts, prominent among whom were the tax collectors, and his attitude to them was offensive to many.

Philip is named in the Gospels of Matthew, Mark and Luke and in Acts as one of the Twelve, but no more is learned of him (Matthew 10:3; Acts 1:13). In the Gospel of John, however, he plays a substantial role. In John's account of the calling of the disciples, Philip was one of the first called, just after Andrew and Simon (Peter). Philip is said to be from Bethsaida in Galilee, but we are not told what he was doing when Jesus called him. He responded immediately, however, found Nathanael, and told him, 'We have found the one Moses wrote about in the Law, and about whom the prophets also wrote—Jesus of Nazareth, the son of Joseph'. When Nathanael asked if any good could come out of Nazareth. Philip said 'come and see' (John 1:43—48). In a later story he is also given an intermediary role. Some Greeks asked to see Jesus. Philip gave the message to Andrew, and together they told Jesus (John 12:20—22).

In John's story of the feeding of the multitude, Jesus asked Philip, 'Where shall we buy bread for these people to eat?', to test him. Philip apparently failed the test, for he responded that even 200 denarii (more than half a year's wages) would not buy enough for each person to have one bite (6:5—7).

John's last reference to him may also be intended to be critical. After the supper at which Jesus explained he was leaving them, both Thomas and Philip asked for more information and Philip asked Jesus 'to show us the Father', explaining 'That will be enough for us'. Jesus, disappointed, asked, 'Do you not know me, Philip...? Anyone who has seen me has seen the Father' (John 14:5—9). All the Gospels emphasize in various ways the incomprehension of the disciples, and John seems to have singled out Philip, along with Thomas, to make the point. It is perhaps intended ironically, in view of Philip's ready response at the beginning.

ANDREW
Andrew was the brother of Simon Peter and, according to John's Gospel, the person who introduced Simon to Jesus. A less stormy character than Peter, he seems to have been a thoughtful and devoutly religious disciple, quietly influencing events in his own way.

Andrew was one of the first disciples called by Jesus. There are two stories of how he became a follower. According to the Gospels of Matthew, Mark and Luke, he was a fisherman who worked with his brother Simon (later called Peter). One day Jesus, walking by the Sea of Galilee, called them to follow him, and they immediately left their nets and followed (Matthew 4:18—20). The impression is that Andrew and Simon worked out of Capernaum (Matthew 4:13), and this is confirmed by the statement that Jesus went to their house in Capernaum with the disciples James and John (Mark 1:29).

According to the Gospel of John, Andrew had a more active role in the beginning of Jesus's activity. Andrew and many others were in the Judean wilderness, at the Jordan river, where John the Baptist was preaching and baptizing. John saw Jesus among the crowd and said 'Look, the Lamb of God' (John 1:36). Two of the Baptist's disciples heard the statement, and they spent the day with Jesus. Andrew was one of these. He then went and brought Simon, telling him, 'We have found the Messiah!' (John 1:37—41). According to John, Peter and Andrew were from Bethsaida, which, like Capernaum, is on the shore of the Sea of Galilee.

Andrew was remembered as one of Jesus's chief disciples, though he was not quite in the inmost group with Simon, James and his brother John. The Gospel of John has two other stories in which Andrew figures prominently. When the crowd following Jesus was hungry, and there was no place to buy food, it was Andrew who told Jesus, 'Here is a boy with five small barley loaves and two small fish'; these proved enough to feed the whole crowd (John 6:5—13). Later, when some Greeks came seeking Jesus, Andrew and Philip played the role of intermediary, conveying the message to Jesus (John 12:20—22).

There is little in the Gospels about Andrew's personality and character, but it seems that he was ready to respond to Jesus in simple faith, and that he was remembered as playing the important role of bringing others to Jesus, including especially his brother Simon.

MARY MAGDALENE
One of Jesus's most faithful followers, Mary Magdalene had enough independence of mind to ignore the damage this would have done to her reputation in an age when women were not expected to travel alone. She remained with Jesus at the crucifixion and was the first to see him after the resurrection.

People of the Gospels

Mary Magdalene, from Magdala (a small village in Galilee) was a follower of Jesus who played a crucial part in the gospel accounts of his death and resurrection.

Of her life we know nothing, except that Jesus had healed her of what was regarded as demon possession (Luke 8:2) probably a type of madness. She followed him during part of his preaching and healing in Galilee, and along with at least two other women (another Mary and the wife of Zebedee), she accompanied him on his final trip to Jerusalem (Matthew 27:56). She saw the crucifixion (John 19:25) and watched the burial and the positioning of the stone at the mouth of the tomb (Matthew 27:61).

On Sunday morning (the morning of the first day of the week), she returned to the tomb. Matthew and John have slightly different accounts of what happened next. According to Matthew, she was with the other Mary and the two women saw the angel roll the stone away from the door of the tomb. The angel told them that Jesus had been raised and that they should tell the disciples to go to Galilee, where they would see him. The women left, half afraid and half joyous, and were met by Jesus himself. They 'clasped his feet and worshipped him'. Jesus repeated the instruction to tell the disciples to go to Galilee (Matthew 28:1—10).

According to John, Mary went to the tomb alone and found the stone already removed. She ran to tell Peter and 'the beloved disciple', who raced ahead to the tomb and found it empty except for the linen wrappings. The disciples returned to their homes, but Mary Magdalene remained at the tomb, weeping. She looked in and saw two angels who told her that Jesus had been raised. Turning around, she saw a man whom she took to be the gardener. Still thinking that Jesus was dead, not yet able to believe otherwise, she asked the 'gardener' where he had put the body. It was only when Jesus spoke her name that she recognized him. He forbade her, though, to touch him. She then found the disciples and told them that she had seen the risen Lord (John 20:1—18).

Behind the slightly conflicting stories, we see the early Christian community's recognition that the first witness to the resurrection was a Galilean woman, one who had been willing to accompany a travelling healer and teacher, even though it may have caused scandal. Mary's willingness to follow Jesus, and her personal devotion to him, make her one of the most memorable of his followers.

Beginning in approximately the sixth century, many fathers of the church identified Mary Magdalene with the unnamed woman of Luke 7:36—50 who washed Jesus's feet with her tears and dried them with her hair. The identification, which sprang from the desire to give names to unnamed characters, continues today, yet there is no reason in the Bible for it. Luke clearly did not have Mary Magdalene in mind when he gave his account of the

MARTHA
Martha is shown in the Bible as a very normal, practical person, busy with the everyday problems of managing a household. Less flamboyant than her sister, Mary, she, too, showed complete faith in Jesus's power.

woman who washed Jesus's feet since he introduced Mary as a new character in chapter 8, after the footwashing incident.

Martha was the sister of Mary of Bethany and Lazarus. She appears in similar stories in the gospels of Luke and John, and from them a fairly clear picture of her emerges, though some of the details vary.

According to Luke 10:38—42, Jesus went to the house of Martha and Mary while passing through southern Galilee or Samaria. Mary sat at Jesus's feet and listened to him, while Martha 'was distracted with much serving'. She complained to Jesus because he allowed Mary to escape the housework, but Jesus replied, 'Martha, Martha, you are anxious and troubled about many things; but only one thing is needed. Mary has chosen what is better and it will not be taken away from her'.

According to John 11:1—12.8, the two sisters and Lazarus lived in Bethany, a village in Judea, near Jerusalem. Lazarus fell ill, and the sisters sent word to Jesus to come. By the time he arrived Lazarus had been dead four days and Martha chided him, saying, 'Lord, if you had been here, my brother would not have died'. She said, however, that she still had confidence that whatever Jesus asked of God would be done and when Jesus said, 'I am the resurrection and the life; he who believes in me, though he die, yet shall he live...' Martha confessed her faith: 'I believe that you are the Christ, the Son of God ...' Jesus went to the tomb and raised Lazarus from the dead.

Later, Jesus returned to their house to eat with them. Again, Martha served, while Mary anointed Jesus's feet.

These stories agree that Martha was the practical one of the two sisters, the one who managed the house and saw that there was food on the table. The account in John's Gospel also shows her as a woman of faith.

Mary of Bethany was the sister of Martha and Lazarus. According to John 12:1–8, Jesus visited their home in Bethany in Judea, where he raised Lazarus from the dead. Later, at dinner Martha served, while Lazarus and others reclined (in the Greek custom) at table. Mary entered, carrying a jar of an expensive perfume, nard. She poured it on Jesus's feet and then wiped them with her hair. Judas Iscariot protested that the money would have been of more use if it had been given to the poor. But Jesus replied that the perfume was for his burial, and he added, 'the poor you will always have with you, but you will not always have me'.

MARY OF BETHANY
Mary stands in the Bible for all those women who recognized Jesus as an outstanding teacher, accepting his words and actions with an emotional response that often brought criticism from more practical followers.

This account seems to be a combination of three similar but distinct stories which appear in the other three gospels. In one, Jesus was dining with Simon the Pharisee, when a woman who was a 'sinner' entered, wet Jesus's feet with her tears, dried them with her hair, and kissed and anointed them with oil (Luke 7:36—50).

In a second story (Luke 10:39—42), Jesus was in a house with Mary and Martha. Mary just sat and listened to the master while Martha was occupied with preparing the meal. When Martha grumbled about her sister's behaviour, Jesus supported Mary, replying that she had chosen the better thing to do.

The third story, in both Matthew 26:6—13 and Mark 14:3—9, is very similar to the first but took place in a different household. According to this, Jesus was in Bethany at the house of Simon the Leper when a woman came to him carrying an alabaster jar of expensive perfume, which she poured on his head. As in John's Gospel, the disciples were indignant, protesting that the perfume could have been sold and the money given to the poor. Jesus's reply was also as it is reported in John's Gospel, but went on, 'wherever this Gospel is preached throughout the world, what she has done will also be told, in memory of her'.

The story of the anointing with oil or perfume has become linked with the name of Mary Magdalene, but she is not mentioned in the gospels as the woman involved. It seems that several women were devoted to Jesus, even though they did not follow him, as Mary Magdalene did. In the story of Mary of Bethany John has combined the characteristics and actions of three women who were drawn to Jesus and his message.

Lazarus, the brother of Martha and Mary of Bethany, is the main figure in the most dramatic miracle ascribed to Jesus and it is striking that the story occurs only in John's Gospel.

According to John 11:1—12, Lazarus and his sisters, Mary and Martha, were close friends of Jesus. Lazarus fell ill, and the women sent for Jesus. He delayed for two days, apparently to make sure that Lazarus would be truly dead when he arrived. When he did come, Lazarus had been in the tomb for four days. Jesus went to the tomb, prayed to God, and cried, 'Lazarus, come out!' The dead man came out, his hands and feet bound with bandages, and his face wrapped with a cloth. He was fully restored to life, and later Jesus shared a meal with the family in Bethany. The raising of Lazarus led many to believe in Jesus, and it was this, according to John, which made the leading Jews decide to have Jesus executed.

The name Lazarus also figures in a parable in Luke 16:19—31. Lazarus, a poor man, is contrasted with a rich man, at whose gate he begs. In the parable, Lazarus died and was taken to Heaven; the rich man died and went to Hades. There he was allowed to see Lazarus's happy state, and he prayed to Abraham that the former beggar be sent to give him water. Abraham refused. The rich man begged that Lazarus be sent to his father's house, to warn his brothers. Abraham refused again, saying, 'They have Moses and the prophets. Let them hear them'. The rich man still pleaded, urging that if a man returned from the dead his brothers would repent. Abraham replied, 'If they do not hear Moses and the prophets, neither will they be convinced if someone should rise from the dead'.

Some scholars have suggested that John developed the story out of the parable, offering a concrete example of a man raised from the dead, whose testimony still was not believed.

Joanna was the wife of Chuza, the steward of Herod Antipas. She is mentioned only in Luke's Gospel. Like Mary Magdalene, she was healed of some illness by Jesus. Luke identified her as one of Jesus's followers in Galilee who helped to support him and his disciples financially (Luke 8.1—3). He also named her as one of the women who came with Jesus from Galilee to Jerusalem, who watched the crucifixion, saw Jesus's body laid in the tomb, and later returned to find the tomb empty. The women were told by angels that Jesus had been raised and passed the news to the disciples (Luke 23:49, 55 and 24:1—11).

Both Matthew and Mark report that there were several unnamed women who followed Jesus in his lifetime and who stood by him in his final agony (Matthew 27:55; Mark 15:40—41). It is assumed that since these were not named, they played no part in the movement after Jesus's death. This may also be true of Joanna for we hear no more about her.

Zacchaeus was a resident of Jericho and a chief tax collector. He was in charge of minor toll collectors such as Levi and he was, as Luke explains, rich. Taxes were collected by 'contractors', wealthy men who pledged the government a certain revenue and were then given the power to tax a region. They employed other sub-contractors: men who promised the chief tax collector a set sum and who then collected as much as they could. The system was obviously open to abuse and in Palestine tax collectors were often regarded as traitors, since they served Rome.

When Jesus passed through Jericho, Zacchaeus, who was short, climbed a tree in order to see him. This attracted Jesus's attention, and he told Zacchaeus to come down and to provide hospitality. The crowd muttered that Jesus would be the guest of a sinner. Zacchaeus, however, chose the moment to renounce his occupation, declaring that he would give half his goods to the poor and promising to restore fourfold whatever he had taken by fraud. (The Jewish law required only an added fifth: Leviticus 6:1—5). Jesus said that salvation had come to his house, adding that 'the Son of man came to seek and to save the lost' (Luke 19:1—10).

This is a touching and colourful account of a main aspect of Jesus's mission. He did not come to call the righteous (for people who are well do not need a doctor), but sinners, prominent among whom were tax collectors and prostitutes.

Simon the Pharisee The Pharisees were Jews who followed the Law most strictly, observing all the laws about diet and behaviour scrupulously. Luke apparently wished to emphasize that Jesus was not always at odds with them, and twice he described him eating at a Pharisee's house. In the first of these stories (Luke 7:36—50; see also 14:1), the Pharisee was named Simon. When Jesus sat down at table, a 'woman of the city, who was a sinner' came in. She had brought an alabaster flask of ointment, and she stood behind the couch on which he reclined. Leaning over, she bathed his feet with her tears, dried them with her hair, and anointed them with the ointment. Simon thought to himself that Jesus was not much of a prophet, otherwise he would have recognized the woman for what she was and rejected her attentions. Jesus justified the situation by telling a parable. The point of it was that the more one is forgiven, the more one loves. He then reversed the 'moral' of the story and applied it to the woman: since she loved much, she was forgiven much. Jesus contrasted her attitude towards him with Simon's own: Simon had not performed the customary courtesies for an honoured guest—he had not given Jesus water for washing his feet, nor greeted him with a kiss, nor anointed his head; but the woman had not only bathed his feet, but also anointed them and kissed them. Jesus then directly addressed the woman, telling her that her sins were forgiven.

Simon here is not depicted as a bad man. He was sincere and wished to learn more of Jesus's message, but he did not treat his visitor with honour and respect. The main reason for including the incident seems to have been to show that Jesus was especially concerned with the salvation of the wicked, including prostitutes. Simon is included as a foil to emphasize the point.

Joseph of Arimathea was from a small village in the Judean hills, but had apparently moved to Jerusalem. There he had become a prominent member of the Sanhedrin, the council of priests. According to Matthew, he was a disciple of Jesus. Having moved, he had to acquire a new tomb (the family burial place would have been in his home village) and he obtained one just outside Jerusalem. After Jesus's death he offered

JOSEPH OF ARIMATHEA
Joseph was a rich merchant who gave his own tomb as a burial place for Jesus. He appears only briefly in the Bible but later legends describe him as a prosperous trader with business connections reaching beyond the Mediterranean to the shores of Britain.

it as Jesus's burial place. Jewish law required that an executed criminal should be buried the same day, and Joseph obviously respected this, as well as wishing to do what he could for Jesus. The law also said that an executed criminal should not be buried in a tomb used for others; since Joseph's tomb was unused, it was suitable.

As a prominent citizen, Joseph had access to the Roman governor Pilate, and he took the initiative of going to him to ask for Jesus's body. Joseph himself took the body (according to John, assisted by Nicodemus), wrapped it, and laid it in the tomb (Matthew 27:57—61; Mark 15:42—47; Luke 23:50—56; John 19:38—42).

Joseph is not mentioned in the Book of Acts, and he seems to have played no further role in the Christian movement, although there is a tradition that he took care of Mary the mother of Jesus. Later traditions describe him as a wealthy trader whose ships sailed as far west as the British Isles. But there is no hint of this in the Gospels. According to these, he was a righteous man, one who 'looked for the kingdom of God' (Mark 15:43), and was obviously attracted by Jesus's message and commitment; but he seems not to have been quite a full disciple.

Nicodemus, who is mentioned only in John, was, like Joseph of Arimathea, a kind of half-disciple of Jesus. These two men probably represent a sizeable group of people who were attracted to Jesus and his message, but who did not become fully committed disciples.

Nicodemus was a leading Pharisee of Jerusalem, called by John 'a ruler of the Jews'. He came to Jesus 'by night', saying that he thought that Jesus must be 'a teacher come from God'. Jesus replied by making a word play in Greek: 'Unless one is born *anothen* he cannot see the kingdom of God'. The word *anothen* means either 'again' or 'from above'. Nicodemus took it in the first sense and answered that it was impossible to re-enter the womb. Jesus's reply showed that he had meant 'from above': 'That which is born of the flesh is flesh, and that which is born of the Spirit is spirit'. Nicodemus here is used as an example of a good, religious person who was interested in learning more but did not quite grasp the significance of Jesus (John 3:1—14).

Later, when the chief priests had just failed in an attempt to arrest Jesus and were debating what to do with him, Nicodemus spoke on his behalf: 'Does our law judge a man without first giving him a hearing and learning what he does?' The priests silenced him by pointing out that there was nothing in the scriptures to indicate that a prophet would ever come from Galilee—and so that it was impossible for one to do so.

Nicodemus, still not fully committed, but still seeing Jesus as someone sent by God, helped Joseph of Arimathea to bury Jesus. Joseph obtained the body, while Nicodemus brought a large quantity of myrrh and aloes to be wrapped with it (John 19:38—42). He does not reappear in the New Testament and so seems not to have joined the Christian movement. He remained one who respected Jesus but who was not fully persuaded that he was God's decisive messenger.

Simon the Leper was the owner of a house in Bethany, which Jesus visited shortly before his final day in Jerusalem (Matthew 26:6—13; Mark 14:3—9). While he was there, a woman named Mary (presumably Simon's daughter or sister) anointed Jesus. When some protested, saying that the ointment could have been sold and the money given to the poor, Jesus replied that 'she has anointed my body beforehand for burying'. (See also *Mary of Bethany.*)

In those days there was not a clear distinction between leprosy as we know it and various other skin diseases. In the New Testament the word 'leper' seems always to refer to someone with a skin disease such as psoriasis or eczema. The symptoms are described in Leviticus 13:40—44 and those who showed them were considered ritually impure. To lessen the risk of infecting others, they had to make their condition obvious, to tear their clothing, leave their hair dishevelled, and cry 'Unclean, unclean'. They also had to live outside settled areas (Leviticus 13:45—46). These restrictions must have caused many people whose disease was not infectious to be separated from society, and it is clear that the Israelite legislators were anxious to safeguard the community rather than the rights of the individual. It only became possible to diagnose leprosy accurately near the end of the nineteenth century.

It is probable that at some time in his life Simon had suffered from a skin disease and retained the word 'leper' from that period. By the time Jesus visited, he must no longer have showed any symptoms.

Cleopas was one of two disciples who met Jesus after his resurrection, on the road to Emmaus, about fifteen miles from Jerusalem. The two were joined by a stranger, who asked what they were discussing. Apparently surprised that there could be anyone who had not heard of the recent events, Cleopas asked if he were the only visitor who had not heard about Jesus, 'who was a prophet mighty in deed and word before God and all the people'. Cleopas then described Jesus's death and burial, as well as the report that women who had visited the tomb had found it empty, but had been told in a vision that Jesus was alive. Jesus then explained that the Christ was intended first to suffer and then to 'enter into his glory'. It was not until they reached Emmaus and sat down to eat that they recognized Jesus—who then vanished. Cleopas and the other disciple (who is not named) returned to Jerusalem, found the eleven disciples and others, and told them 'what had happened on the road, and how he was known to them in the breaking of the bread' (Luke 24:13—35).

Jairus was the ruler of a synagogue, presumably in Galilee, whose daughter fell ill and who came to Jesus seeking his help. Before anything could be done, news came that the girl had died. Jesus nevertheless went to Jairus's house, and asked the mourners, who had already gathered, why they mourned, saying that the child was not dead but only sleeping. He then went in, took her hand, and commanded her to rise. She did so, and he ordered that she be given food (Mark 5:21—43).

It is not absolutely clear in the original text whether the reader is supposed to think that the child had really died or whether she was still at the point of death. It is probable, however, that the authors intend this story to be read as an account of raising the dead. (See *Lazarus.*)

Bartimaeus, whose name is given only by Mark, was a blind man who begged on the outskirts of Jericho. When Jesus passed through the city, Bartimaeus heard the crowd and caught Jesus's name. He cried out, 'Jesus, Son of David, have mercy on me!' Some told him to be quiet, but he called out all the louder. Jesus heard him, stopped, and asked what he wanted. He requested his sight. Jesus replied, 'Go your way; your faith has made you well', and his sight was restored (Mark 10:46—52).

Malchus was a servant of the High Priest. All four Gospels report that, when Jesus was arrested, one of his followers drew his sword and cut off the ear of the High Priest's servant (Matthew 26:51; Mark 14:47; Luke 22:50; John 18:10). Luke, wishing to make Jesus look as little like a revolutionary as possible, reports that Jesus healed the man (Luke 22:51). Only John identified the two men involved: it was Peter himself who used his sword, and the servant was Malchus.

Barabbas was an insurgent who had been arrested some time before Jesus's own arrest and trial. There had apparently been a small uprising against the Romans at about the time Jesus and his followers arrived in Jerusalem for Passover. Several people had been arrested, among them the two men with whom Jesus was crucified. The term 'robber', (which is used in Mark 15:27) was especially used for bandits who were more revolutionaries than common criminals.

The Roman Prefect, Pontius Pilate, had the custom of releasing one prisoner during the principal Jewish holy days. This time he offered the Jerusalem crowd a choice: he would release Barabbas (who was said to have committed murder during the uprising) or Jesus. Pontius Pilate knew Jesus was not himself part of the uprising but seems to have assumed that the crowd would prefer the gentle teacher, Jesus, to the insurrectionist Barabbas. The crowd, however, urged on by the chief priests, demanded that he release Barabbas, which he did.

Simon of Cyrene was 'passing by' when Jesus was being taken by the Roman soldiers to be crucified and they compelled him to carry the cross. This would have been only the horizontal cross beam, to which the arms were attached. The vertical beam would have been already in place.

Mark (15:21) tells us that Simon was the father of Alexander and Rufus. The family may have been living in Palestine at the time, or they may have been on a pilgrimage from Cyrene in North Africa. From the casual way in which the names of the two sons are mentioned, it may be that they were known to readers of the gospel as members of the Christian movement. A Rufus is mentioned by Paul (Romans 16:13), but his brother Alexander is not otherwise referred to. Perhaps the family became interested in the man into whose destiny they had unexpectedly been drawn.

BARABBAS
Barabbas was a revolutionary bandit rather than a common criminal and had been arrested for murder during an uprising against the Romans just before Jesus was captured. There was continual resistance to the Roman occupation and Barabbas may have been a local resistance hero.

The chief priests

While Palestine was under Roman rule, the priests were the natural leaders of the people. Various members of the Herodian family governed parts of the country at different times, but they were seldom spokesmen of the people, and they do not seem to have had much moral authority. The priests, on the other hand, were seen as God's appointed ministers, the intermediaries between him and his people.

The priests not only served in the Temple in connection with sacrifices and other services, they were also responsible for seeing that the Jewish law was kept. Their duties included general supervision of the people, the trial of cases of litigation and the punishment of those condemned for breaking the law.

In practice, the High Priest and his council had very extensive authority, for the Roman Prefect lived not in Jerusalem but in Caesarea on the coast, coming to stay in Jerusalem only during the holy days when the city was choked with people and the chances of riots were high. Otherwise, the priests were in charge of both religious and civil law. They could not execute people (only the Roman rulers could do this) but they could arrest, interrogate and flog offenders.

At the head of the priesthood was the High Priest. By tradition he was chief spokesman for God among the people, especially since there was no longer a descendant of David on the throne. In first century Palestine the High Priest was appointed either directly by Rome or by one of the Herodians, to whom Rome sometimes delegated the authority. There were a few aristocratic families among the priesthood (though we do not know how many), and the High Priest was always chosen from among them. The other priests from these families were called collectively 'the chief priests', and the High Priest generally used these men as advisors. He could also call on other powerful and wealthy men (called 'the elders' in the Gospels) for advice. When formally convened, these advisors became 'the

CAIAPHAS
Jerusalem under Roman domination was a turbulent city, susceptible to anti-Roman riots and periodic outbreaks of religious fervour. It was the responsibility of the High Priest to maintain order and Caiaphas successfully did so for eighteen years—longer than any other High Priest. He was shrewd, tough and decisive.

Sanhedrin', the official Jewish court.

Not all the chief priests were worthy of the power they held and many were involved in political scheming. The High Priest, however, had a very difficult task. He had to mediate between Rome and an often rebellious population, and by necessity he had to be a man of compromise. If he resisted Rome too much, revolution would break out and many people would die. On the other hand, if he did not resist enough, he was resented by his own people. The mass of the population probably harboured at least some hostility towards the priestly aristocracy. Yet the priests belonged to the family of Aaron, which God had set apart for his worship. Since they had been chosen by God, they retained authority even though some of them were corrupt.

Annas was appointed High Priest by Quirinius in the year AD6 or 7 and served until AD15. According to Josephus, he had five sons who were High Priests (Antiquities 20:197—198), and according to the New Testament he was the father-in-law of another, Caiaphas (John 18:13).

According to Luke 3:2, Jesus began his ministry when Annas and Caiaphas were High Priests: later Peter and John were brought before Annas 'the High

Priest' and Caiaphas, as well as the other chief priests (Acts 4:6). According to John 18:12—14, Jesus, when arrested, was taken first to Annas, who interrogated him and had him bound, and then sent him to Caiaphas. All these passages make Annas seem to be the real authority, though we know that Caiaphas was actually High Priest during and immediately after Jesus's public ministry. The evidence that Annas continued to be influential after he had been deposed is only found in the New Testament and is not confirmed by Josephus.

Caiaphas Joseph Caiaphas was High Priest from about AD 18 to 36, managing to retain the office longer than anyone else during the hundred years of direct or indirect Roman rule. The New Testament shows Annas as exercising a great deal of influence while Caiaphas was High Priest, which may be true. It would appear, though, that Caiaphas was himself a man of considerable foresight and ability.

It was Caiaphas and his advisors who decided that Jesus should be arrested (though not in view of a crowd, since a riot might break out—Matthew 26:5), it was in Caiaphas's house that Jesus was tried (Matthew 26:57; John 18:24, 28), and it was on Caiaphas's instructions that Jesus was led to Pilate. Matthew 27:1 mentions 'all the chief priests and elders', but Caiaphas's word would have been decisive.

In the Gospel of John, Caiaphas explains his motive for having Jesus executed: 'It is expedient for you that one man should die for the people, and that the whole nation should not perish' (John 11:50). John believed this referred to Jesus's death as a spiritual act of atonement, but it is the language of political necessity under Roman rule. Jesus preached that a new 'kingdom' was imminent, and his words might easily incite a crowd to riot, leading to direct military intervention. It was much better to kill the charismatic prophet than to run the risk that he would stir up the crowd. This is the sort of decision that would be made by a man shrewd enough to serve for so many years under Roman domination.

Rulers of the State

The Herods were rulers of all or part of Palestine during the years 37 BC—AD 66. When Jesus was born, Herod, called 'the Great' because of his exploits and the scale of his building programme, was king over all of Palestine, though ultimately he was answerable to Rome. Jesus grew up and carried out most of his ministry in Galilee, which was governed by one of Herod's sons, Antipas. During the growth and development of the early church parts of Palestine were governed by other descendants of Herod, Agrippa I and Agrippa II. All, like Herod himself, were puppets who maintained their office at Rome's pleasure.

Herod the Great was King of Judea at the time of Jesus's birth. He was only half Jewish. His father came from Idumea, just south of Judea. When the Romans conquered Palestine in 63 BC, they restored the ruling family, the Hasmoneans, to the throne. However, they divided the kingdom and gave administrative and military control to Herod's father, Antipater. Antipater appointed his son Herod Governor of Galilee. In a series of Roman civil wars and Hasmonean intrigues, Herod skilfully backed the winning side and was eventually appointed King of Judea by the Romans. They considered he was strong enough to control the most unruly part of their empire, a part which they had conquered but not occupied or administered.

Herod combined extraordinary vigour with personal bravery, tactical skill, ruthlessness, and administrative gifts. By the year 25 BC he had won for himself a sizeable kingdom, covering Palestine and some of the area east of it. The Romans continued to trust him and he continued to back the winning side in the various civil wars.

However, signs of the paranoia which became a prominent feature of his later life, began to emerge. He had always feared the Hasmoneans, whose throne he had usurped. He knew that they had the support of many of the Jewish people, and although he had married a

Hasmonean princess, he knew that marriage into the family was not enough to secure him the loyalty of Jewish Palestine. He even suspected his wife, Mariamne, of plotting against him and had her killed. Herod's mental stability seems to have declined from this point on.

In spite of this, he remained a strong and successful ruler. He launched one of the greatest building programmes ever undertaken by a minor king. He had the Temple in Jerusalem built on a scale never known before and had other large buildings, including several impregnable fortresses, constructed.

As he grew older, he became more and more suspicious and eventually accused even his own sons of plotting against him. Three were executed, two in 7 or 6 BC, the third in 4 BC.

It was during the last period of Herod's life that Jesus was born and Herod's actions recorded in the Bible match other accounts of his behaviour at this time. According to Matthew 2:1—12 wise men came from the east, seeking the coming king. Herod, learning of a 'king' to be born, ordered the wise men to report his whereabouts. They were warned in a dream not to do so and they returned to the East. Herod then ordered a slaughter of all the male children in Bethlehem and the surrounding area who were two years old or younger (2:16—18). Joseph, however, had been forewarned by an angel, and had taken Mary and the infant Jesus to Egypt (2:13—15).

Herod died in great physical agony in 4 BC, which was probably the year of Jesus's birth. He was succeeded in Judea by Archelaus and in Galilee, where Jesus grew up, by Antipas.

Herod Antipas was a son of Herod the Great and inherited from him a quarter of his kingdom, receiving the title 'tetrarch', 'ruler of a quarter'. His lands included Galilee and some of the territory east of Samaria and Judea. He ruled Galilee from 4 BC to AD 39, during which time Jesus grew to maturity and was executed. He is referred to in Mark 6:14 as 'King Herod' and in Matthew 14:1 and Luke 9:7 as 'Herod the Tetrarch'.

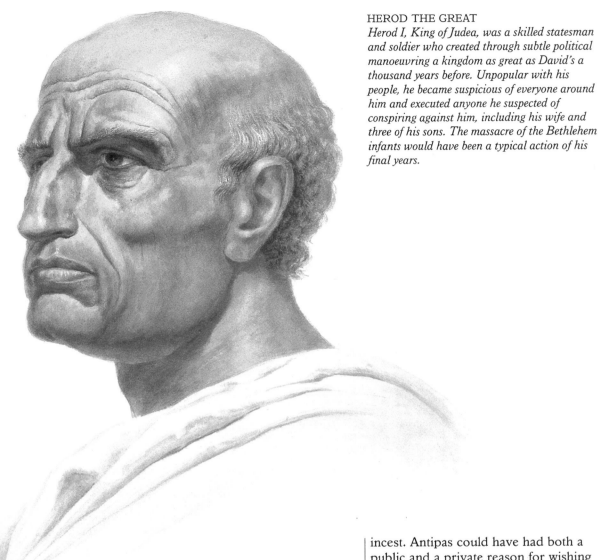

Antipas's reign was on the whole peaceful, though during its last decade its tranquillity was disturbed when he became infatuated with Herodias, whom he met on a trip to Rome. Both were already married and were also related to each other (see *Herodias*). Antipas and Herodias resolved to marry despite these obstacles.

Antipas's chief contribution to biblical history was that he executed John the Baptist. According to Josephus (Antiquities 18:116—119), this was because he feared that John's preaching would lead to uprisings. The gospels have a more salacious story: John had objected to Antipas's marriage to

Herodias. Antipas feared John's power with the people, and so could do nothing to harm him. He was finally forced to kill him, however, when he made a promise to Herodias's daughter, Salome, that he would give her anything she wished. At Herodias's urging, Salome requested 'the head of John the Baptist on a platter', and the Tetrarch ordered that it be done (Mark 6:14—29).

The story in the New Testament contains at least one error: it calls Herodias the wife of Antipas's brother Philip (Mark 6:17). She was actually the wife of Antipas's half-brother Herod II. It was Salome who was married to Philip. The story itself is not impossible, and it shows knowledge of Antipas's weakness. It is also quite possible that John the Baptist had denounced him for

incest. Antipas could have had both a public and a private reason for wishing the Baptist's death.

In AD36 the father of Antipas's first wife invaded Antipas's kingdom to avenge his daughter's honour and defeated his army. Antipas lost face, not territory and his ruin was not completed until Herodias persuaded him to go to Rome to ask for a higher title than 'tetrarch'. Instead of receiving the hoped for title of king, he was banished to France, where Herodias joined him. Antipas died in exile.

Herod Archelaus was one of Herod the Great's sons, and one who was fortunate enough not to be suspected of treason against his father. When Herod died in 4BC there was much confusion about the succession. He had left two wills; and, besides, Rome had the power to honour them or not. The emperor

Augustus decided to divide the kingdom into two halves. Archelaus received Judea, Idumea and Samaria, and the title 'ethnarch', 'ruler of the nation'. The second half was itself divided into halves, one going to Philip and one to Antipas.

Archelaus's career as ethnarch was not a success. Delegations of both Jews and Samaritans accused him of brutality and maladministration, and Augustus banished him to France in AD6, where he died. His territory was then directly administered by Rome, by an official called first a Prefect, later a Procurator.

Archelaus is mentioned once in the New Testament. When Joseph, Mary and the infant Jesus returned to Palestine, after the flight to Egypt to avoid Herod, Joseph was warned in a dream to beware also of Archelaus (Matthew 2:22), and the family moved on to Nazareth in Galilee.

Herod Philip After the death of Herod the Great, one quarter of his kingdom was given to Philip, one of Herod's surviving sons. He is named in the New Testament, incorrectly, as having been married to Herodias. In fact he married her daughter, Salome (see *Antipas*).

Philip died without children in AD 34. His territory was first attached to Syria, and then given to his half-nephew Agrippa I in AD 37.

Herodias was the daughter of Aristobulus, the half-brother of Herod II and Antipas. In spite of her relationship to them, she married first Herod II and later Antipas—both her half-uncles. According to the Gospels she was instrumental in causing the death of John the Baptist: she urged her daughter Salome to ask for his head on a platter as a gift from Antipas.

The marriage of Antipas and Herodias led to difficulties. Firstly, the father of Antipas's first wife invaded his kingdom and defeated his army. Secondly, Herodias persuaded Antipas to go to Rome to ask for a higher title than 'Tetrarch'. Instead of granting his request, the Emperor Caligula banished Antipas to France and gave his territory to Agrippa I. Herodias chose, however, to follow Antipas into exile,

HERODIAS
Herodias, the wife of Herod Antipas, was an ambitious intriguer who was indirectly responsible for the execution of John the Baptist. Later, her husband lost his throne as a result of her scheming. Herodias herself was given the chance of a life in Rome but chose to follow Antipas into exile in France.

and she lived out her days with him.

Herodias was ambitious, lustful and unscrupulous—but also proud. Further, she may truly have loved Antipas. At any rate, having caused his ruin, she decided to stay with him.

Salome was the daughter of Herodias (by her first husband Herod II) and the wife of her own half-uncle, (Herod) Philip. While John the Baptist was in prison, Salome danced for Antipas (her mother's second husband). Inflamed, he offered to give her anything she asked. John the Baptist had denounced Herodias's marriage to Antipas and Herodias now urged her daughter to ask for his death. Salome asked for and received John's head. Of her further life nothing is known.

Pontius Pilate was the Roman Prefect of Judea from AD 26 to 36, and the man who ordered that Jesus be crucified.

Pilate is barely mentioned in Roman sources, but he is described extensively by Philo and Josephus, his Jewish contemporaries. Josephus tells several stories which represent him as callously trampling on Jewish sensibilities. One is that he used funds from the Temple treasury for the construction of an aqueduct. When a crowd of Jews protested, he had his soldiers silence them with bludgeons (War 2:175—177). On another occasion he apparently ordered his troops to bring Roman standards with the image of the Emperor on them into Jerusalem. According to Jewish law it was an offence to make a 'graven image' of anything. The Jews considered the soldiers were breaking the law and made a large but peaceful demonstration which finally forced Pilate to remove the standards (War 2:169—174).

Philo describes him as 'unbending and recklessly hard'; in his administration there were 'corruptibility, violence, robberies, ill-treatment of the people, grievances, continuous executions without even the form of a trial, endless and intolerable cruelties' (Legation to Caius 38).

Since he served as Prefect for ten years, he was evidently not completely without administrative ability. Yet many of these charges must be true. After a massacre of Samaritans, Vitellius, the Roman legate in Syria, dismissed Pilate and sent him to Rome to answer for his conduct. There is no information about what happened to him after this.

The Gospels portray Pilate as a man of good intention, but weak and easily cowed. According to Matthew, Pilate wanted to release Jesus and was even urged by his wife to do so. Because of pressure from the chief priests and elders, however, he resorted to a stratagem. At Passover he had the custom of releasing a prisoner chosen by the crowds, and he offered them the choice of Jesus or an insurgent, Barabbas. The crowd, urged by the chief priests, cried out for Barabbas to be released. Pilate reasoned with them, asking, 'what evil has he done?', but

PONTIUS PILATE
Pontius Pilate was the Roman Prefect who governed Judea from AD 26 to 36. It was on his orders that Jesus was crucified. His rule was so callous, bloody and brutal that he was eventually dismissed and recalled to Rome in disgrace.

they were insistent. Finally he washed his hands, saying that he was innocent of Jesus's blood. The crowd cried, 'His blood be on us and on our children'. Pilate released Barabbas, had Jesus scourged, and then ordered him crucified (Matthew 27:11—26).

The Gospel of John brings out this aspect of his character more strongly. Pilate tried to have a philosophical discussion with Jesus, asking him 'What is truth?', and plainly told the crowd 'I find no crime in him'. He repeated this after the crowd had chosen Barabbas, but this time they cried 'Crucify him'. A third time he attempted to release Jesus, but the crowd warned 'If you release this man, you are not Caesar's friend; every one who makes himself a king sets himself against Caesar'. These words finally forced him to order crucifixion (John 18:29—19:16).

The early Christians were eager to claim that nothing about their movement was hostile to Rome, that Roman officials had always realized this to be the case, and that Jesus (as well as his subsequent followers) was punished and executed only because of the malice of the Jewish leadership.

For this reason the Gospels make a point of showing Pilate as favouring Jesus's release. However, their description does not match the portrayal of Pilate offered by Josephus and Philo, as a man who was callous, bloody and brutal. It is doubtful that Pilate actually had the custom of releasing anyone demanded by the crowd and he probably did not require much urging to have the trouble-maker from Galilee executed. The general picture in all the Gospels, however, according to which it was the chief priests who most wanted Jesus to be killed, is probably accurate. They later persecuted the Christian movement, and a subsequent High Priest, Ananus, had James the brother of Jesus executed (AD 62) without Roman permission—for which he was deposed.

Augustus Caesar Augustus was supreme head of the Roman Empire when Jesus was born (Luke 2:1). Originally named Gaius Octavius, he lived from 63 BC to AD 14 and was the chief architect of the Roman Empire.

In the political and military scrambling that followed Julius Caesar's death, Octavian gradually established himself in complete control. In 27 BC the Roman Senate conferred on him the title 'Augustus' (Revered), and formally granted him vast powers. Though he possessed virtually absolute power, he did not abuse it, and he preserved the forms of the Roman Republic, avoiding the trappings of kingship and modestly taking the title 'princeps' (first citizen). He established the *pax Romana*, bringing at last peace and prosperity to a world which had been in constant war and tumult for over 200 years. He was popularly regarded as having performed superhuman accomplishments and after his death he was deified by the senate.

Tiberius Claudius Caesar Augustus is the emperor referred to in the gospels as 'Caesar'. He was the son of Livia, the wife of Augustus, and her first husband. Augustus adopted Tiberius as his heir. The Senate elected him princeps (first citizen) after Augustus's death in AD 14. He died in Capri, almost insane, in 37.

According to Luke 3:1 Jesus began his public life in the fifteenth year of Tiberius, that is, about the year AD 29. It was the image of Tiberius that was on the coin about which Jesus asked, 'Is it lawful to pay taxes to Caesar?' (Matthew 22:15—22; Mark 12:13—17; Luke 20:20—26). According to Luke 23:2 and John 19:12—15 Jesus was accused of making himself king and thus opposing Caesar.

Quirinius was a distinguished Roman who had been consul of Rome in 12 BC. In AD 6 he was appointed Legate of Syria, where he served for several years. He died in AD 21.

The Legate of Syria had general jurisdiction over Palestine and, according to Luke 2:1—2, a census was held during Quirinius's term of office. It required Joseph and Mary to go to Bethlehem to be enrolled for tax purposes. However, according to both Luke and Matthew, Herod the Great was king when Jesus was born; and since Herod died about ten years before Quirinius became legate, there is some confusion about the dates.

Luke seems to have confused them because of riots: when Herod died in 4 BC there were riots (as there often were after the death of a king). Ten years later Herod's son, Archelaus, was removed from his position as 'ethnarch' and ruler of Judea, and Judea was placed under direct Roman government. There were again riots and we know from historical records that Rome ordered a local census, as it often did when the government changed. This census was conducted under the direction of Quirinius, then legate in Syria. The uprisings and the census seem to have run together in popular re-telling, so that Luke, writing over 70 years later, put the census in the same year as the first period of riots, rather than the second.

The Acts of the Apostles

The Acts of the Apostles was written by the same person who wrote the Gospel according to Luke. Acts falls roughly into two halves: the first (Acts 1—12) deals principally with the Jerusalem church, with Peter at its head; the second part (13—28) with Paul's activities. Acts is the only source of information that exists on the early Jerusalem church and is thus invaluable. For Paul's mission, however, there is also the direct evidence of Paul's letters. Acts and these letters disagree on two or three major and several minor points. When compared with Paul's letters, it is clear that Acts must be used with care, but also that it is generally accurate with regard to people and places. In the following entries evidence from Paul's letters, where it exists, has been treated as the most reliable source but information from Acts has been freely used.

Theophilus is the only person to whom a book of what is now the New Testament was dedicated and both the Gospel of Luke and Acts were dedicated to him (Acts 1:1).

There is no information about who Theophilus was. The name means 'friend of God', and some have suggested that it refers not to an individual, but to 'all readers who wish to be friends of God'. The contents of Luke and Acts show that their author intended to present Christianity in a favourable light to a well-educated and prosperous middle class. It is Luke who again and again pointed out the social and economic standing of converts, supporters and benefactors of Christianity. Luke also especially emphasized the degree to which Jesus went to sinners and outcasts, but these stories seem to be addressed to more prosperous readers in order to inspire them to good deeds. It may be, therefore, that Theophilus was either an imaginary person who allowed Luke to write at the level he wanted or else a real man who belonged to the group whom Luke wished to address: well-intentioned, solid citizens, who were open to a nobler form of religion than any they knew.

Leaders of the early church

Barnabas was one of the earliest and most important converts to the Christian movement. Though he was from Cyprus (Acts 4:36) he was living in Jerusalem and was converted in the first months after the resurrection. Like many Greek-speaking Jews he had returned to Palestine, the homeland of his people and his faith. He appears to have been prosperous, since he sold a field and gave the money to the common fund of the Christian community. The early disciples practised a form of voluntary communism, and the apostles received money derived from selling houses and fields and distributed it to needy members (Acts 4:36—37).

Barnabas also distinguished himself by speaking in Paul's favour when Paul first met the Jerusalem apostles, who were naturally suspicious of the man who had been their persecutor (Acts 9:26—27).

In the early days of the movement, Barnabas went to Antioch, where he became the leader of the Christian community. This was then, and remained for some time to come, the principal church except for Jerusalem. It was also Paul's 'home base' (Acts 11:22; 13:1), and it was from there that Barnabas, Mark and Paul set out to preach in Cyprus (Acts 13:2—4). Acts

mentions Barnabas first of the three, and it is probable that he was considered the leader.

From Cyprus they went to the southern coast of Asia Minor, preaching in Perga, Antioch of Pisidia, Iconium, Lystra and Derbe. At Lystra, Paul healed a cripple, and this led to loud acclaim, as people cried, 'The gods have come down to us in the likeness of men!' The author of Acts explains that they called Barnabas Zeus and, because Paul was the chief spokesman, they called him Hermes, the messenger of the gods. Again, Barnabas appears to be the leader, since he was taken for Zeus, the chief of the Greek gods. Presumably he appeared striking and impressive.

Paul and Barnabas were, of course, distressed at being identified with pagan deities. They tore their clothes and preached about the One God. Jewish opponents then made trouble, and in the end Paul was stoned and left for dead (Acts 14:8—20). Paul recovered, however, and he and Barnabas soon returned to Antioch.

Acts does not relate any further missionary trips shared by Barnabas and Paul, but possibly they worked together in Greece. Paul referred to Barnabas when he defended himself against the charge that since he supported himself financially he was only a second-rate apostle. Replying that he had the right to be supported by the church but chose not to claim it, he asked, 'Is it only Barnabas and I who have no right to refrain from working for a living?' (1 Corinthians 9:6).

There are two very different accounts of the next major events of Barnabas's life. According to Acts, disciples from Judea came to Antioch and insisted that Gentile Christians should be circumcised. This led to a conference in Jerusalem which Barnabas and Paul attended as the chief representatives of Antioch. The subject was Gentile converts and whether or not they should be obliged to keep the Jewish law. James the brother of Jesus proposed the solution: Gentiles should abstain from food offered to idols, from blood, from what is strangled, and from sexual immorality; that is, they should keep some of the Jewish dietary laws,

avoid even the appearance of believing in idols, and follow Jewish sexual ethics, but need not accept circumcision. This agreement was to be circulated to all the churches.

When the two men returned to Antioch, Paul proposed another trip to Barnabas, but Barnabas insisted on taking Mark. Paul refused and the two quarrelled. Barnabas and Mark sailed alone to Cyprus—and the author of Acts drops Barnabas from the story (Acts 15).

The second version of events comes from Paul's letter to the Galatians. According to Galatians 2:1—13, it was Paul who insisted on the Jerusalem conference and he attended it with Titus. He does not mention Barnabas. Paul wrote that the conference ended with an agreement, but not one about food laws: James and Peter agreed that Paul could continue his mission in his own way ('they added nothing to me'), and Paul promised in return to take up a collection for the support of the Jerusalem church from his Gentile churches in Asia Minor and Greece. The agreement that Gentiles did not need to observe the Jewish law ran into difficulty, however, when Peter came to Antioch. At first he ate with the Gentile Christians; but then James sent a message, and Peter withdrew, taking the other Jewish Christians with him. Paul adds, distressed, 'Even Barnabas was carried away by their hypocrisy' (Galatians 2:13).

Both versions, therefore, agree that Barnabas and Paul had a disagreement in Antioch, but give different reasons. According to Acts, it was a dispute about Mark, whom Paul regarded as not reliable enough. According to Paul, it was over whether Jewish and Gentile members of the movement should eat together—presumably at the Lord's Supper.

Of Barnabas, in either case, we hear no more. Acts 15:39 reports that he sailed to Cyprus, and as Paul referred to him when writing to the Corinthians, he probably continued to be a missionary, but no further details are given. Nevertheless, it can be said that his contribution to the movement was immense: he was a major supporter of the apostles and their followers in

Philip the Evangelist In the earliest days of the Christian movement there was some conflict in Jerusalem between Greek-speaking and Aramaic-speaking Jews. The Greek-speakers complained that their widows were being left out when food was distributed (see *Barnabas*). The apostles responded by choosing seven Greek-speakers to organize the distribution. Two of these, Stephen and Philip, played important roles in the spread of the Christian message (Acts 6:1—6).

Philip was the first to evangelize Samaria, where he had considerable success, around 34—35, converting many people, including Simon Magus (Acts 8:4—13). He then returned to Jerusalem and was directed by the Spirit to walk towards Gaza on the coast. There he met an Ethiopian, a eunuch who was in charge of the treasury of Candace, queen of the Ethiopians. The eunuch was reading Isaiah, apparently in Greek, and had come to the passage 'He was led like a sheep to the slaughter . . .'(Isaiah 53:7—8). He asked Philip what it meant. Philip seized the opportunity to tell him about Jesus, saying that this was the person Isaiah had foretold. They walked on together and when they came to some water, the eunuch asked to be baptized. Philip then went on to Caesarea (Acts 8:26—40).

Apparently he continued his work there, for when Paul and his companions landed at Caesarea on their way to Jerusalem for the last time, they stayed with Philip and his four daughters, who were prophetesses.

Jerusalem; he was leader of the principal church outside Jerusalem; and he did substantial missionary work.

As is the case with many other figures in the New Testament, we know about Barnabas principally because he associated with Paul. The two sources for knowledge of the early movement—Acts and Paul's letters—are both dominated by Paul and his immediate colleagues. It is impossible to estimate the full contribution of other leaders of the early church but at least with Barnabas we know something of his actions between about AD 32 and 52.

BARNABAS
Barnabas was a Greek-speaking Jew from Cyprus, living in Jerusalem at the time of Jesus's death and resurrection. He became one of the earliest converts to Christianity and one of the first to accept Paul as a genuine follower of Jesus. He led the Christian community in Antioch and travelled with Paul on his first missionary journey—to Barnabas's home country, Cyprus.

James, the brother of Jesus, is one of the most interesting and also most puzzling leaders of the early Christian movement. He and other brothers of Jesus are mentioned in Mark 6:3 ('Isn't this Mary's son and the brother of James, Joses, Judas and Simon?') and Paul refers to the fact that the 'other apostles and the Lord's brothers and Cephas' travelled with their wives (1 Corinthians 9:5). We therefore know that more than one of Jesus's brothers served in the early Christian movement. Yet they do not seem to have been disciples during Jesus's lifetime.

JAMES, THE BROTHER OF JESUS
After the resurrection, James became one of the principal leaders of the church in Jerusalem. His good sense, diplomacy and firmness kept the early Christians together in a period when there was no established dogma and conflicts arose about the best way to spread the new beliefs.

Paul's list of people to whom Jesus appeared after his resurrection probably explains this puzzle. He wrote that one appearance was to James alone (1 Corinthians 15:7). This James was probably Jesus's brother, since Paul had already mentioned the appearance to the Twelve, including the other James, the son of Zebedee (1 Corinthians 15:5). It was presumably this experience which convinced James that his brother was the Messiah of Israel and which turned him from a sceptic into a believer.

Whatever the reason for his change of heart, James soon took a substantial and in some ways the leading role in the early church. Paul recounts that three years after his own conversion he went to Jerusalem to meet Peter and saw 'none of the other apostles except James, the Lord's brother' (Galatians 1:19). On a subsequent trip he met James, Peter and John. On this occasion they agreed that Paul should continue to admit Gentiles to the movement without circumcising them (Galatians 2:6—10). (See *Barnabas*.) This did not however, immediately settle all the questions relating to Gentiles and James continued to be involved in the discussion. In Antioch, following the agreement with Paul, Peter ate with non-circumcised Gentile converts but withdrew when a message came from James (Galatians 2:11—14). From this it seems that although James was willing to recognize Gentiles as members of the church he did not want the Jerusalem apostles to associate too closely with them. He may have feared that if they did so, Jews would reject their message since it conflicted with the strict observance of the law.

There is little in Acts to help fill in the picture of James and his rise to leadership in Jerusalem. We first meet him in Acts 12:17. Herod Agrippa I had executed James the son of Zebedee and arrested Peter. Peter was miraculously released and went to the house of John Mark's mother. There he told the servant girl, Rhoda, to 'tell James and the brothers' that he had been freed (Acts 12:1—17). Acts does not give James a speaking part until the conference with Paul about the admission of Gentiles is reported (Acts

15:13—29). He is mentioned one last time, as leading the elders who received Paul when he made his last trip to Jerusalem (Acts 21:18).

The Jewish historian Josephus provides information about his fate. When there was no Roman Procurator in Palestine, the High Priest, Ananus, convened the Sanhedrin (the Jewish governing body) and had James executed. This seems to show that the chief priests remained hostile to the Christian movement which at this time received some protection from Rome.

Stephen was a Greek-speaking Jew, resident in Jerusalem, who was an early convert to the Christian movement. He became the first Christian martyr. Along with Philip and others, he was appointed to a position of leadership and he attracted attention by the 'signs and wonders' he performed. He was opposed by the Synagogue of Freedmen. This was composed of Greek-speaking Jews from various parts of the Mediterranean who had moved to Jerusalem, perhaps after having been freed from slavery (Acts 6:1—10).

They complained to some of the elders about Stephen and Stephen was accused before the Sanhedrin of saying that Jesus would return and 'destroy this place' (the Temple) and 'change the customs' decreed by Moses. Acts says that these charges were made by false witnesses, but the charge about predicting the destruction of the Temple may well have been true. Jesus had predicted that it would be destroyed (e.g. Mark 13:2) and in Acts Stephen made a speech against the worship carried out in the Temple. Near the end of the speech, he said, 'The Most High does not live in houses made by men' (Acts 7:48). Finally he accused the leaders of the Sanhedrin of persecuting the prophets and the members themselves of murdering the Righteous One (Acts 7:51—53).

Stephen's words were infuriating and the members of the Sanhedrin dragged him outside and stoned him. The witnesses against Stephen laid their outer robes at the feet of Saul (later to be called Paul). Stephen died praying that they be forgiven (7:54—60).

STEPHEN
Stephen was a young assistant to the apostles who was selected to distribute gifts to the widows of Jerusalem. He was eager to spread the news of Jesus's resurrection and infuriated the elders of the Temple by predicting that it would be destroyed. When they condemned him to death by ritual stoning (the traditional punishment for blasphemy), he became the first Christian martyr.

John Mark There is a mixture of traditions about John Mark, but he remains rather a shadowy figure. He may have been one of the most important members of the early Christian movement—companion of Barnabas, Paul and Peter and possibly the author of the earliest Gospel.

He is first mentioned in Acts 12, where 'John who is called Mark' appears in a story about Peter. At the time of the first persecution of the Christian movement by a secular ruler, Agrippa I, James the son of Zebedee was executed and Peter was arrested. Peter, however, was miraculously released. He went to the house of Mary, the mother of John Mark. Since 'many' disciples were there, and since a servant (Rhoda) opened the door, we may assume that she was a woman of some wealth (Acts 12:12—13). Later, Mark accompanied Paul and Barnabas first to Antioch, then to Salamis, on the eastern side of Cyprus. He is described as their 'helper', so was probably a young man, not a full partner in the missionary work (Acts 13:5).

The missionaries crossed Cyprus to Paphos and from there sailed to Perga, on the southern coast of Asia Minor. There Mark, for reasons not given, left and returned to Jerusalem (Acts 13:13).

Paul soon returned to Jerusalem himself, and when he was ready to leave to revisit the cities where he had worked, he asked Barnabas to accompany him again. Barnabas suggested taking Mark, but Paul refused. It now becomes apparent that Mark's departure from Perga had been important for some reason, because the disagreement between Paul and Barnabas led to a break between the two leading missionaries outside Palestine. Paul returned to Asia Minor, but Barnabas and Mark went to Cyprus (Acts 15:36—41).

From the letters by or attributed to Paul, however, there is no hint that such dramatic events took place. In Philemon, Mark is mentioned as a 'fellow worker'. Colossians 4:10 mentions Mark as with Paul—and also says that he was Barnabas's cousin. In 2 Timothy 4:9—11, Paul asks Timothy to bring Mark, adding that 'he is useful in

JOHN MARK
John Mark may have been the young man described in the Gospel of Mark as a witness to Jesus's arrest. After the resurrection, the apostles met at his mother's house and he himself accompanied both Paul and Peter on missionary journeys. The Gospel which bears his name was the first to be written and may have been based on Peter's own recollections of the life of Jesus.

serving me'. It seems from these references that the breach between Paul and Mark was made up. If, as is possible, the two passages were written after Paul's death, they certainly show that Paul's followers regarded Paul and Mark as having been on good terms.

There is also a tradition which relates Mark closely with Peter. 1 Peter 5:13 calls Mark 'my son', and the close relationship to Peter was later to be strongly emphasized. In the fourth century the church statesman and historian Eusebius quoted Papias (who wrote about the year 140), as saying that Mark became Peter's interpreter and 'wrote accurately, though not in order, all that he remembered of the things said and done by the Lord'. Papias continues, 'he had neither heard the Lord nor been one of his followers, but ...he had followed Peter...' Papias's comment is usually taken to refer to the Gospel according to Mark, or to an early version of it.

Those who believe that Mark's Gospel was based on Peter's preaching point out that it contains details which could come only from an eye-witness. Thus in Mark 1:43 Jesus is said to have 'expressed violent displeasure', and in 3:5 to have 'looked around with anger'. Others believe that these expressions of emotion were added to make the narrative more colourful. A more convincing argument is the case of the nameless young man who fled naked when the soldiers who arrested Jesus attempted to seize him (Mark 14:51). It is tempting to see here a private reminiscence on the part of one particular young man—perhaps the one who wrote the Gospel.

Most modern scholars, however, do not think that the Gospel of Mark as we now have it is a direct report of Peter's preaching, although it may well contain some of Peter's recollections and eye-witness accounts. It is now impossible to assess the role of John Mark in this process, but there is no reason completely to exclude him.

Matthias Jesus was known to have had twelve special disciples during his ministry. He was betrayed by one, Judas, who then himself died, possibly

CORNELIUS
Cornelius was the first non-Jew to be converted to Christianity. For both Peter, who baptized him, and Cornelius himself, this must have been a decisive step, for Cornelius was a Roman soldier, a potentially dangerous man to welcome into the movement. The Roman empire, however, allowed freedom of religion as long as the state was not threatened and in the early years of the church apparently gave Christianity some protection.

by his own hand. According to Acts, after Jesus's resurrection the disciples decided to choose another man to make up the number twelve. They determined that the man must have been a follower 'beginning from the baptism of John until the day when he (Jesus) was taken up'. They found two candidates, Joseph Barsabbas and Matthias. After prayer, lots were cast, and the lot fell to Matthias, who was then considered as the twelfth apostle (Acts 1:20—26). Nothing else is known.

Early converts

Dorcas was the Greek name of a disciple in Joppa, called in Aramaic 'Tabitha'. Both words mean 'gazelle'. She was known for her good deeds, especially in helping the poor. When she fell ill and died, the other disciples sent to Lydda, which was nearby, and asked Peter to come at once. He found her being mourned by those whom she had helped, including widows wearing the clothes she had made for them.

Peter prayed and then commanded her to rise. She did so and Peter presented her to the disciples, alive and well. The event caused a sensation and led to further conversions (Acts 9:36—43).

Mary the mother of John Mark Mary had a house in Jerusalem which was large enough to serve as a meeting place for many of the disciples, and in which she had servants (see *Rhoda*). When Peter was miraculously freed from prison he went there and sent word to James and others that he was free (Acts 12:12—17).

Rhoda was a servant in the house of Mary the mother of John Mark. In about the year 41, King Agrippa I had James the brother of John executed. He then arrested Peter, whose life was evidently also in danger. An angel appeared to Peter and released him from prison and he hurried to John Mark's mother's house. When he knocked at the door, it was Rhoda who answered and recognized Peter's voice. She was overjoyed and ran to tell the others, in her haste leaving the door locked. At first no-one believed her but finally the door was opened and Peter was admitted.

This is the only mention of Rhoda but it is interesting because it gives an indication of Mark's social standing.

Cornelius The story of Cornelius occupies the whole of Acts 10. The author of Acts makes him the test case and the first major instance of a Gentile who converted to the Christian movement. Since this involved, on the part of the early church, the decision not to make Gentile converts follow all Jewish laws, the story of Cornelius is of major significance.

Cornelius was a Roman centurion, officer of 'a hundred'. He was stationed on the coast, in Caesarea. An angel appeared to him with a specific message: send men to Joppa and return with Peter (who was staying there with Simon the tanner). Meanwhile, in Joppa, Peter had had a vision of his own. While praying on the roof, he had seen a vision in which a large sheet was let down from heaven, containing all

kinds of four-footed animals, as well as birds and even reptiles. A voice commanded Peter to kill and eat. Peter is depicted in this story (as in some others) as being a bit obtuse. The vision had to be repeated twice more to make him see the point and even then it was not entirely clear: when the messengers from Cornelius arrived, he was still wondering.

Peter accompanied the soldiers to Caesarea and there met Cornelius, who described his vision. Peter then fully grasped the issue and spoke clearly, 'God does not show favouritism, but accepts people from every nation who fear him and do what is right'.

The vision had meant that Jewish food laws need not be kept by Gentile converts to the Christian movement. The question whether Jewish converts should still observe them would later lead to a major dispute between Paul and the Jerusalem apostles. The immediate consequence of Peter's vision, however, was that he could accept a Gentile who worshipped the one God and believed in Jesus without any further requirements such as circumcision, dietary restrictions, and sabbath observance.

While Peter was talking, the Gentiles (Cornelius and his household) began to speak in tongues, and Peter ordered that they be baptized. Thus Cornelius, who had already 'feared God'—that is, had worshipped the one God of Israel—became the first Gentile fully to convert to Christianity.

Simon the tanner owned a house in Joppa, on the Mediterranean coast. He was probably an early convert and Peter stayed with him for 'many days'. It was at Simon's house that Peter saw the vision of all kinds of food let down on a sheet and was told 'kill and eat', and it was at Simon's house that the messengers from the Roman Cornelius found Peter (Acts 9:43; 10:6,17—32).

It may not be accidental that the tanner plays an indirect role in the admission of Gentiles to the Christian movement. Tanning was an unsavoury occupation, and tanners were considered outside the bounds of normal society. The fact that Peter

stayed there shows that he was willing to go to outsiders. The tanner's house was an appropriate place for Peter to see the vision which made all foods clean and which thus made it easier for other outsiders, the Gentiles, to join the Christian movement.

Ananias and **Sapphira** figure in one of the most unpleasant stories in the New Testament. The earliest Christian congregation in Jerusalem held their goods in common (Acts 4:32). A married couple, Ananias and Sapphira, sold some property but put only part of the proceeds at the apostles' disposal. Peter rebuked Ananias, pointing out that he could have kept the property or, having sold it, could have disposed of the money in some other way: communal ownership was not compulsory. But Ananias, Peter continued, had lied to God. Ananias fell to the floor dead.

Sapphira soon came in, not having heard about the fate of her husband, and a similar scene was played out. She directly lied about the amount of money realized by the sale of the property and she, too, fell at Peter's feet and died (Acts 5:1—11).

Simon Magus Simon was a Magus in Samaria who was attracted to the Christian movement by the signs and wonders performed by Philip. 'Magi' were astrologers and sorcerers, originally Zoroastrians from Persia but including others who learned their arts. The three wise men from the East who, according to Matthew 2 visited the infant Jesus, were Magi. Simon was already known for his sorcery, so that some thought he was 'the divine power known as the Great Power'; but he wished to learn still further miracles.

When Peter and John came from Jerusalem to reinforce Philip's message in Samaria, Simon came to them to be baptized. He asked the apostles to give to him the power to pass on the holy spirit and he offered them money. Peter rebuked him, saying, 'May your money perish with you', and urging repentance. Simon then asked Peter to pray for him 'so that nothing you have said may happen to me'. (Acts 8:9—24).

SIMON MAGUS
Astrologers and sorcerers were common in the first-century, many claiming supernatural powers from the ancient Persian traditions. Simon was already a successful and famous magus but, recognizing that the Christians had discovered a far greater power than his own, he tried to buy the secret of the Holy Spirit.

No more is learned from the New Testament about Simon Magus, but the later Church credited him with starting one of the Gnostic heresies which plagued second-century Christianity.

Ananias of Damascus was an early member of the Christian movement and the man who baptized Paul. After the vision which led to Paul's conversion, he was for some time without his sight and was taken to Damascus where Ananias lived. The Lord appeared in a dream to Ananias and told him to go to 'the street called Straight' and ask there for the house of Judas, where he would find Paul. At first Ananias did not wish to obey, recalling how Paul had persecuted the church. He was told, however, that Paul had been chosen to preach the Gospel. Everything happened as the dream foretold. Ananias went to the house of Judas, laid his hands on Paul and told him that he was acting on the Lord's instructions and that Paul would regain his sight. 'Something like scales' immediately fell from Paul's eyes and he was baptized (Acts 9:10—18).

Agabus was a prophet in the early Jerusalem church who made two dramatic predictions. Shortly after Paul's conversion, while Paul and Barnabas were working in Antioch, Agabus arrived from Jerusalem and predicted that there would be a famine over the entire Roman world. This led the disciples in Antioch to send aid to Jerusalem (Acts 11:27—30). There was in fact a famine in Judea in the year 46—47 and this is probably the one to which the story refers.

Agabus's second prophecy came near the end of Paul's career. Paul had finished his work in Asia Minor and Greece and was returning to Jerusalem with the money collected from the Gentile churches for the Christians in Jerusalem. Agabus came from Jerusalem to meet him in Caesarea. When they met, Agabus took off Paul's belt and tied his own hands and feet, and said that the belt's owner would be tied in the same way (Acts 21:10—11). Paul was arrested shortly afterwards and never regained his freedom.

Rulers and priests

Claudius succeeded Caligula as Roman emperor in AD 41 and ruled until 54. He is known in the New Testament chiefly for 'expelling' the Jews from Rome, an act which brought Prisca and Aquila to Corinth (Acts 18:2). The popular Roman biographer Suetonius wrote that 'he expelled from Rome the Jews, who were constantly rioting under the leadership of Chrestus' (Claudius 25:3). The most likely explanation of this statement is that there were disturbances in the Jewish community because of the preaching of Jesus as Christ, and that the Romans did not follow the internal squabbling of the Jewish community closely enough to know just what was going on. Claudius solved the problem by forcing many or most Jews to leave.

It is known that the decree did not directly expel the Jews, but rather forbade them from assembling. This meant that they could not worship and in effect forced them to leave Rome; so Suetonius and Acts could rightly refer to the action as 'expulsion'.

Gallio (Junius Gallio Annaeus) was a member of a distinguished and wealthy Roman family. His brother was Seneca, the Stoic philosopher and tutor of Nero.

An inscription shows that he was Proconsul of Achaia, the part of Greece which includes Athens and Corinth, in either the year AD 51—52 or 52—53. Paul was brought before Gallio in Corinth on the charge that he taught people to worship in a way that was 'contrary to the law', apparently the Jewish law. Gallio took this to be only an internal Jewish dispute and dismissed the case (Acts 18:12—17).

Gallio ended his life by suicide. He had participated in a plot against Nero which failed, and he was ordered to kill himself. This was considered less disgraceful than a public trial and execution. The same plot had earlier claimed the life of his brother Seneca as well, and in the same way.

Felix was Prefect of Judea from AD 52—60. By his brutality and maladministration he did much to speed the country to full revolt, which in fact broke out six years after his recall. His behaviour was so bad during his time in office that when a deputation of Jews complained about him to Rome, it took all the influence of his brother, one of the most powerful men in Rome, to prevent him from being banished from Rome as well recalled from Judea.

After Paul was arrested in Jerusalem and taken to Caesarea, it was Felix before whom he was tried. According to the account in Acts, Felix was very favourably disposed towards Paul, listening to him with interest, though perhaps only because he hoped for a bribe (Acts 23:24—24:27). The author of Acts, however, consistently declines to criticize Roman administrators and always represents them as friendly towards the Christian movement. The way Felix is described helps to show Rome as on Christianity's side and to attribute all difficulties to Jewish malice. Whatever his attitude towards Paul, however, Felix did not dispose of the case, but left Paul in prison to be dealt with by his successor, Festus.

Drusilla was the third daughter of Agrippa I. She became the lover of Felix (the Roman Prefect who first tried Paul in Caesarea), and bore him a son (Josephus, Antiquities 20:142—144). Acts 24:24 refers to her as Felix's wife and mentions her as with him in Caesarea.

Festus Porcius Festus was Prefect (or Procurator; at about this time the title was changed) of Judea from AD 60—62.

When he assumed office, Paul was in prison having been left there by Felix, the retiring Prefect. Festus offered Paul the opportunity of being tried in Jerusalem, but Paul knew he would not get a fair trial there and instead appealed to his right as a Roman citizen to be tried before Caesar. This was granted by Festus (Acts 25:1—12).

Sergius Paulus was the Roman Proconsul at Paphos, on the island of Cyprus during Paul's first missionary journey, around the mid-forties. When Paul and Barnabas passed through, he asked them to come to him to explain their message. A sorcerer, Elymas, was present at their meeting and he opposed Paul. Paul quite literally sent him into a fog, and this display of power convinced Sergius Paulus, who became a believer himself (Acts 13:4—12).

Claudius Lysias was a 'Chiliarch', which means 'commander of a thousand'. He was in Jerusalem when Paul was arrested on suspicion of taking a Gentile into the inner courts of the Temple. The alleged act aroused great hostility and a few men formed a plot to assassinate Paul when he was taken for trial before the Sanhedrin. Paul's nephew, however, overheard the plot and reported it to Paul, who managed to pass the information to Claudius Lysias.

The commander's action was prompt. He ordered two centurions to prepare their troops and to escort Paul to Caesarea, where he could be tried before the Roman Procurator, Felix. In a letter he explained the situation, adding that he had ordered Paul's accusers also to go to Caesarea, to present their case. The prompt action was successful and Paul was safely escorted to Caesarea to await trial (Acts 23:12—35).

Publius was the chief official on Malta, although we are not told his precise title (Acts 28:7—8). He offered hospitality to Paul and his companions during their trip from Caesarea to Rome. They had been shipwrecked and the residents of Malta, especially Publius, were generous in their assistance.

Herod Agrippa I was a grandson of Herod the Great and is referred to simply as 'Herod' in Acts 12:1. Agrippa was born about 10 BC and spent many of his early years in Rome. After a not-very-successful sojourn in Galilee, as an administrator under Herod Antipas, he returned to Rome. There he succeeded in becoming friendly with Caligula, the Emperor Tiberius's heir apparent. When Caligula came to power (AD 37) he gave Agrippa the tetrarchy that had belonged to his uncle Philip. The Emperor also bestowed on Agrippa the title 'king'. Agrippa's arrival in Palestine as 'king', though over only a small and relatively poor part of the country, led to jealousy on the part of Antipas, his uncle and former employer. In the bickering which resulted, Caligula again befriended Agrippa. He banished Antipas to France (39) and bestowed Galilee on Agrippa (40).

In the next year the wily Agrippa, who was back in Rome, helped Claudius to gain power. As a result Judea and Samaria (which had been directly governed by Roman officials) were added to Agrippa's kingdom, and thus he reigned over virtually the entire area once ruled by Herod the Great. He enjoyed his eminence for only three years, dying in the year 44.

During his brief reign he committed one act which made an impression on the Christian movement: for unknown reasons, he executed James the brother of John. It is usually supposed that this took place in about the year 41, after Agrippa took power in Judea, since Acts 12 seems to imply that the events took place in Jerusalem. It is possible, however, that James had fallen foul of Agrippa in Galilee, since he plays no role in descriptions of the early church.

Herod Agrippa II, the son of Agrippa I, is referred to as 'Agrippa the king' in Acts 25:13. He was a minor when his father died, and so could not succeed to the throne. Judea was returned to direct Roman administration. During the next few years, however, Agrippa II was given small parts of Syria. His kingdom was later enlarged, so that he ruled over part of Galilee, part of the country east of Galilee, and a small area around Abila in Judea. He was also given the right to appoint the High Priest.

According to Acts, Agrippa and his sister Bernice (with whom he seems to have had an incestuous relationship) came to Caesarea while Paul was in prison there, and Paul was brought before him. Paul asked, 'King Agrippa, do you believe the prophets? I know that you believe', and Agrippa replied, 'In a short time you think to make me a Christian!' Agrippa agreed with Festus that Paul could have been set free had he not appealed to Caesar (Acts 25:13–26:32).

The Jewish revolt against Rome broke out a few years later, and Agrippa sided with Rome. Little is known of the king's final years. The last of the Herodian dynasty, he died around AD 100.

Ananias was High Priest from about AD 48–58. When Paul was arrested on the charge of bringing a Gentile into the Temple (a capital offence), he was first brought before the Sanhedrin, with Ananias at its head. Paul said that he had 'lived before God in all good conscience up to this day', and at once Ananias ordered him struck. Paul reviled him, but apologized when he was told that he was speaking against the High Priest (Acts 23:1–5). Apparently Ananias was not wearing his robe and so Paul had not recognized him. Ananias subsequently came to Caesarea to accuse Paul before the Procurator Felix (Acts 24:1).

According to Josephus, Ananias was a man of great wealth, some of it acquired dishonestly. His servants, for example, stole for his benefit the tithes of grain which were intended for the ordinary priests. Since the devout priests, following the biblical law, would not eat ordinary food, some starved to death (Josephus, Antiquities 20:181; 20:205–210). He was also friendly with the Roman Procurator, Albinus, who accepted bribes and governed badly. Finally Albinus was recalled and Ananias was deposed. Despite this he continued to exercise influence, as was often the case with former High Priests, who even retained the title (Josephus, War 2:441).

When the Jewish revolt against Rome broke out in AD 66, Ananias hid. He knew that his support of the Roman occupation and his abuses of power made him a marked man. The revolutionaries, however, hunted him down, killed him, and then burned his house (War 2:441).

Gamaliel The Gamaliel mentioned in Acts is Gamaliel I, the grandson of the great leader of the Pharisees, Hillel, and probably leader of the Pharisaic party in his own day. The Pharisees were a small but influential party in Judaism. They were principally interpreters of the law, and they wished to modernize some aspects of Judaism. This they sought to accomplish through their theory of 'traditions' handed down by the elders, which supplemented the written law. One of the main traditions was belief in the resurrection.

The dominant party was the Sadducean, which was the party of the priestly aristocracy. The Sadducees rejected the idea of tradition in favour of keeping the written law only, and they also denied the resurrection.

After the destruction of the Temple in AD 70, the successors of the Pharisees, taking the title 'Rabbi', began a reformation of Judaism which finally became effective towards the end of the second century AD, and which has endured to the present day. Gamaliel I was, at the time of Jesus, a leading figure of this great movement.

When the chief priests and other members of the Sanhedrin interrogated the apostles, Peter offended them by saying, 'We must obey God rather than men', clearly implying that he and not the High Priest knew the will of God. Peter continued by accusing the Sanhedrin of executing Jesus. Many wanted to mete out the same punishment to Peter and the others, but Gamaliel spoke on their behalf, 'Keep away from these men and let them alone; for if this plan or this undertaking is of men, it will fail; but if it is of God, you will not be able to overthrow them. You might even be found opposing God!' His counsel prevailed, and the apostles were released after being flogged (Acts 5:17–42).

According to Acts 22:3, Paul stated that he was educated 'at the feet of Gamaliel'. It is possible that Luke attributes this statement to him in order to associate Paul positively with the most famous Pharisee of the day. When Paul writes in his letters about his achievements as a Pharisee he does not mention Gamaliel (Galatians 1:13–14; Philippians 3:4–6), and his early career as persecutor of the Christians does not fit well with Gamaliel's tolerance. Paul also claims to have been unknown by sight to the churches in Judea (Galatians 1:22); if he had studied under Gamaliel for a long time, this would not have been likely.

Paul and his Mission

Paul was a Jew from Tarsus, a city near the south-east corner of Asia Minor. The date of his birth is unknown, but he was probably born about the same time as Jesus. The years during which he accomplished deeds which would indelibly write his name in history were approximately AD 40—60. Most scholars put his death in Rome in 62 or 64.

Paul is known to us through two sources: letters which he himself dictated and the Acts of the Apostles. These agree on many points, but there are also substantial conflicts. According to Acts, for example, he travelled to Jerusalem five times. According to his own sworn testimony ('Before God, I do not lie!', Galatians 1:20) he had made the trip only two times when the letter was written. Shortly after writing Galatians he made a third trip to Jerusalem, taking money which he had collected for the aid of the Jerusalem church. It was on this third trip that he was arrested and eventually sent for trial to Rome. Scholars disagree about the relative merits of the two sources for such things as dates, but there is no doubt that the letters better capture the spirit and mind of the man—the flash and fire, the passion and vigour, the wit and charm, the fear and trembling—and this account will rely almost entirely on the letters.

The basic outline of his career is quite straightforward, although some of the details of places and dates are either uncertain or disputed. Paul's letters show him to be a man of solid middle-class upbringing. His Greek is clear and forceful, but not elegant; unlike his contemporary, Philo of Alexandria, he had not had a private tutor from Athens. He could speak Aramaic (or Hebrew, or both; Acts 21:40), and he may have known Latin, but his main language was one of the greatest international languages of all time: *koine* (common) Greek. According to Acts, he was a Roman citizen.

He had learned a trade, called 'tent making' in Acts 18:3, which perhaps included also leather-working or even sail-making. He boasted that, as a missionary, he supported himself by working with his own hands (1 Corinthians 4:12). This is revealing: the poor do not find working with their hands to be worthy of special mention. Paul had probably been trained for ownership or management. He knew how to use a secretary, and he dictated his letters. He also knew how to organize and plan. Most of the time he had more than one assistant (see *Timothy, Titus, Silas*); and he could send one here, another there, while himself going elsewhere, and rejoin them to assess the situation and make further plans. He was no materialist, and he often lived in poverty, but that was by choice (1 Corinthians 4:11). He knew how to be 'abased' and how to 'abound' (Philippians 4:11—12), and his commitment to causes often meant that materially he did not 'abound'.

Paul was at first a Pharisee and when he is first mentioned in Acts, was an active persecutor of the early Christian movement. In approximately the year 33, while he was on his way from Jerusalem to Damascus to organize punishment for Jewish members of the Christian movement, Christ appeared to him. In Acts Paul describes this revelation as a bright light which left him temporarily blinded (Acts 22:6—11), but in his letters, he says only that 'God revealed his Son to me' (Galatians 1:16). This experience turned him into an apostle for the very cause that he had persecuted. He felt himself not only called to serve Christ, but to accomplish a special task: the conversion of Gentiles.

For the rest of his life, he was to devote himself to this task. During the next 20 years he steadily worked his way west from Antioch, establishing churches all across Asia Minor, in Macedonia, and in Greece, especially in substantial cities. He visited Jerusalem twice for special reasons. His own view of his mission was that he was independent of the Jerusalem church, having been directly appointed 'apostle to the Gentiles' by God. He saw his task as being the establishment of churches in Asia Minor, Greece and Rome, and he was pressing steadily west. Acts has a different view: he was commissioned by the Jerusalem apostles to work in Asia Minor and Greece, but periodically he had to report back before making another missionary journey. The evidence from Paul's own letters does not reflect the idea of missionary journeys punctuated by return trips to Jerusalem.

Paul's two visits to Jerusalem were significant. The first time he wanted to meet the Jerusalem apostles and make sure that they were all preaching the same message. He met Cephas (Peter), but he 'saw none of the other apostles except James the Lord's brother' (Galatians 1:18—19). 'After fourteen years'—whether fourteen years after the first visit, or fourteen years after his call is uncertain—he went again, to fight out the principal theological issue of his career. He took Titus, a Gentile convert and valued assistant, who became the object of controversy (Galatians 2:1).

The situation was this: Paul, regarding Jesus as the Messiah, and having read the prophetic predictions that 'in the last days' Gentiles would join Israel (Isaiah 2:1—2), thought that it was time Gentiles joined the messianic movement. The Jerusalem apostles agreed, but there was an obvious question: did the Gentiles have to accept the Jewish law—represented by circumcision—or not?

Paul thought not: they could join the movement simply by professing faith in the Messiah (in Greek, the Christ) and by being baptized. That made them 'heirs of the promises to Abraham'

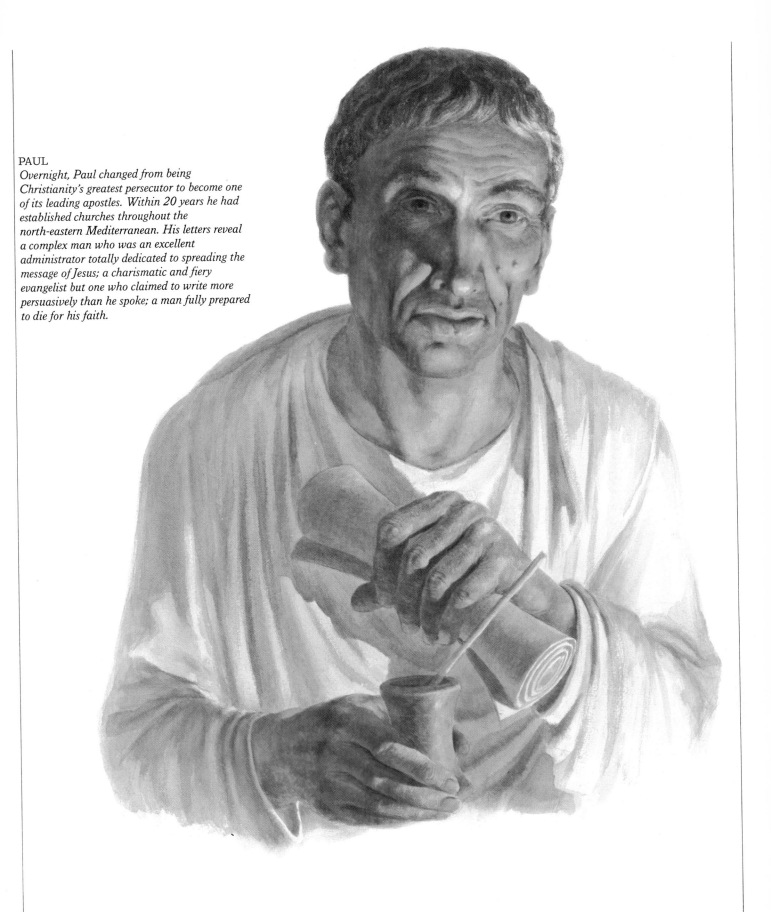

PAUL

Overnight, Paul changed from being Christianity's greatest persecutor to become one of its leading apostles. Within 20 years he had established churches throughout the north-eastern Mediterranean. His letters reveal a complex man who was an excellent administrator totally dedicated to spreading the message of Jesus; a charismatic and fiery evangelist but one who claimed to write more persuasively than he spoke; a man fully prepared to die for his faith.

(Galatians 3:15—18, 23—29). Some in Jerusalem—called by Paul 'false brethren' (Galatians 2:4)—thought that Gentile converts must accept the Jewish law, and they even attempted to force Titus to be circumcised (Galatians 2:3—4).

The Jerusalem 'pillars'—James, Peter and John—finally sided with Paul. They themselves would not convert Gentiles unless they accepted the law, but Paul could, and they would recognize his converts. But he was to take up a collection from his Gentile churches in order to show their solidarity with the Jerusalem church (Galatians 2:6—10).

Despite the agreement with Peter, James and John, some would not let the matter rest, and they attempted to convince the members of the churches founded in Galatia that they should be circumcised. Paul felt that if admission to the movement, and ultimately salvation, depended on accepting the Jewish law, 'Christ died in vain' (Galatians 2:21).

The conflict with 'false brethren' in Galatians led him to his most enduring theological position, the one which has proved to be Christianity's most potent argument: humans are righteous only by God's grace, not by 'works of law'.

After coming to the agreement with the Jerusalem leaders, Paul spent the rest of his active career on the collection, and he delivered it himself—though he was tempted to send it (Romans 15:25—29; 1 Corinthians 16:3—4). He knew that he faced danger in Jerusalem, but finally he put aside his fears and some time between 52 and 55 he carried out his last free act in order to show that the body of Christ was one, though its members were diverse (1 Corinthians 12:12) and he made his third and final trip to Jerusalem.

The fears, however, were well founded. The collection was accepted by James, and so Paul's worry about a rupture caused by the 'false brethren' came to nothing. His other enemies, however, mounted an attack which was ultimately successful. He was accused of taking a Gentile into the Temple; that is, farther in than the court of the Gentiles. This led to some tumult, Roman troops intervened and Paul was arrested and imprisoned in Caesarea. He was there for several years. The successive Roman prefects, Felix and Festus, seem not to have known what to do with him, and finally Paul settled his own fate by exercising his right as a Roman citizen to be tried by Caesar (Acts 21—28). He was sent to Rome and was in prison there for at least two years (Acts 28:30—31). The author of Acts ends the story there. Some scholars think that Paul was eventually released and went to Spain, where he wrote 1 and 2 Timothy and Titus. Most are of the view that these letters were written by a follower after his death, and that he was martyred in Rome. It is simplest to think that Acts ends the story because Paul's career had come to its conclusion, and the author chose not to describe what may have been a ghastly end. The first readers would already know that Paul had perished in Rome.

It is often supposed that both he and Peter died in the first Roman persecution of Christians. Rome had suffered a major fire in July, 64. Nero had been away, but it was rumoured that he had planned the fire to make room for ambitious building schemes. He needed someone to bear the blame, and he settled on the new 'superstition'. This is the description of Tacitus, a Roman historian:
'Their execution was made a matter of sport: some were sewn up in the skins of wild beasts and savaged to death by dogs; others were fastened to crosses as living torches, to serve as lights when daylight failed. Nero made his gardens available for the show and held games in the Circus, mingling with the crowd or standing in his chariot in charioteer's uniform.' (Annals 44:3—8)

If Paul did so end his days, he would not have been surprised. He expected Christians—and especially apostles—to suffer, and he saw suffering as sharing the suffering of Christ. And he believed he and the others would be 'fellow heirs with Christ, provided we suffer with him in order that we may also be glorified with him' (Romans 8:17). Throughout his career he saw himself as being always 'given up to death for Jesus's sake' (2 Corinthians 4:11), but suffering—and, no doubt, death itself—he met with this confidence: 'Who shall separate us from the love of Christ? Shall tribulation, or distress, or persecution, or famine, or nakedness, or peril, or sword?...No, in all these things we are more than conquerors through him who loved us. For I am sure that neither death, nor life...nor anything else in all creation, will be able to separate us from the love of God in Christ Jesus our Lord.' (Romans 8:35—39.)

Paul's letters reveal many personal traits and also something about his life. Paul, destined to become Jesus's most influential spokesman, never met him, and he first met the leading disciples only three years after his own conversion (Galatians 1:18). The contrast between Paul, on the one hand, and Jesus, Peter and the other Galileans, on the other, could hardly have been greater. Jesus was from a very small village and was closer to the peasants who worked the land than to the merchants who traded in Jerusalem; and he seems never to have travelled enough to have compared different cultures and to have experienced different societies and their values. Paul, on the other hand, was a city-dweller and a cosmopolitan, moving easily throughout the Graeco-Roman world.

Paul possessed many of the standard values of Graeco-Roman society, especially as modified by the Jewish communities. He regarded it to be against nature for men to have long hair and immodest for women to pray with heads uncovered (1 Corinthians 11:4—16). He appears himself to have been celibate (1 Corinthians 7:7), but he urged married partners to engage in sex regularly (7:5). He frowned on divorce, but he could tolerate it (7:10—16). Unlike pagans, but like Jews, he abhorred homosexuality (Romans 1:26—27). He did not favour excessive displays of charismatic gifts (1 Corinthians 13:1—14,19), and he worried that his congregations were not orderly enough (14:26—40). 'All things should be done decently and in order' so as not to make outsiders think that the Christians were mad (14:23,40). Speaking in tongues and prophesying should not get out of hand.

His beliefs contained the seeds of social revolution. He thought that, 'There is neither Jew nor Greek, there is neither slave nor free, there is neither male nor female; for you are all one in Christ Jesus' (Galatians 3:28). Yet the only part of this that he tried to achieve socially was the union of Jew and Gentile. Slaves were full 'brothers' in Christ (Philemon 16), but they should not seek freedom from ownership (1 Corinthians 7:21—23); and to women he accorded in many ways equality (7:4; 11:8—12), yet the usual distinction of sexual roles was to be maintained (14:33—36). It seems that Paul thought 'the appointed time (had) grown short' and that 'the form of this world (was) passing away' (7:29—31). There was not time to remake society.

In short, Paul combined zeal with sobriety, good judgement, and administrative skills; an innovative and challenging theology with social practicality; and religious fervour with concrete planning. He was the ideal apostle for a new religion in the Graeco-Roman world.

During approximately the first half of his life Paul was a Pharisee, and for a few years a persecutor of the Christian movement. During the second half he was an apostle of Jesus Christ. At both periods he was fully and totally committed to the course to which he felt called by God; at each task he was, by his own modest estimate, the best there was: 'If any other man thinks he has reason for confidence in the flesh, I have more: circumcized on the eighth day, of the people of Israel, of the tribe of Benjamin, a Hebrew born of Hebrews; as to the law a Pharisee, as to zeal a persecutor of the church, as to righteousness under the law blameless.' (Philippians 3:4—6)

His descriptions of his first career are matched by his estimates of his second. When he was in danger of losing control of the Corinthian church which he had founded, and when other Jewish apostles were telling his converts that he was a second-rate and second-hand apostle, he shrewdly began by appearing to agree, but then scored his point: 'For I am the least of the apostles, unfit to be called an apostle, because I persecuted the church of God. But by the grace of God I am what I am, and his grace toward me was not in vain. On the contrary, I worked harder than any of them' (1 Corinthians 15:9—10). He humbly added that 'it was not I, but the grace of God', but he gave himself no little credit.

As both a Pharisee and as an apostle, Paul could boast that he was among the best, and there is no reason to doubt it.

The letters to the Corinthians bring out another aspect of Paul: he was apparently not a great speaker or a physically commanding figure. Comparing himself with Apollos, he wrote, 'I was with you in weakness and in much fear and trembling; and my speech and my message were not in plausible words of wisdom' (1 Corinthians 2:3—4). His opponents could say that 'his letters are weighty and strong, but his bodily presence is weak, and his speech of no account' (2 Corinthians 10:10), and he had to grant the point.

He countered these attacks in two ways. First he claimed that, though he did not preach with the eloquence and wisdom of Apollos, he was in fact not deficient, for he spoke the 'wisdom of God', which is foolishness to humans (1 Corinthians 2:2, 7, 10—16). His second ploy to defend himself was more effective and shows even better his quickness and resourcefulness: he turned his defects into virtues, and his weakness became his strength. "Three times I besought the Lord about this (the 'thorn in the flesh'), that it should leave me; but he said to me, 'My grace is sufficient for you, for my power is made perfect in weakness." (2 Corinthians 12:8—9)

The 'thorn in the flesh' was apparently some bodily ailment which is never specified—see 2 Corinthians 12:7; 4:10; Galatians 4:13—14. He was also the victim of persecution and danger: '. . . with far greater labours, far more imprisonments, with countless beatings, and often near death. Five times I have received at the hands of the Jews the forty lashes less one. Three times I have been beaten with rods; once I was stoned. Three times I have been shipwrecked; a night and a day I have been adrift at sea; on frequent journeys, in danger from rivers, danger from robbers, danger from my own people, danger from Gentiles, danger in the city, danger in the wilderness, danger at sea, danger from false brethren; in toil and hardship, through many a sleepless night, in hunger and thirst, often without food, in cold and exposure' (2 Corinthians 11.23—27).

What was Paul doing by means of these extraordinary efforts, which led him into such conflict and danger, including even attacks from fellow Christians ('false brethren'), and which entailed suffering and finally death?

Near what was, even by his own estimate, the end of his career, he looked back on it this way: 'I will not venture to speak of anything except what Christ has wrought through me to win obedience from the Gentiles, by word and deed, by the power of signs and wonders, by the power of the Holy Spirit, so that from Jerusalem and as far round as Illyricum I have fully preached the gospel of Christ' (Romans 15:18—20).

Paul's travelling companions

Timothy was a young Gentile boy (though according to Acts 16:1 his mother was Jewish) who lived in Lystra in Asia Minor. He was one of Paul's first assistants, being named in the earliest letter in the New Testament (1 Thessalonians) as Paul's aide. Apparently, Paul had sent him to Thessalonica where the Christians were suffering in some way which is not specified. Timothy's mission was to 'strengthen and encourage' them. Timothy had returned and had reported that his mission had been successful (1 Thessalonians 1, 3).

When substantial conflict arose between Paul and the Corinthians, Paul sent Timothy to Corinth to help settle the trouble (1 Corinthians 4:17). Here it appears that Timothy was not successful. Paul himself made another trip to Corinth and wrote a harsh letter. He then sent Titus, who seems finally to have resolved the problem (2 Corinthians 7:5—7).

Timothy, however, was not disgraced or discouraged by his partial failure and he appears in two of Paul's later letters as still one of his companions and as still one who could be sent on a mission in Paul's place (Philippians 2:19; Romans 16:21).

A follower of Paul, writing in his name, urged Timothy not to let others look down on him because of his youth (1 Timothy 4:12). This indicates that the young man, though he had not been able to solve the problems in Corinth, remained a valued member of the early Christian mission in Asia Minor and Greece.

We do not know who wrote the books now known as the Letters to Timothy and we do not know precisely when they were written. Parts may have been by Paul but other sections may have been written by a follower of Paul writing in his name. Some sections may even have been written after Timothy himself was dead.

Eunice was a Jewish woman, the wife of a Gentile and mother of Timothy. She was converted during Paul's first journey through Derbe and Lystra. She is mentioned gratefully in a letter to Timothy: 'I am reminded of your sincere faith, a faith that dwelt first in your grandmother Lois and your mother Eunice' (2 Timothy 1:5).

Titus was a Greek and was one of Paul's chief colleagues, although less is heard of him than of Timothy. He figures in only two places in Paul's letters, but his part is significant.

In around the year 50, when Paul went to Jerusalem to discuss his mission to the Gentiles with Peter, James and John, Titus went with him. Some of the Jerusalem disciples wanted Gentile converts, including Titus, to be circumcised. They argued that to be Christian one must also be Jewish. Paul resisted, and the 'pillars' of the Jerusalem community took Paul's side. Titus was not circumcised and Paul won a significant victory (Galatians 2:1—10).

Titus took a more active part in Paul's controversy with the Corinthian church. A 'party spirit' had developed, some

claiming to be 'of Paul', some 'of Cephas'. Paul wrote what is now 1 Corinthians, urging them to unity, sent Timothy (1 Corinthians 4:17) and made another visit himself. All these efforts were unsuccessful. Unhappy, he left Corinth and travelled north, at some point sending Titus as his representative (2 Corinthians 12:18), and then a harsh letter (probably 2 Corinthians 10—13). He travelled on to Troas but was too anxious about Corinth to remain there and so recrossed the Hellespont to Macedonia. Here Titus met him, bringing news that the Corinthians had received him with obedience, fear and trembling. Paul, greatly relieved, wrote what is now 2 Corinthians 1—7 (see 2 Corinthians 2:13; 7:6—16). Since Titus had established good relations with Corinth, Paul sent him back to help with the collection for the Jerusalem church (2 Corinthians 8).

A later author, writing in Paul's name, speaks of Titus as active in Crete so it seems that his work was not limited to Corinth even though it was there that he had his greatest success (Titus 1:5).

Silas, also called Silvanus, was one of Paul's principal colleagues, apparently taking on this position after Paul broke with Barnabas. In Paul's earliest letter, 1 Thessalonians, Silvanus is mentioned along with Timothy as sharing in the greetings and message of the letter. The same two are mentioned in 2 Corinthians 1:19 as having preached with Paul in Corinth. These letters show that Silas was associated with Paul during his principal activity in Macedonia and Greece, on what is traditionally known as 'the second missionary journey'.

This general picture is confirmed by Acts, which also includes more details about Silas. According to Acts Silas first came to prominence after the 'Jerusalem conference', when Paul hammered out the details of the admission of Gentiles with the leaders in Jerusalem. Silas was appointed to help carry the agreement to Antioch (Acts 15:22). After this Paul and Barnabas parted. Barnabas and Mark went to Cyprus, while Paul returned to Asia Minor with Silas (15:40).

They continued through Asia Minor and crossed the Hellespont to Macedonia. In Philippi they met with trouble. They were followed there by a slave girl who was regarded as possessed by a demon or spirit. She had made money for her owners by fortune-telling. As she followed them, she said that the message of Paul and Silas was true. Paul rebuked the demon which possessed her, and she was healed. The owners, however, seeing that her profitable fortune-telling was finished, charged Paul and Silas with encouraging illegal customs. This was a plausible accusation, since Gentiles who converted to Christianity gave up up worshipping at the pagan temples, including those of the gods of the city and empire. The two missionaries were brought before a magistrate, stripped, beaten with rods, and imprisoned. In the night there was an earthquake, and the doors opened. The jailer, thinking that he had lost his prisoners and would be punished, was about to kill himself when Paul called out that they were still there. The jailer was converted on the spot.

The next morning the magistrate saw that the hue and cry was over and ordered Paul and Silas to be released. Paul, however, pointed out that his rights as a Roman citizen had been infringed by the hasty punishment and imprisonment; he demanded and received an apology from the magistrates (Acts 16:16—40).

Silas continued to work with Paul and Timothy in Thessalonica and then Boroea. In both cities they won some converts but also had more difficulties. In Thessalonica they were accused of opposing Caesar because they preached another king, Jesus. Some of their converts were arrested but released on bail. Paul, Silas and Timothy left, but some of their opponents followed them from Thessalonica to Beroea. They stirred up the crowds against Paul and the others, and this time Paul was forced to leave. He went on to Athens, but later sent for Silas and Timothy. They caught up with him in Corinth and continued their joint work there (Acts 17:1—18:5).

We hear no more of Silas during the

Paul had converted him there. He was involved in one of the more dramatic events in the early missionary effort. In Ephesus a silversmith, Demetrius, was disturbed because the Christian preaching was harming his business, which largely depended on the sale of replicas in silver of the temple of Artemis. Demetrius rallied the other craftsmen who were in a similar situation and they created a disturbance. They seized Aristarchus and Gaius and rushed them to the theatre, where a crowd gathered. Paul was advised by local officials not to appear; Alexander attempted to quieten the crowd but failed. The city clerk appealed to them to proceed in an orderly manner and bring charges in the courts. The appeal was successful, the men were released and Paul and his companions soon afterwards travelled to Macedonia (Acts 19:23—41).

Aristarchus is mentioned one other time; he apparently continued to travel with Paul, for he is mentioned as accompanying him on his last trip, from Caesarea to Italy, where he was to appear before Caesar (Acts 27:2).

Tychicus was a Macedonian who joined Paul's mission in Ephesus and then sometimes travelled with him (Acts 20:4). In the letter to the Colossians Paul or one of his followers wrote that Tychicus would come to Colossae, calling him 'a dear brother, a faithful minister and fellow servant in the Lord'. He would bring news about Paul, which may mean that he was especially close to him (Colossians 4:7—8). There are further references to him as one of Paul's travelling assistants in 2 Timothy 4:12 and Titus 3:12.

Trophimus was a Gentile convert in Ephesus who is named in Acts 20:4—5 as one of Paul's travelling companions. Although apparently a minor member of Paul's entourage, Trophimus was destined to play a very important role.

Paul had arranged a collection in Asia Minor and Greece and he and some of his Gentile converts travelled to Jerusalem to deliver the money and to demonstrate the solidarity of the Gentile and Jewish wings of the church;

TIMOTHY
Timothy was a young Gentile from Lystra, Asia Minor. He became one of Paul's earliest assistants despite his youth and was sufficiently trusted to be sent on independent missions in Paul's place. He succeeded in encouraging the

Christians in Thessalonica when they were in difficulties, but failed in Corinth where Paul had sent him to end a controversy within the Church. Nevertheless, Timothy remained one of Paul's most trusted and reliable companions on his missionary journeys.

rest of Paul's career. In the letter known as 1 Peter, however, he is associated with Peter. The letter concludes by saying, 'By Silvanus, a faithful brother . . .I have written briefly to you' (5:12).

Most scholars think that Peter himself did not write the letter but that it was written in his name by one of his followers after his death. The letter is written in excellent Greek, certainly

beyond a Galilean fisherman. Those who believe that it was by Peter say that Silas did more than take dictation, but composed the letter at Peter's direction.

Aristarchus is mentioned in the letter to Philemon as one of Paul's fellow workers (vs.24) and in Colossians 4:10 he is named as Paul's 'fellow prisoner'. He was a Macedonian, and apparently

Trophimus was one of the party. He and Paul were seen together, perhaps near the Temple, and from this arose the charge that Paul had taken a Gentile 'into the Temple'. The Temple had a court of the Gentiles into which they could enter; but a notice, which has survived, stood between the Court of the Gentiles and the Court of the Israelites, forbidding Gentiles to go further on pain of death. It was this prohibition which Paul and Trophimus were accused of transgressing (Acts 21:29). The blame fell on Paul, who was regarded as the responsible party, and it was this accusation which led to his arrest in Jerusalem and thus ultimately to his death in Rome some years later.

Most scholars assume that Paul did not actually take Trophimus into the Temple and that the charge was false. He had, however, claimed that his Gentile converts were true 'heirs of Abraham' (e.g. Galatians 3) and this could well lead to the belief that they should be able to enter the Court of the Israelites. It is not known what happened to Trophimus.

Luke was a companion of Paul, though not one of his major aides. He is mentioned along with others as a 'fellow worker' in Paul's letter to Philemon (24). In Colossians 4:14 he is referred to as 'the beloved physician'.

Since both of the references appear in letters sent to Colossae, Luke was probably a local assistant of Paul's in Asia Minor. He is not mentioned in any of Paul's letters to churches in Macedonia and Greece.

Some time in the course of the second century, the Gospel which is now called 'According to Luke' and the Book of Acts were attributed to Luke. Both works were written anonymously and the titles were supplied later. Both were certainly written by the same person. Their introductions are very similar and both Luke and Acts were dedicated to Theophilus. The theology and literary style of the two works are in very close agreement. The question is whether or not the author can be identified with the Luke who was one of Paul's companions.

One of the reasons why some

LUKE
The author of the Gospel according to Luke was an educated man who had studied Greek writings, knew the Hebrew scripture in Greek translation and could write in the style of the authors of Biblical history. Believing in repentance, forgiveness and good deeds, his Gospel dwells sympathetically on stories about women, sinners and the poor and includes the most memorable of Jesus's parables.

scholars think that Luke wrote both books is that parts of Acts are written as an eye-witness account, perhaps a travel diary of one of Paul's companions. Instead of saying 'they went', the author occasionally writes 'we went' as if he was there in person.

This happens for the first time shortly after Paul and his companions had passed through Phrygia, the province in which Colossae is located (Acts 16:6—12). It has been suggested that

Luke joined the missionaries in Phrygia and travelled with Paul to Macedonia and that he only started to keep his diary when the travellers took ship for mainland Europe (Acts 16:11). This is speculative, though barely possible. One argument against it is that the author of Acts did not understand Paul's theology very well and he also made mistakes about Paul's journeys.

Whether or not the physician Luke was the author of Luke and Acts, it is possible to say a considerable amount about the man who wrote them. He was literate and the structure of the books shows that he had studied Greek writings. He also knew the Hebrew scripture (later called 'the Old Testament' by Christians) in Greek translation and could write in the style of the authors of biblical history when he wished.

Luke's theology was less complicated and also less powerful than that of Paul; his picture of Paul is more pedestrian than the Paul of the letters. Luke believed in repentance, forgiveness, kindness and good deeds. In the Gospel he dwelt on stories about women, sinners and the poor, showing sympathy for them and emphasizing that Jesus accepted them. It is thanks to Luke that we have the most memorable of Jesus's parables, such as the Parable of the Prodigal Son and the Good Samaritan. The author of Luke and Acts may not have been Luke 'the beloved physician' but he fulfilled the noblest aspirations of the medical profession.

Companions and converts

Andronicus and **Junia** are mentioned only once, in Romans 16:7. They deserve to be saved from obscurity, and this is especially so of Junia. Because of what is said about this couple, there is a long tradition of representing her as a man. This is based solely on a name which is almost identical for male and female. In Greek the gender of the name is indicated simply by an accent mark, and the early manuscripts are written without accents. Most modern editors and translators have chosen the masculine form of the name although this does not appear in ancient literature and inscriptions while the feminine form is common. Modern scholars consider that Andronicus and Junia were a married missionary couple, like Aquila and Prisca, who are mentioned in the same passage (Romans 16:3).

Dionysius the Areopagite was a member of the Areopagus, the city council in Athens, and the only one named as converting after Paul's speech there (Acts 17:19—34).

Romans The last chapter of the Letter to the Romans includes an unparalleled list of names. These are people known to Paul in the church to which he writes, or who are nearby and can be greeted, or who are travelling to that church. Further, Paul mentions several people with him at the time, and his secretary names himself. If the letter was in fact sent to Rome, the extraordinarily long list of people to be greeted would mean, as one scholar put it, that virtually everyone whom Paul knew had moved there. Many scholars have therefore suggested that Romans 16 is part of another letter, written as an introduction for Phoebe, the Deaconess of Cenchreae (16:1—2), and sent to a church where Paul had many friends and to which Phoebe was travelling—probably Ephesus. When, probably in the nineties, Paul's letters were edited for publication this short message was attached to the book of Romans. Paul doubtless wrote numerous such letters, but the rest have disappeared.

Many of the people mentioned here have separate entries and these appear in *italics*. Paul names as those with him who send greetings, *Timothy*, one of his main companions, and six others: three Jews, Gaius his host, *Erastus* the city treasurer, and Quartus. The scribe, Tertius, adds his own greeting (16:22—23). Paul was therefore writing from a city which had a mixed congregation, partly Gentile and partly Jewish, which included some people of prominence. One was prosperous enough to provide a room for Paul, as well as a meeting room for the church, and one was a city official.

The list of those greeted is even more interesting. The letter singles out 27 people and two families. Two couples stand out: *Prisca* and *Aquila*, and *Andronicus* and *Junia*. Women were obviously active in Paul's groups, for besides the two wives and *Phoebe*, the deaconess whom the letter introduces, there are six more women: Mary, 'who has worked hard among you'; Tryphaena and Tryphosa, 'workers in the Lord'; Mother of Rufus, 'his mother and mine'; Julia and the sister of Nereus, 'greetings'.

The list of men is also interesting. *Aquila* and *Andronicus* are members of important missionary husband-and-wife teams. Urbanus is 'a fellow worker', and Persis has 'worked hard in the Lord'. Epaenetus is distinguished as the first convert in Asia (that, is the Roman province of Asia, in western Asia Minor). Rufus is 'eminent in the Lord'; Apelles is 'approved'; Ampliatus and Stachys are 'beloved'. Only one, Herodion, is Jewish.

The rest receive just 'greetings', as do nameless others who are 'with' some of those named, probably as members of house churches. The lack of public buildings for meetings of Christians made large congregations impossible, and the names here show how they were divided into small groups.

Eutychus On the evening before Paul left Troas on his way to Jerusalem for the last time, about AD57, Paul preached and discussed late into the night, apparently trying to cover a lot of ground before his departure. The group of Christians was meeting in 'an upper room', probably two floors above ground level. (Thus American translations will say 'on the third floor'.) Eutychus was seated in a window, becoming drowsier as the talk went on and he finally fell to the ground. Paul rushed down and lifted him. It is not clear if the narrator intends to say that Eutychus had been killed. He writes, Paul 'lifted him dead', but then says that Paul at once cried out, 'His life is in him'. In either case, the young man lived and even managed to stay for the rest of the discussion, being taken home the next morning (Acts 20:7—12).

Enemies and opponents

Hymenaeus Hymenaeus and Alexander are named as false teachers in 1 Timothy 1:20, and Hymenaeus is linked with Philetus in the same capacity in 2 Timothy 2:17. The author of 1 Timothy says that he had turned Hymenaeus and Alexander 'over to Satan' so that they would learn not to blaspheme. This is similar to the phrase used by Paul about a man who was committing incest in Corinth: he was to be delivered 'to

Satan', so that his body would be destroyed but his soul saved (1 Corinthians 5:1—5). Presumably 'turn over to Satan' means 'expel from the church'. In both instances the intention was to help rather than to destroy. The author of 1 Timothy hopes that the false teachers will learn better.

It is difficult to say what the false teaching mentioned in 1 Timothy was. The author writes that these men 'rejected conscience' but we do not know in what way. In 2 Timothy, however, the erroneous doctrine is specified: Hymenaeus and Philetus held 'that the resurrection is past already' (2 Timothy 2:18). They believed, in other words, that Christianity consisted of an inner renewal, and that there would be no physical resurrection at the end of time. Paul himself had preached that those in Christ became a 'new creation' (2 Corinthians 5:17), and language such as this might lead some to think that the new creation had already come, and that there would be no life after death. Paul always looked forward, however, to a resurrection of the body, and he wrote about it in 1 Corinthians 15.

Hymenaeus and Philetus probably taught that those who were baptized possessed the Spirit and were no longer constrained by the normal restrictions of the world. They may also have been 'charismatic' enthusiasts, boasting of their ability to speak in tongues and seeing this as proof that they had already become new beings.

Elymas, apparently also named Bar-Jesus (son of Jesus) was a *magos*—that is an astrologer and magician in Cyprus. Roman officials and others were often advised by astrologers and this appears to have been the case in Cyprus. The proconsul, Sergius Paulus, summoned Paul and Barnabas to explain the gospel to him. Elymas tried to persuade him not to accept it. Paul called him 'son of a devil' and said that he would be blinded and 'unable to see the sun for a time'. Immediately he was surrounded by mist and darkness so that he could not see. Sergius Paulus was persuaded by the miracle and accepted the Christian message (Acts 13:4—12).

The Letters

The church at Corinth

Apollos was a Jew from Alexandria, Egypt, who came to Ephesus in Asia Minor. He had already accepted baptism by disciples of John the Baptist, but the two Christians Prisca and Aquila 'expounded to him the way of God more accurately', and he went to Corinth to continue work there. He was noted for his eloquence (Acts 18:24—28).

Paul had founded the church in Corinth (Acts 18:1), but he was not there when Apollos arrived. We do not know how long Apollos stayed in Corinth, for he apparently travelled further as an evangelist. Some time later, Paul (who was then in Ephesus) learned that factions were developing in the church at Corinth: some members claimed to belong to Paul's party, some to Cephas's (Peter's), some to Apollos's (1 Corinthians 1:10—13). Paul wrote attacking both factionalism and eloquent wisdom (1 Corinthians 1:10—4:9). He did not, he wrote, speak eloquently or with worldly wisdom himself (2:3—4), but, by the Spirit, he did speak the wisdom of God (2:1—16).

Paul made it quite clear what was worrying him and directly warned Apollos to be careful how he built on the foundation which he, Paul, had laid: the 'building' would be tested by fire. If it were 'wood, hay or straw' it would be destroyed and the builder would be punished. Only gold, silver and precious stones would endure (3:10—17; 4:6).

Yet Paul had to grant that Apollos had done good work and wrote that he had encouraged him to visit Corinth again (16:12). Nothing more is heard of Apollos. He must have been one of numerous travelling evangelists at work for the Christian cause, most of whom remain entirely unknown. Because he crossed Paul's path, his name is mentioned in the only surviving evidence for the missionary activity of the early church, the letters of Paul and the Book of Acts.

Chloe, whose name means 'blond', was a prominent woman in the Corinthian church, which Paul had founded in approximately the year AD49. She sent some of her 'people', either slaves or freed dependants, to Ephesus, where Paul then was, to let him know that dissension had arisen in the Corinthian church (1 Corinthians 1:11). The Book of Acts mentions the conversion of prominent women at Thessalonica (Acts 17:4), and here we have the name of such a woman at Corinth.

Stephanas was one of Paul's converts in Corinth and one whom Paul personally baptized (1 Corinthians 1:16). Paul writes that he baptized 'the household' of Stephanas, so he presumably had not only a family but also a household staff of slaves or freedmen. Stephanas and his household had the distinction of being the first converts in Achaia (1 Corinthians 16:15).

Stephanas, with others, later visited Paul in Ephesus, and they may have been the ones who told Paul about the arguments in Corinth (see *Apollos, Chloe*). It is clear that Stephanas remained loyal to Paul, for Paul urged the church in Corinth to follow 'such men', as well as his own fellow workers.

Phoebe Romans 16 was written to introduce Phoebe, called 'a deaconess' or 'a minister'. The chapter may originally have been part of another letter now lost, and so we cannot be sure to which church Phoebe was

CHLOE
Chloe was a leading convert to the church in Corinth, apparently a woman of authority. She once sent a message to Paul about the growing dissension within her group, acting decisively and independently in a difficult situation.

travelling. She was from Cenchreae, near Corinth. Since the church at the time did not have set titles for offices (except the term 'apostle' for the major travelling missionaries), we do not know exactly what Phoebe did. The Greek word *diakonos*, which implies 'service', was used for many church workers, and in 1 Corinthians 3:5 Paul applies it to Apollos and himself. In 1 Corinthians 12:28 Paul names different kinds of tasks. He puts first being an apostle, then a prophet. He then lists teaching, healing, helping others, administering and speaking in tongues. As 'a minister'

Phoebe could have performed any of the functions from prophecy downwards. Paul explicitly says that she helped others, and she may also have taught or prophesied.

Phoebe was travelling alone (though possibly with a servant or freedman) to a strange city, and she needed a letter of introduction to the Christians there. Letters of introduction played a substantial role in giving the widely separated churches a feeling of belonging to a unified whole. The Christians made great efforts to stay in touch with one another (see

Epaphroditus). Since she travelled alone, she was probably of mature years and some wealth. Paul, in fact, calls her a 'patroness of many and of myself as well'. This may mean that she subsidized some of his work and other aspects of the Christian movement. Phoebe must represent numerous people whose names are lost, but who worked hard in the early Christian churches.

Crispus was one of Paul's converts in Corinth, one of only three people Paul is known to have baptized himself (1 Corinthians 1:14). According to Acts, Crispus was an important convert, for he was the head of the synagogue in Corinth and was baptized into the new faith with all his household (Acts 18:8).

Sosthenes succeeded Crispus as ruler of the synagogue in Corinth, after Crispus was converted to Christianity. He and others attempted to persuade the proconsul of Achaia to punish Paul and when the proconsul threw out the charge, the Jews turned on Sosthenes and beat him. This Sosthenes is probably not the same as the one mentioned in the letter Paul sent from Ephesus to Corinth (1 Corinthians 1:1).

Erastus is named in Romans 16:23 as sending greetings and is described as 'the city's director of public works'. If this chapter belongs with the main Letter to the Romans, we know that it was written from Corinth, so Erastus was a city official in Corinth. It may be, however, that the chapter was originally a separate letter, written from another city; in this case we do not know were Erastus worked. Although Acts frequently points out the roles and positions of the converts, Erastus is one of the few named by Paul as having any kind of public responsibility.

Another Erastus is named in Acts (19:22). He was sent by Paul from Ephesus to Macedonia and in 2 Timothy 4:20 he is said to have been left by Paul in Corinth. This Erastus seems to have been one of Paul's minor assistants so it is unlikely that he was the same person as Erastus the public official.

The church at Ephesus

Demetrius of Ephesus was a silversmith in Ephesus whose trade consisted in part of the sale of silver shrines to the goddess Artemis. He created trouble for Paul and his colleagues because their message was damaging his trade. Two of the Christians, Gaius and Aristarchus, were dragged into the theatre by a tumultuous mob. The intention may have been to accuse them and make them answer in public, but the noise was too great for anyone to be heard. The anger of the crowd seems to have been directed against both the Christian missionaries and the resident Jews (who also, of course, opposed idolatry). A non-Christian Jew named Alexander tried to speak in defence of his people, but he was shouted down. It was finally the city clerk who calmed the crowd (Acts 19:23—41).

Alexander of Ephesus was a Jew who tried to defend his people when the crowd attacked them and Paul's group of Christians (see *Demetrius*). Two other Alexanders are mentioned. The first, in 1 Timothy 1:20 was a false teacher (see *Hymenaeus*). The second was a coppersmith who did Paul 'great harm' (2 Timothy 4:14). There is no indication of what this harm was.

Gaius Several people with this name are mentioned in the New Testament as it was a common name of the time. The first was a Macedonian who served Paul as an assistant in Ephesus. When Demetrius the silversmith roused a crowd against the missionaries, Gaius was one of the two men who were seized and taken to the theatre. The crowd was quietened and the men released and Paul and his companions returned to Macedonia (Acts 19:29). Some have suggested that this Gaius was the same man as 'Gaius from Derbe' in Acts 20:4. This is simply because he is mentioned in the next chapter of Acts, but there is no good reason to make the identification. Derbe itself was about 200 miles from Ephesus.

Another Gaius was a convert in Corinth, baptized by Paul himself (1 Corinthians 1:14). A Gaius is mentioned again in Romans 16 and if this letter was sent from Corinth to Rome, he may be the same man. In verse 23 he is said to 'offer hospitality' to Paul and 'the whole church', which would mark him as a man of some means. If he were prominent, it would also explain why he was baptized by Paul himself.

The letter known as 3 John is also addressed to someone called Gaius.

Artemis is the name of a Greek goddess, whom the Romans identified with the Latin goddess Diana. The worship of Artemis in Ephesus resulted in considerable danger to Paul and his colleagues (see *Demetrius*). In Ephesus the goddess Artemis (Acts 19:23—41) was not in fact much like the original Greek goddess or the Latin Diana, who were principally goddesses of the hunt and of childbirth. Artemis (or Diana) of the Ephesians was a fertility goddess adopted from an earlier religion of Asia Minor.

Onesiphorus According to 2 Timothy 1:15—18 Onesiphorus had come from Asia to give comfort to Paul, who was in prison in Rome. The principal church in the Roman province of Asia was Ephesus, and so it is likely that Onesiphorus was from there.

At the end of the letter Paul sends greetings to the household of Onesiphorus (2 Timothy 4:19), which may imply that he had remained in Rome with Paul.

The church at Philippi

Clement is mentioned in Paul's letter to Philippi as a 'fellow worker', and as one whose name is written 'in the book of life'. Two clues make us suppose that Clement was a convert in Philippi and Paul's 'fellow worker' while he was there. One is simply that Clement is not otherwise named in the New Testament, and so he seems not to have travelled with Paul. The other is that he is mentioned just after Euodia and Syntyche, who are quarrelling, and who obviously are in Philippi: Paul 'entreats' them to agree (Philippians 4:2—3).

There is no reason to identify the Clement of Philippi with Clement of Rome, a bishop who, in the nineties, wrote a letter to Corinth (1 Clement).

Epaphroditus was sent from Philippi to Paul when he was in prison, bringing gifts and staying to be of what service he could. It is not known exactly where Paul was imprisoned at the time but several messages passed between him and the church at Philippi. The Philippians had heard of Paul's imprisonment, and had sent Epaphroditus; Epaphroditus had fallen ill; the Philippians had heard of it and Paul had learned that they were concerned. So at the time the letter was written, there had been four trips and the sending of the letter, carried by Epaphroditus, made the fifth (Philippians 2:25—30; 4:18). Paul looked forward to three more: he hoped that Timothy could go and return and that he himself would be able to make the trip (2:19—24). Acts refers to only two substantial imprisonments, one in Caesarea, the other in Rome. Both these places seem too far from Philippi for so many messages to have been exchanged. Paul, however, said of himself that he was often in prison (2 Corinthians 11:23) and it has been suggested that on this occasion he was in Ephesus, only about 250 miles from Philippi (about ten days journey) and thus within relatively easy reach.

Paul is unstinting of his praise of the young man. He calls him 'my brother, fellow worker and fellow soldier', and he urges the Philippians to honour such men. Ephaphroditus had 'almost died for the work of Christ' (Philippians 2:25—30).

Epaphroditus joins Onesimus (in the Letter to Philemon) as one who helped Paul in prison; and like him, he inspired one of the warmest and most personal letters which we have from antiquity.

Lydia was a merchant in Philippi, in Macedonia. Her trade was in 'purple cloth'; that is, cloth dyed with the rare and expensive Tyrian purple dye which is painstakingly derived from certain shellfish. The dye was generally reserved for the clothing of rulers. The higher Roman officials in Philippi may

ONESIMUS
Onesimus was a slave who was in prison with Paul in Ephesus. He had run away from his master, Philemon, and Paul wrote a letter in his support, asking Philemon to forgive him. In about AD *110, the Bishop of Ephesus was a man named Onesimus. There is no evidence that this is the same person, but it is tempting to imagine that the runaway slave returned to Paul's service and became a leader in the church.*

have worn the purple on official occasions.

Lydia's trade apparently prospered. She was head of a household which probably contained both slaves and freedmen who were still dependent on her. Acts (16:13–15) tells us that she was a 'worshipper of God'. That is, she was a Gentile who was on the fringe of the synagogue, attending and worshipping the god of Israel, but not formally converted to Judaism. Acts indicates that Paul was especially successful among such people.

When Paul and Silas were visiting Philippi they were arrested but soon released. They then went to Lydia's house where they met other converts to the Christian gospel (Acts 16:40). Lydia must have been one of the leading members of the church in Macedonia: she was prosperous enough to have meetings of the church members in her house and she assisted the new movement in various other ways.

The church at Thessalonica

Jason was a prosperous man in Thessalonica in the late 40s who had joined the Christian movement and had accepted Paul and his companions into his house. Perhaps the church also met there. The Jews of Thessalonica objected to Paul telling Gentiles that Jesus was the Jewish Messiah and that the Gentiles could belong to the Jewish messianic sect (not then called Christianity) without accepting the law of Moses. They attempted to accuse Paul and Silas and went to Jason's house to look for them. Finding them gone, they seized Jason and others instead, brought them before the city officials and accused them of serving another king than Caesar—potentially a charge of treason. Jason had adequate funds and posted bond. Paul and his companion Silas left by night for Beroea (Acts 17:5–10).

Acts does not say what eventually happened to Jason but his troubles may not have been over. In his letter to Thessalonica Paul speaks about the sufferings which are part of following Jesus (for example 1 Thessalonians 1:6) and in that letter he also includes a virulent attack on the Jews for impeding his work with Gentiles (2:13—16). Acts presents the Jews of Asia Minor and Greece as stereotypes, always in opposition to Paul and creating trouble for him. In Thessalonica it appears that they really did so.

In Romans 16:21 Paul sent greetings from Jason, his 'kinsman' (fellow Jew), but it is not known whether or not this is the same Jason.

The letter to Philemon

Philemon was a prosperous Christian convert who lived either at Laodicea or Colossae. He was the man to whom the letter to Philemon was addressed. His slave, Onesimus, had run away and had come to Paul in prison. Paul sent Onesimus back to Philemon with a letter which asked not only that Onesimus be forgiven, but also sent back to Paul to serve in his ministry.

Onesimus is the subject of Paul's letter to Philemon, which was written while Paul was in prison. We do not know which of Paul's imprisonments this was but it was probably one in Ephesus—though this is not mentioned by name in Acts.

While in prison, Paul met Onesimus, a slave who had apparently run away from his master, Philemon. Whether Onesimus intended to come to the prison to seek Paul's help, or had been arrested as a runaway, is not known. In any case Paul wrote to Philemon asking that the slave be forgiven. Paul, however, wanted more. The name 'Onesimus' means 'useful', and Paul plays on the meaning, saying that he had been 'useless' to Philemon, but was now 'useful' to both of them.

Paul said that he would have liked to keep Onesimus, but was sending him back, though it was like sending his heart. And, he added, Philemon should remember how much he owed Paul—'you owe me your very self'—presumably his soul, saved by conversion. He concludes 'I know that you will do even more than I ask'.

This is a subtle request that Onesimus be returned to Paul, to work in his service. About the year 110, we learn

from the letters of Ignatius that an Onesimus was Bishop in Ephesus. It is tempting to think that the runaway slave did return to serve Paul and rose to leadership in the church.

Epaphras was in prison with Paul when the letter to Philemon was written, and Paul names him as sending greetings (Philemon 23). He is also mentioned in Colossians, where it appears that he was a native of Colossae (Colossians 4:12) and that it was he who established the church there ('as you learned it from Epaphras'—1:7). Colossae was a very small town near Ephesus, and Paul probably used people such as Epaphras to establish churches in smaller places while his own work kept him in the main city. Epaphras, however, had not remained in Colossae, but had returned to Paul with news of the church there (1:8). We do not know where Paul and Epaphras were in prison, but it may have been in Ephesus itself. (See also *Epaphroditus* and *Onesimus*.)

Demas is mentioned in Philemon 24 as a 'fellow worker' and in Colossians 4:14 as sending greetings. In 2 Timothy 4:10, we read that Demas, 'in love with this present world', has deserted Paul and gone to Thessalonica. This section of the letter may be a fragment of the original letter by Paul, but if it was written after his death, like the rest of 2 Timothy, it shows that Demas's desertion was remembered as a significant event.

Letters of John

The three short letters which bear the name John were written around the end of the first century, probably in Asia Minor. 1 John in particular is very close in style to the Gospel of John, though it was probably not written by the same person. 1 John 4:7—21, on love, is one of the high points of early Christian literature: 'He who does not love does not know God; for God is love...In this is love, not that we loved God but that he loved us...' 1 John is especially concerned to deny *docetism*, the view that Christ was not fully human. Thus it emphasizes that those who have the

spirit of God will confess that 'Jesus Christ has come in the flesh' (4:2).

There were, however, other 'spirits' abroad, and travelling evangelists claiming to be inspired by the spirit, were spreading versions of the Christian message which the authors of our epistles opposed. 2 and 3 John deal with what attitude should be taken towards such people. 2 John proposes a strict limitation on hospitality towards wandering preachers: if someone denies that Jesus came in the flesh, he should not be received or even greeted (vss. 7—11). 3 John redresses the balance: it stresses the need for hospitality, though it does not say whether or not any limits should be imposed.

Demetrius is commended in 3 John 12 as having 'testimony from everyone, and from the truth itself'. The author adds that 'I testify to him too'. The 'testimonies' probably mean that his views are to be followed. The references to church leaders and strife in 2 John and 3 John are very obscure, and it is difficult to say why Demetrius is being praised. It may have been for offering hospitality to visiting preachers and prophets (5, 9—10).

Diotrephes was the opponent of the Elder who wrote 3 John. He is said 'to like to put himself first' and not to acknowledge the author's authority. It appears that his fault was that he did not welcome visiting Christians, but rather 'put them out of the church' (9—10). The author of the letter sided with Demetrius against Diotrephes.

Gaius was the last Christian leader to whom 3 John was addressed. Since we do not know where or when the letter was written, it is impossible to guess whether or not he is identical with the other men named Gaius mentioned in Paul's letters and Acts (see *The church at Ephesus*).

Dates
in the
Bible

Fixing definite dates for the people of the Bible is not a simple matter. It is hard for us to imagine what it was like without a world time scale, but in Bible times, no standard method of establishing precise dates existed. Most ancient calendars were based on the phases of the moon and because these vary slightly from month to month, it was impossible to establish a truly accurate year length. Dates were recorded in different ways, often in the form seen in, for example, Luke 3:1, 'In the fifteenth year of the reign of Tiberius Caesar...' Hundreds of years after an event such as this, it would have been very difficult to determine accurately the precise year that it took place and therefore how many years had elapsed since that time.

For the biblical period before Saul became king, there is still no universally agreed time scale, and doubts grow the further back we try to reach. It is, however, possible to agree dates for the kings of Israel, using the records of the Assyrians and the Egyptians.

The Assyrians lived in what is today northern Iraq and founded an empire which eventually absorbed the kingdom of Israel. They named each year after a different state official. Lists of these officials survive, showing who was king and what notable events occurred. In the year when a man called Bur-Sagale held office, the ninth year of king

Ashur-Dan III, a solar eclipse is recorded. Astronomers calculate this occurred 15 June 763 BC and from this many of the Assyrian kings can be dated. The Egyptians also provided lists of kings, with the lengths of their reigns and astronomical information. On a certain date during the seventh year of Sesostris III, the star Sirius was said to have risen simultaneously with the sun. It was exceedingly rare for this to happen on that date and astronomers pinpoint the year as 1872 BC. From this Sesostris III and his predecessors and successors have been dated. Where Assyrians and Egyptians refer to one another, the dates can be cross-checked.

Israel comes into the system through references by the Assyrian king Shalmaneser III. He names the Israelite king Ahab among his opponents in his sixth year (853 BC) and received the tribute of the later Israelite king Jehu in his eighteenth year (841 BC). Taking the names of the kings of Israel and lengths of reigns recorded in the Bible, we can work back to Solomon, who reigned approximately 961—922 BC.

Dating the earlier events recorded in the Bible is less certain. According to 1 Kings 6:1, the Exodus took place 480 years before the foundation of the Temple, in Solomon's second year. This brings the Exodus to about 1440 BC. 480 (12 x 40) is, however, a suspiciously round figure. The phrase 'forty years' is common in the Bible—as the length of the wilderness wanderings, the periods of peace inaugurated by three of the Judges, the ministry of Eli and the reigns of David and Solomon. Many suspect that often it simply means a generation. Most modern commentators in fact place the Exodus in the thirteenth century BC and both the Bible and archaeology support this date. In Exodus 1:11, the Israelites built a stone city called Raamses, a project which could well have been one of those undertaken by the ambitious warrior and builder Ramesses II, who reigned during the thirteenth century. And archaeologists have dated the remains of various Canaanite cities which could have been destroyed by the Israelite conquest, to the second half of the thirteenth century BC.

Dating becomes even more difficult as we move back to the times of the patriarchs. According to Exodus, the Israelite bondage in Egypt lasted for 430 years (but the Bible also states that it lasted four generations, which would have been a far shorter period) from the time of Jacob's death. Jacob's death in turn ended the era of the patriarchs, which lasted 307 years (Abraham begat Isaac at the age of 100, Isaac begat Jacob at the age of 60, and Jacob lived 147 years). Few, however, take these biblical figures literally, and recent suggestions for the date of Abraham based on archaeological evidence cover most of the range 2000—1500 BC. The patriarchs and the Exodus could have been dated more precisely if the Bible had named the kings of Egypt who met Abraham, Joseph and Moses. However, they are all called simply by the title 'Pharaoh' (meaning Great House). The first Pharaoh actually named in the Bible is Shishak, in Solomon's day.

The biblical figures place the Flood 29 years before Abraham's birth and the Creation 1656 years earlier still. On the basis of these reckonings, the Jewish calendar divides the year 1987 between 5747 and 5748, reckoned from Creation, a universal starting point. The biblical figures, however, seem not to be intended literally but rather to enshrine a symbolic meaning, now forgotten.

The New Testament

There are many uncertain points in early Christian chronology but it is possible to give approximate dates to important events and some of the books.

Reckoning by our modern calendar, Jesus was born about 4 BC. This puzzling date comes from an ancient mistake. Both Matthew and Luke represent Jesus as having been born about the time Herod the Great died. Herod's death, in turn, can be fixed in terms of the Roman calendar. The Christian calendar dates from the sixth century, when a monk, Dionysius Exiguus, calculated and placed the start of the Christian era in the wrong year, about four years out. His calendar was accepted in England in 664 and eventually spread throughout the west. The scientific fixing of ancient dates by modern scholarship still continues but most of the work was done by earlier generations of scholars, and a sixth century monk would have had little chance of getting it precisely right.

Index

Italic numbers refer to illustrations.
Bold numbers refer to maps.
Inset maps are indicated by the letter i.

St. John's Episcopal Church
322 South Greer
Memphis, TN 38111

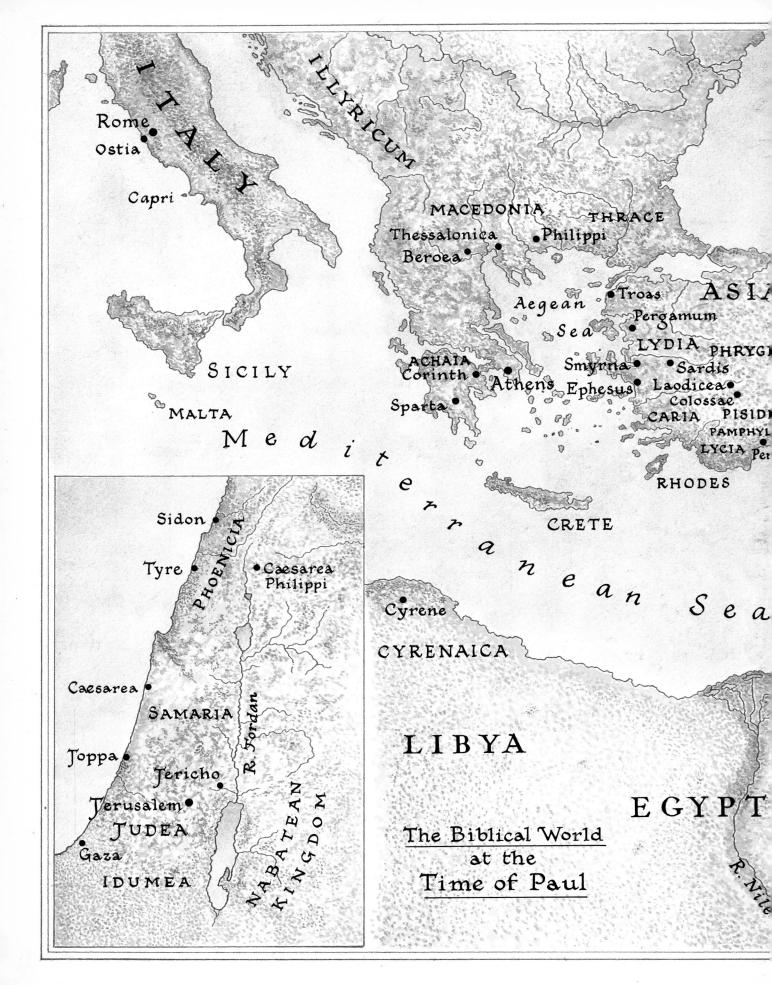

ITALY

Rome
Ostia

Capri

ILLYRICUM

SICILY

MALTA

MACEDONIA

Thessalonica
Beroea

Philippi

THRACE

Aegean

Sea

Troas

Pergamum

ASIA

LYDIA

PHRYGI

Smyrna
Sardis

ACHAIA
Corinth
Athens
Ephesus
Laodicea

Sparta

Colossae

CARIA

PISIDI

PAMPHYL

LYCIA

Per

RHODES

CRETE

Sidon

Tyre

PHOENICIA

Caesarea
Philippi

Cyrene

CYRENAICA

Caesarea

SAMARIA

R. Jordan

Joppa

Jericho

Jerusalem

JUDEA

Gaza

IDUMEA

NABATEAN KINGDOM

M
e
d
i
t
e
r
r
a
n
e
a
n
Sea

LIBYA

EGYPT

R. Nile

The Biblical World
at the
Time of Paul